AN AMERICAN CRISIS:
Veterans' Unemployment

Stand by Them | How You Can Help | Solutions

MARK BAIRD

*This book is dedicated to America,
its armed forces and their families,
and to patriotic citizens and companies
across our country.*

Contents

Preface

M A R K   B A I R D

America is in crisis. We need to regain our national unity, identity and pride. What are the fundamental mores, beliefs and principles that are the fabric of America? What makes us strong and resilient to decay and destruction? What must be done to preserve us and to provide safety and security and stability for generations to come?

Respect for national institutions, traditions, elected authorities, law enforcement, and US military veterans are all crucial to the perpetration of a democracy and to our nation America in particular. Like all humans, these man-made societal systems are flawed. But that by no means permits us to disregard or to disrespect their essential value to our continuation as a sovereign people. Our obligation is to be always vigilant and to repair the breaches to these walls of protection that are the bulwarks of any nation that endures. And that is the overriding theme and purpose of the *An American Crisis* books: the preservation and security of America.

Whether you are blue, red or some other spectrum like me, this book should be read. It shares the American voices and ideas and answers from people in a variety of ethnicities, fields, and experiences about one of these foundational pillars of our society: US military veterans.

It is time for a comprehensive and permanent solution to US veteran unemployment to be put into place for perpetuity. The technology of the 21st Century allows us to do so. But the answers will not be implemented effectively if we leave it to our politicians and government bureaucracy. They have already had more than 200 years. So the intent and purpose of *An American Crisis: Veterans' Unemployment* is to gather some of the leading visionaries and participants in veteran unemployment and to begin the construction of a viable and permanent pathway to full employment for US veterans. This book is a forum of chapters authored by Americans dedicated to this end.

We care about US veterans because many of them are the most extraordinary men and women that our country possesses. We also care about them and work tirelessly on their behalf because they are crucial to the endurance of our American civilization. Maintaining their morale is of paramount importance! The 1,000-year world domination of Rome ended when its citizens no longer would enter the military because there were no benefits or employment safety net for them when their term of service ended. Instead, Roman veterans frequently became paupers. Hence, Rome had to rely on mercenaries that eventually turned on them and destroyed their empire. It is national suicide for any country that disrespects and disregards those valiant citizens who defend it.

An unfortunate reality of the world since the dawn of history is that we must defend ourselves from each other. We have police, judges, political representatives and state militias to protect and defend us within our borders. And we have multiple US military bases filled with Marines and sailors and soldiers and airmen all across the country that provides us a national fortress against attack. Without such citizens we would quickly fall into anarchy, and be conquered and consumed by another culture and people. The light with which God has blessed our country and that has been a beacon to the world for over 235 years would be extinguished.

In order to create 'a more perfect union' and to ensure our country's continuance, it is time to construct a better support mechanism for those citizens that offer their bodies as weapons of war in our defense.

From having served US veterans and their families for many years, I can tell you many personal stories of my association with them that poignantly represents their particular patriotic passion and value. However, to offer a more comprehensive solution, I have collected a host of US veterans to assist me.

Authors from every branch of our military have contributed, both men and women. These are US veterans who have successfully reintegrated into civilian society from the 'other world' of the US military. They share their personal experiences and trials in finding employment, creating income, and establishing a secure foundation for themselves and their families. But these particular US veterans are also still devoted to serving other members of our military. Although they are no longer on active duty, they have chosen to continue serving by turning and helping others leaving the military to avoid the hardships and struggles they and others have gone through. They are walking point for their military brothers and sisters.

Our united purpose is to present answers to US veteran unemployment. Our intent is to assist those in need of immediate solutions and to prepare a passage for future veterans. Each of our authors is convinced that it is our national responsibility to provide this successful pathway back into the civilian world for citizens that serve in our military.

Congress on occasion passes new bills to support veterans, especially during and following wars in which we engage and suffer severe and numerous causalities. The funding allotted by these bills is administered almost solely by the Veterans Administration (VA). And the people paid by the VA to administer these government financed programs for the large part are dedicated to providing the best assistance as possible. But the VA is a bureaucracy, and as such is limited by its own size and costs to rapidly deploy its resources where needed. So it is necessary for US companies, organizations and citizens to stand in the gaps. We cannot relegate the entire responsibility of caring for these men and women to our government. We all must share in fulfilling this national obligation.

There are a variety of needs that veterans have, especially if they served actively in combat or if they were harmed physically or psychologically. But for every one of them the major objective is to stand on their own two feet (or prosthetics) and to be able to support themselves and their families financially. This is the foundation veterans must have in order to address other issues and to once again participate as productive civilians and to pursue the prosperity and happiness available to all Americans.

An American Crisis: Veterans' Unemployment provides a variety of answers for US veterans and our nation. It is our attempt to stimulate more discussion and thought about this vital issue. But more importantly, it contains real-life solutions to be acted upon right now.

This is not a book just for US veterans. Every American needs to participate—from students to senior citizens—in order for our nation to maximize the utilization and benefits of this particularly valuable national resource: US veterans. We all must do our part.

Within these pages you will be able to hear the hearts and souls of the men and women who dare to put themselves in harm's way for our sakes. But nothing can replace meeting and getting to know your local US veterans personally.

Recently, I met a Navy corpsman who was returning to combat for his 7th deployment. I asked if he was frightened that his luck was running out. "Sir," he responded, "my family came to this country from the Philippines. They knew no-one, had nothing, and could not speak the language when they got here. Since then, my mother and father have built a business that has made it possible for them to raise 7 children. They have earned several million dollars and have put all of their children through college and provided for their grandchildren to do so too. I am the exception, because I joined the military instead. And there is nothing else in my life that I want to do, and nothing that is more important. America has given my family everything we have. I love my country. And if my time is up, I have no regrets. I keep US Marines alive! I make sure that their time isn't up. And so I have told my family and friends not to lament my death if that should come. I will gladly give my life for this country that has already given me and mine so much!"

So this is the question: When US veterans like this corpsman return home and leave the military, can we permit them to be unemployed and have their families sink into poverty? Or do they deserve a better break?

The Americans that enlisted to fight in Iraq and Afghanistan, as well as all other US veterans, should be held in highest esteem. The men and women who choose to fight wars on our behalf do so with tremendous excitement and patriotic pride. It gives their lives purpose and direction. And they are eager to train and become professional warriors in order to defend us from our enemies. But their choice to do so is also very difficult and requires complete commitment. They must put their military responsibilities ahead of family, friends and self. They are often sent to sea or to bases in foreign countries for months and years.

When these veterans return and re-enter our civilian world they stand out. They are mature beyond their years. And they anticipate an opportunity to use their US military education and experience to better America and to build a future for themselves and their families. But when they are prevented from achieving their employment or entrepreneurial visions due to a lack of concern and willingness from those for whom they sacrificed so much, it is hurtful and disillusioning.

Veterans really do not expect anything more than the opportunity to give it their all and to succeed. They are particularly focused and driven individuals. However, they need some assistance in restarting their civilian lives. And that begins with our respecting their stalwart service to us. This should also extend to their spouses who provide exceptional support during those military years. And it is my conviction that most Americans do possess sincere, patriotic concern for them.

In the armed forces, veterans have responsibilities and duties to perform every day. Leaving the military and having no job to take the place of that work becomes debilitating if it continues for very long. Inertia is not healthy for anyone; but, it is particularly harmful to those whose way of life has been purposeful activity. Our veterans that actually experience live-fire combats are especially susceptible. A critical part of their recovery process is to stay busy. This is even more important for those who have been seriously wounded and gone through rehabilitation.

But since the founding of our nation no established pathway for veterans to reintegrate quickly into civilian society has been created. There are a variety of programs and efforts by the VA and nonprofit organizations and even veteran-hiring programs instituted by businesses. But far too many US veterans never find a way back into the world they left: our world.

It is our hope that this book will help US veterans, and inspire all Americans to take great pride in these courageous citizens. But that would not be enough. This book must also light a fire within you to act. So join your voice with ours, declare your support for our troops publicly, and encourage others to read this book.

Every brick in a building is essential to its strength and permanence. Let's all do our part to secure America's future!

1: The HirePatriots Story

MARK BAIRD

My name is Mark Baird. I am the author of this book and the founder of HirePatriots.com and its 501(c)(3) Patriotic Hearts. My mission, calling, and purpose in life is and has been to serve US veterans and their families. My particular goal is to enhance the respect, honor, support, and appreciation given to these exceptional US citizens.

I, along with 23 other contributing writers, formed a collaborative effort to solve this problem. An Army general, an Army colonel, the president of VetJobs, a chaplain, a Congressional Medal of Merit recipient, a sergeant major, a wounded warrior, a military spouse, a Fortune 500 VP, and others contribute insightful and poignant chapters with the purpose of getting veterans back to work expediently, or to assist them in becoming successful entrepreneurs. Contributing authors from every branch of our military have provided material for this book.

I grew up in a particularly patriotic period of American history. We had just won World War II and were considered the greatest country and military power on Earth. General Eisenhower, the recent commander in chief of European Allied Forces, was the US President. He was followed by another war hero, John F. Kennedy. Audie Murphy, the highest decorated veteran in World War II, was a movie star. I pledged allegiance to the flag of the US every morning at school and sang songs about America and patriotism. There was even a Bible reading time. And at the local drive-in, before every movie, they showed a family kneeling in prayer with these words: "The family that prays together stays together."

My father was a submariner during WWII. He had an unlocked trunk in the garage, and I would often lift the big pirate's chest-like lid and peer in. There was a bayonet, medals, a Japanese flag, ribbons, pictures—a history of my father I never heard anything about. It fascinated me.

Then there was my uncle Jake. He was a square jawed, ruddy faced Marine, just like in the recruiting posters. He had a big smile, big shoulders, a big laugh, and was full of life. If ever there was a "man's man," that is what he was to me then and still is now.

Jake had stormed a dozen beaches in the South Pacific. He was a sergeant and led a platoon. I listened to him recount what seemed to be every step of his military career whenever all the relatives got together. After dinner, the men would go into the den and close the door while the women cleaned up in the kitchen. I got to go with the men: my grandfather, a Marine; my other uncle, a fighter pilot; Jake; my dad and me. Jake liked to talk, and he had great stories, so we sat entranced and listened. When we all met at Jake's, which we frequently did, I would end up laced with his war souvenirs: necklaces of teeth and ears taken from the enemy. So many dead bodies piled up in front of his 'hole in the sand' that he did this to pass the time, since it was impossible to sleep.

Jake saw half of his own boys killed every time they stormed a beach. And he stormed a dozen beaches. Imagine being given forty 18 to 19-year-old boys and leading them through deep surf towards an enemy beach with 500 hundred machine guns! And seeing at least half of them die horribly before you even get to the sand! And then you get replacements and it happens all over again and again and again...

Like almost all US veterans, Jake was God fearing and moral man. The necklaces were a disconnect; but, understandably so.

Jake was a real life John Wayne to me, an American hero. "If only I could grow up and be like him," I said to myself every time I saw him

In 1968, when the Vietnam War was about to explode with the Tet Offensive, I got my chance. I was out of high school, so I joined the US Marines. But to my grave disappointment, they found that I had a rare blood type that made me ineligible for service. However, years later, after I had graduated from college, married and had a child, I joined the Marines again to become an infantry officer. (This was before computers, and no-one discovered that I was actually listed as "4-F.") They scheduled me to go to the East Coast and enter Officer Candidate School at Quantico. But destiny had a different plan. I got kicked in the groin while playing soccer, went to the hospital for surgery, had an infection transmitted to me in a blood transfusion, and was deemed unfit for military service again. I am sorry, Jake. Despite all my efforts, it just was not God's will.

After finishing at Westmont College, a Christian institution, I was a pastor at a storefront church in Isla Vista, the student community for UC Santa Barbara. It was a time of student unrest and demonstrations against the Vietnam War. In Isla Vista, the students went on a rampage and burned many buildings, including the Bank of America. The buildings on both sides of my little church were destroyed, but our windows and doors were left totally unmolested. When a huge, unruly crowd, throwing rocks through all the store front windows, came to our church a loud clear voice came from somewhere out of the din of rioting: "No, not them. Leave them alone!" They did. And I am still convinced that it was an angel who spoke.

Being a new pastor, I decided to visit all 20,000 student residences in Isla Vista and meet my neighbors, share the Gospel, and see if they would fellowship at my church. This effort changed my life in an unexpected way. About every hundred doors that opened to my knock were recent Vietnam veterans. Some had been discharged based on a military assessment of their being psychologically unfit because of the severity of their combat trauma.

Their doors opened slowly and revealed an atmosphere of darkness, oppression and horror. I did not have any idea what these war veterans had experienced. They were my age and living in a nightmare that consumed their lives. They often had threatening countenances filled with anger and disdain. They knew about a reality of humanity that I had never experienced, and they had no respect for my opinions about God and eternal life because I had not seen what they had.

I began attending Vietnam Veterans Association meetings and events to try to understand. I ended up in a camouflaged tent representing Point Man Ministries at their veteran gatherings. Veterans would come inside my tent if they wanted prayer. But I was unprepared for their confessions. Indeed, I heard stories about Hell on earth. And metaphorically, these veterans were Hell's burn victims.

I prayed for every one of them. Oftentimes I still do. But each one bared their soul to me and burdened my heart to breaking. I realized I had to do more.

Being a pastor did not pay my family's bills, so I began a business. I bought a homemade carpet cleaner in the garage of the guy who later developed Rug Doctor and went to work. My business grew quickly and created the necessity for me to train and hire employees. By that time I had moved south next to two Marine bases, El Toro and Tustin. I recruited those Marines to work with me, which gave them a way to make money and make their lives a bit easier. This made me happy. And I knew that the military gave them experience in making and keeping things exceptionally clean.

The Vietnam War was over by then, so I had a mixture of war veterans and civilians. There was a major and noticeable difference. The US Marines, especially the Vietnam veterans, had maturity, confidence and drive that was unlike anyone I had hired before.

The Marines that began cleaning banks and real estate and insurance offices for me did such meticulous work and were so respectful to my clients that soon I began to receive compliments and referrals. Their professional work ethic and attitudes caused my business to explode. Within two years my small town business covered the entire state. I literally had more new client requests than I could handle.

I began selecting my best US veteran employees and putting them in charge of regional areas. They were in charge of supervising cleaning crews and providing customer service for my clients within those regions. And for the entrepreneurial minded I made this offer: they could buy the accounts under their charge from me and begin their own business maintenance company.

This was a good idea for several reasons. These US veterans were excellent leaders and respected and liked by those they supervised. They took charge and were trusted by my clients. They paid me 20% of their net profits for a year, and then those clients became their own new business. Some of these veteran entrepreneurs went on to become building maintenance millionaires. They exceeded anything I was able to do.

I also met a lot of Marines during the start of Saddleback Church: The megachurch created by Rick Warren, author of the bestseller *A Purpose Driven Life*. I began attending the church's Vietnam veterans meetings. The veteran who took me there was Greg E., a three-tour

Vietnam War Army veteran. He was well over six feet tall and had a prophet's beard.

Greg had lived in trash dumpsters since his honorable discharge in 1973. He lived for just one reason when he returned 'home' to the States: to stay drunk. The police knew Greg well. As a courtesy, every Christmas they would arrest Greg so that he could get medical attention and a good meal in the county jail. But in 1990 Greg had a life-changing experience.

On Christmas Day, 1990, Greg, a decorated Vietnam War veteran, was arrested by the Tustin Police Department. They knew he was harmless. Sometimes he broke into abandoned buildings, urinated in parks or fell asleep on bus benches. But he always showed the police respect and never caused any trouble when they took him into custody.

They took Greg to the Orange County Jail. Greg was grateful. He always looked forward to this annual Christmas arrest. He got to see a doctor and dentist, and get a shower, a cot, blankets and a warm meal.

The jail doctor knew Greg from frequent visits over the years. The doctor had been monitoring Greg's liver. This year he gave Greg the news that the doctor had known was inevitable. Greg told me that this is what he was told: "Greg, you are going to die soon. Your liver is destroyed. I am going to have the Sheriff release you. Go and get a bottle and then have your last drink. You probably won't live through the week."

Later that day, Greg found an abandoned gas station and broke a window to get inside. He had panhandled for enough money to buy a fifth of vodka. But as he sat on the floor, opened the metal cap and lifted the alcohol to his lips, Greg had a vision. He told me that he suddenly saw Jesus Christ appear in the dilapidated station with him. Jesus held out an arm. "Take my hand. I will save your life and use you to save the lives of many others." Greg never drank that bottle.

And so when I first met Greg, he was not the person I have just described. He was a supernova! His countenance was brilliant. He was the embodiment of God's love and joy.

Greg also saved me. My pastoring of Vietnam veterans and the numerous nightmarish stories—which were told in exact detail—affected me beyond my ability to cope. I began dreaming their nightmares. Their realities became mine too. I got lost in a maze of hellish memories. I began experiencing vicarious post-traumatic stress disorder (PTSD). This resulted in me publishing a poem about my pseudo-reality in the local newspaper. Greg read it and somehow found me.

I heard several loud knocks on my apartment door. The depression I was experiencing unwisely led me to begin drinking from morning to night. I opened to the brilliant light of the sun flooding in and the outlined figure of a large being on the threshold of my home. I thought Greg was an angel that had come to take me to heaven.

"Did you write this poem?" he asked abruptly, holding out a copy he had cut from the newspaper. I recognized the first line and nodded agreement. The next thing I knew, Greg grabbed me by the arm and was pulling me down the stairs. He took me straight to an Alcoholics Anonymous (AA) meeting and became my sobriety sponsor.

Greg was a transformed person. He had been completely sober ever since Jesus appeared to him. He now was an elder in a local recovery church and a regular preacher at the county rescue mission. Greg was also the founder and leader of the Saddleback Church veterans group. Every year he found enough funding to take Vietnam veterans who were having difficulty reintegrating to civilian life after the trauma of Vietnam back to the bases at which they were stationed 'in country.' This was amazingly therapeutic for them.

One of the Vietnam veterans that went on these trips had been blown up on his third day in Vietnam. Both of his legs and an arm were blown off and he lost an eye. He was 18 years old when it happened, but he was 40 when Greg took this US veteran back to the outskirts of the village where this had occurred.

Of course, for the last 22 years this Army veteran had lived in a motorized wheelchair. When they showed up at the remote village, the sight of this elaborate wheelchair attracted a lot of attention. An elderly woman came up and began asking questions. Then she went to her hooch and returned with a US Army helmet. It had that veteran's name still visible on it. She had recovered it after the explosion that ripped his truck apart and used it as a flower planter in her home since that fateful day.

That veteran and this former enemy hugged and cried. They were both sincerely sorry for the suffering each had caused to the other and their loved ones.

Greg was not a public speaker. He could talk forever with veterans, alcoholics and substance abusers one-on-one. But Greg was nervous when he had to get on stage. I had been a preacher for many years, so I was comfortable speaking in front of groups. Greg and I formed a bond.

We traveled together from here to there sharing Greg's testimony and my calls to repentance and a new life.

The Assemblies of God Church sponsored Greg as a speaker and sent him across America to their churches and rallies. They even gave Greg a scholarship to earn a master's degree in theology at Vanguard University, their college in southern California.

Greg and I were as close as any brothers have ever been. Then, in 2004, two Vietnamese young adults who were members of a church Greg planted outside Saigon invited him to be the Master of Ceremonies at their Christian wedding. It was a secret event, because belief in Christ is punishable by imprisonment in that country. And so this celebration was held in the midst of a jungle to protect those who attended from prosecution.

Unexpectedly, as Greg was ministering on the temporary stage a thimble of alcohol was offered to him as part of the traditional Vietnamese ceremony. He paused for a moment. He had not tasted any alcohol for more than a decade. But he decided not to interrupt the wedding and drank the very small amount.

In AA it is taught that alcoholism is a 'progressive disease.' So although Greg had not tasted any alcohol for years, that simple thimble released a generation of unsatisfied desire. That night, after the Christian wedding, Greg went into Saigon. He bought alcohol. Then he purchased drugs. Then he purchased prostitutes. Greg died a few months later from a massive overdose. There was no way I could stop him. The Vietnam War finally caught up and killed him.

A few months before this occurred, Greg introduced me and my wife to a wealthy Vietnam veteran who was the sole sponsor of a Vietnam veterans' recovery center. The owner asked Greg if he knew of a pastor who would hold services for the 25 men it housed full-time. Soon afterwards, my wife and I were holding Sunday services and counseling during other days of the week. By 'counseling,' I really mean 'listening.'

We quickly learned that we were strangers in a strange land. We were not one of them and we never would be. Even a suggestive hint from us of what they should or should not do (drinking, drugs, violence, etc.) was immediately obvious as being the wrong way to go. Instead, I preached about God's forgiveness and love. I shared about how their service and sacrifices mirrored the sacrifices and attitude of Christ. I praised them and told them of the glory and honor their trails had earned them. I encouraged them, and implored them to turn their bad experiences into positive channels, like helping other veterans.

I admitted to them that my wife Tori and I knew nothing about the experiences and losses they suffered. But like a doctor and a nurse in a hospital, my wife and I were there to listen and to offer a healing of their psyche, heart and soul, if they wanted it.

We remained at that facility for many months. One by one, the US veteran residents who lived and worked there when we came in felt ready to move on. They left our facility with our hugs and prayers. Then it was time for other ministers to take our places and to be used by God in this difficult but precious calling.

At this time, my wife's mother had fallen into the final dementia stage of Alzheimer's. She needed constant supervision and care. We sold all that we had and purchased outright a three bedroom, two bath home so that we and Tori's mom could live together. This house was right outside the fence that encircled the Camp Pendleton Marine Corps base. Taking care of my wife's mother was another ministry God wanted us to do. This time it was my wife who took the lead. My appreciation, respect and love for Tori grew beyond what I ever imagined as I watched her patiently and tirelessly care for her mother's every need. One day, her mom fell and broke her hip. "Annie" slipped quickly after that and passed away in her bed in our home.

Now here is the starting point of a miracle that has benefited thousands of US veterans and their families, as well as transformed my life and Tori's. It has helped just as many US civilians too. Since this event, it has been as if Tori and I have fallen into a fast-flowing river. Its current has taken control of our destiny.

HirePatriots.com

Where we chose to buy a home, US Marines lived all about us. And everywhere we went in town, we saw dozens more. I relished this. I love the United States Marine Corps. Whenever my wife and I took walks, pushing her mom in her wheelchair, we always said hello to every Marine we saw. Within a few weeks, they knew who we were and greeted us by name. It was delightful being their neighbors and friends.

So one day, we were pleased to answer the door and to see a Marine in fatigues whom we had not seen before. "Sir," he said, standing straight but slightly off center due to injuries, "I need your help." Hearing those words from an injured US Marine, standing on my very doorstep, still grips my heart and pushes tears out of my eyes.

"Sir, I just got home from Iraq maybe an hour ago. I discovered that my wife was laid off soon after I deployed. She had not let me know. I just found out when I got home that there was no electricity or heat in the house. Sir, I have two small children. I want them to be warm tonight. Is there any work that I can do for you around your home or yard so that I can earn enough to get my family's utilities turned back on today?"

My voice cracked as I replied. "Son," I answered as I shook his hand, "please let me just give you the money you need. It is the very least I can do for what you have already done for me." But he adamantly refused. His honor would not abide it.

That stalwart man, this United States Marine, worked for me for five hours doing whatever I asked. He cleaned my house. He repaired the timing on my carburetor. And he fixed my favorite chair that I was about to throw out. I paid him $100. He got his utilities turned back on.

After that we took several thousand dollars from our savings and we paid for a website and job board to be built for local residents and businesses in case they might also want to hire a local Marine (or their spouse) to help them with chores, or as a new employee. We guessed that there might be a few more Marines who might need a way to earn some extra income to pay bills, etc. It was called HireMarines.com. It later became HirePatriots.

com when the Admiral of the Navy for the Southwest called and asked us to change the name of our job board so that his sailors could use the site to get jobs from it too. That site soon began receiving 10,000 visitors a week.

Now to be honest, this number of visitors did not show up all by themselves. It took a bit of leg work. My wife and I printed up business cards and fliers. We checked on all of the dates of Chamber of Commerce "sundowners" (events where businesses congregate to network) in the multiple cities within San Diego County. We attended these and shared with the dozens of business people at each about our free website. They loved it!

Soon, the people we met at these chamber events began posting jobs. They were overjoyed with the experience and we began receiving multiple emails every day about how extremely pleased they were with the veterans they hired. Everyone thanked us profusely for creating this opportunity to hire and to get to meet and know the Marines and sailors we all saw every day in our communities. The US armed service members and their spouses in San Diego were overjoyed too.

We contacted every local newspaper, TV, and radio news affiliate and told them our story and sent them the replies we received from our site's users. Soon, they began showing up at our house with photographers, cameras, and reporters. Almost overnight we were recognized wherever we went. Our truck had a HirePatriots banner on both doors and the back. When we went to the store, there often were veterans and their families waiting at our vehicle after we shopped in order to thank us. They hugged us and told us what a "lifesaver" our simple job board had been to them. Their appreciation has been enough for us to dedicate the rest of our lives and all that we have to this mission. Serving them has been the centerpiece and the fulfillment of our lives since.

In 2008, the local newspaper, serving the communities around Camp Pendleton, declared us the number one news story of the year. The chamber gave us their "Extra Mile" award. The county supervisor, Bill Horn, a former US Marine, gave us $25,000. Dick Cheney, the US Vice President, called and asked if he could have a picture taken with us. President Bush gave us the Congressional Medal of Merit. The National Chairman of the Republican Party made us Honorary Chairmen of the California Economic Council. A colonel from the Pentagon made a video about HirePatriots. We were on the most popular radio show in San Diego, the Roger Hedgecock Show, every week for about 20 minutes. The TV news stations kept having us on to tell more of the heartwarming stories created by the people who hired US veterans on our website. FOX National Business News interviewed us on Veterans Day. 400 San Diego businesses and 1,500 executives held a dinner for us and presented us with the county's most significant business award, The LEAD Award's "Visionary Trophy" for creating economic development. And HirePatriots has been featured in *PEOPLE* Magazine as "Heroes Among Us" in their April 1, 2013 issue. And their PEOPLE First initiative has selected us as their charity of choice.

We were known and beloved by generals, admirals, enlisted ranks, veterans, military spouses, CEOs, entertainment personalities, news producers, newspaper editors, residents, senior citizens, and by everyone else. Both political parties contacted me to run for office. Neither my wife nor I sought after nor in any way expected such a response. We were overwhelmed. All of the ideas and plans that we had thought would take us to the end of our lives completely changed. It was a seismic shift, equal to the state of California having an earthquake and ending up between the continent and Hawaii.

Job Fairs

But Tori and I had to find a way to earn money. The life savings we had put away were decreasing rapidly. There were posters, flyers, business cards, bumper stickers, new phone bills, employees, advertising and website expenses that we had not considered. We created a plan to use the grant County Supervisor Bill Horn had given us to create military job fairs. It would help our local veterans, and it might get more companies to purchase banners from our website and create enough income to keep us going.

We had never held a job fair before. We just did it. US veterans are more accustomed to this. They have always told me that the key to survival is to "adapt and overcome." We attended a few job fairs, took a guess at how it was done, and then gave it our best try. Here is a motto I learned growing up: necessity is the mother of invention. We applied it.

We had difficulty at first getting permission to host a job fair on Camp Pendleton. It is always safer to say no than yes in the military. But I went to the local Chamber president, who played golf with all of the top brass on the base. He spoke with the commanding general and we were given permission.

It is very labor intensive to host a job fair. Besides reserving the hall, the tables, the tablecloths, the coffee, and all of the basics, most importantly we had to get companies and veterans to attend. We stayed on the phones all day every day for two months. We spoke with and left messages for over a thousand HR people.

We acquired 132 companies with job openings to fill to attend our first event. All of these companies also paid to have a presence on our website, so we were able to turn a little profit.

The day after our first job fair on the base there was a picture of a Marine paraplegic coming out of our job fair. She was a captain who was blown up in Iraq. Her severe injuries caused her to stay in a coma for months. When she awoke, she discovered that the doctors delivered her firstborn child during the time that she was unconscious. Unfortunately, she also discovered that her husband, also a Marine, had been killed in Afghanistan. She discovered she was a new mom and a widow in one day. I remember seeing her coming into the job fair. She was in a motorized wheelchair and had her baby in her arms. She looked very distraught. But the picture on the front page of the *North County Times* the next day showed a happy, beaming woman. She was holding up several job offers as she left our event. The quote said that she went in thinking that her "life was over" and she had no idea how she would support herself and her child. But now she knew that companies still wanted her and life looked a lot better. She believed that she just might make it after all. That one Marine captain made all of our hard work and effort completely worthwhile.

After a couple of hiring events we noticed that many of our veteran job seekers were not talking to any recruiters. They would just gather info and leave. We then began enlisting the help of volunteers, mostly from those posting chores on our site. These citizens, mostly senior citizen ladies, met the job seekers at the door. They would take them in hand and lead them into the fair. While doing so, they would ask what kind of job they hoped for. Then they would take them to the appropriate recruiter and introduce them by name. From then on we did not see any more quick exits. Thank you, dear ladies!

After that, we held eleven more job fairs. But as our efforts to help veterans increased with new programs, the time consumption, cost and risk of hosting these events became overwhelming. However, we have been honored by having a retired general recently join HirePatriots. He is about to host two day-long hiring events: "Warriors to the Workforce." He already has donations from companies that have pledged to support his effort and attend. We have made his new job fair initiative a program of Patriotic Hearts, HirePatriots' 501(c)(3) nonprofit. Several job fairs are already planned this year, and more may be on the schedule soon.

Military Marriage Retreats

An article that appeared in the local newspaper claimed that the "multiple deployed enlisted rank marriages" were taking a huge toll. It claimed the divorce rate was as high as 90% for that group on Camp Pendleton Marine Base. The article said the wives on Camp Pendleton referred to the numbers of marriages that were breaking up as "the Plague." This broke our hearts to read.

We knew many Marine wives. We worked with the family readiness officers (FRO) at Camp Pendleton. They were dear military wives who loved and supported their Marines with all of their hearts and souls.

We had to take action. Something had to be done. These dear families did not deserve this. But the stress, separation and hurt feelings created by military life and compounded by two wars and months or years of not seeing each other created severe misunderstandings and distance when troops returned home. These patriotic young couples and citizens did not know how to deal with their mixed-up emotions. They did not know how to reconnect and reignite their romance and love. That frustration was causing their families to split up despite their mutual love.

I wrote to San Diego supervisor Bill Horn again. Each county supervisor is given a yearly stipend to grant to people and organizations that they feel help San Diego be a better place. I told supervisor Horn about what I had read and asked if he could help us to host a marriage retreat for the veterans in San Diego. He responded with $20,000!

Just as we had never held a job fair before, we had never hosted a marriage retreat either. Once again, we were "flying blind." But once again, *necessity* was compelling us to do so.

Across the street from the main entrance to Camp Pendleton is a beautiful gem of a boat harbor. At its very tip, jutting out towards the Pacific Ocean is a wonderful luxury resort, Marina Inn Suites. We rented 22 amorous suites facing the harbor or ocean. Each was a richly furnished suite that had a separate bedroom with a canopy bed, kitchen and hot tub. We placed a romantic gift basket on each bed and strewed rose petals all over the covers and floor.

Then we made reservations at the fine restaurants in the harbor. Everyone we asked was glad to participate. They gave us discounts when they could and greeted our veteran couples with great cordiality when we arrived.

It was easy to enlist couples. Our website, HirePatriots.com, had 10,000 military members a week from San Diego visiting it. Within a few days the marriage retreat was filled. We even had two military couples from the East Coast sign up to attend.

Military members who have been in combat feel particularly hardened and are difficult to get to come to a retreat for help with their marriages. We asked everyone for three positive confirmations that they were definitely attending the retreat. And we made a call to everyone the evening before the retreat to get final confirmations. Nevertheless the next day some of the veteran couples who confirmed did not show up.

But 16 combat experienced veteran couples did show up. On the first evening, as couples arrived and greeted us, the wives were open and vocalized their feelings first. Some could not resist expressing the hurt and anger they felt. Their military husbands, on the other hand, were mostly like emotionless blocks of ice.

It is sometimes challenging to get the couples in the right frame of mind for these retreats. And since then we have found a simple way to make that happen.

There is enough room for all of our couples to fit into our master suite at this Inn. Most sit on the floor. The husbands lean against a wall, and because of limited space the wives naturally sit in front of their husbands and rest against their chests. The husbands respond by putting their arms around their wives. For some couples, this might be the first time that they have been this close since returning from combat. It is like watching ice melt on a sunny day. Tears begin to flow.

We spend Friday, Saturday and Sunday morning watching the *Love & Respect* videos and discussing each. We believe love best motivates a woman and respect most powerfully motivates a man. The narrators in the DVDs are a Godly couple who have been married for over thirty years. Their personal testimony and teaching, particularly about the innate need for respect, resonates well with veterans.

Local veteran groups, mostly retired people, volunteer to help us. They bring delicious home cooked meals. Then they sit and talk with the young troops. Sometimes we get World War II veterans who have been married for more than 60 years. Thank God for their enduring affection and wisdom. It is so encouraging and convincing.

For the conclusion of our retreats, we present each couple with a collage of pictures taken of them during the retreat. We frame the pictures. In the middle of the frame, surrounded by all the pictures, is a big picture that we take of them cutting a wedding cake beneath a flowered bower and with the ocean in the background. On the back of that picture is our personal contact info. Whenever these couples have a bad fight or difficulty, they are to take down the picture and call us. In eight years, not one couple has split up. They are all still married and together. I do not state this to praise ourselves. But I think we have proven that at least the majority of endangered military marriages and families can be saved. It requires small peer groups. It cannot happen nearly as effectively in large auditoriums.

The US military chaplains have received many millions to host marriage retreats. We have attended some. They do their best. They rent out fabulous hotels we could never afford, they bring in a hundred couples from nearby bases, and they run an excellent government sponsored video seminar of the basic truths of successful marriages. But their effectiveness does not come close to using our historically proven method of recovery: <u>Let people who have witnessed the same trauma heal each other.</u>

No doubt about it, HirePatriots was having a tremendous effect upon veterans in San Diego County. But as these military members would get transferred to other bases in the country, we would hear from them. "Hey, where is HirePatriots in my area? I need to earn some extra money!" Their need created the necessity for us to create a plan for expanding across the country in order to serve veterans everywhere as we were doing in San Diego.

Cause Marketing

Companies that wanted to hire veterans purchased banners on our website. We had over a hundred of their emblems scrolling on HirePatriots, but we really did not have any more of a relationship with these companies after that. Of course, the hope and goal of these businesses was to have veterans click their banners, go to their webpage, find the jobs and apply for them. And that worked sometimes, but not often enough to fill all of these companies' positions. They needed banners on a lot of websites in order to get enough clicks from job-seeking veterans.

Then one day the thought occurred to me, "What if they had their own customized HirePatriots website and job board?" Ours was now getting visited by 40,000 veterans a month. What if they could get that many too? They probably would be able to fill all of their jobs.

I realized this could also provide a solution to our own dilemma. If we could select a business in each location that is near an active US military base to represent us with their own HirePatriots site and job board, then we could help veterans all across America. And we would not have to disappoint our local military who get restationed to other parts of the country.

I wrote up our *Steps to Success*. This is a detailed account of what we did in San Diego to make our site so popular. It plainly lays out the path to follow in order to spread the news and to regularly get on TV, radio and press. And it explains how to turn the residents who post jobs into avid volunteers. In other words, this document tells how to become the most popular business in your region, and especially well known by every veteran in your area.

So we began contacting businesses that were located near US military installations all across America. We offered them a customized

HirePatriots website, job board and blog. Anyone who came to their site to post or to search jobs would find out all about their business. Plus, they would have the contact information for all of those job seekers, because to use our site all users must create an account and register. Hence, they could recruit from within their own database and get tremendous media advertising for free, and save many thousands of dollars each year. What a deal! Better than that, they would also be offering essential support to the US veterans and their families within their network.

Soon, our corporate supporters were much more than advertisers. They were HirePatriots regional and local leaders. They had their own HirePatriots web address. We were working together synergistically. We were spreading the news about them, and they were spreading the news about us. It was a hand in hand relationship. We promoted them through our website with banners, blog posts and links to their own HirePatriots site. They spoke on TV, radio, and at local clubs and conventions about HirePatriots, while passing out fliers with a link to their own HirePatriots URL. They became famous in their area, and so did we. Most importantly, the more they followed our steps, the more veterans found out about HirePatriots' job openings and were hired.

It was a synergistic relationship. They solved their recruiting problems at a fraction of what they were spending before. They also sold more products as their reputation and fame grew. And we had a spokesperson and representative who was going around that region spreading the word about HirePatriots.

Cause Marketing Examples

If Wally from Wally's Widgets buys advertising on a TV or radio station, his message will basically be this: "Hi everybody, if you need widgets come to WallyWidgets.com and buy yours today!" He may also mention how much better his widgets are than his competitors' and offer a special deal. There are a million pitches like this in the media every day. That is why TV remotes have fast forward.

But instead, what if Wally asked the TV station if he could come on not on his behalf, but on behalf of the local active duty troops, veterans and their spouses? If he tells them that he has a free job board for the communities within that region to help veterans find jobs or earn extra money by helping residents, they will put him on for free. And what will these tens of thousands people see when they go to his site to post and search? They will see everything that has to do with Wally's Widgets. Plus they will leave their contact information for his newsletter.

Wally will definitely sell more widgets, and he will not have to pay to advertise. He will be making a lot more money. At the same time, he will be stimulating the economy in his area by getting thousands of veterans hired, for a day or for a career. He will be providing a way for local citizens to support their troops in a practical and meaningful way. Wally will be known and loved as an exemplary patriot, and that will be good for his business too.

Recently, we had a veteran-owned franchise join us. A few days later, I put a key executive of that company on the radio with me. He got to introduce that franchise as a new HirePatriots leader in his state, and to introduce himself and share about their turnkey opportunity. We received a call a few days later. That radio interview resulted in him getting more franchise requests in a week than he had ever had before.

Here is the comment that company's development director wrote on my LinkedIn page: "I recommend Mark and the HirePatriots higher cause marketing system with no reservations. Mark is the rarest of animals, an honest person that cares about and delivers results. Mark has been outstanding! It's been a pleasure working with and getting to know him both personally and professionally."

A trucking school became a member. They were frustrated because a nearby base allowed a competitor to bring their truck into the base and recruit for their school, but they would not let this trucking company do so. They asked how being a HirePatriots member might help their case.

We put one of their instructors on a couple of radio and TV stations in that area when that base was about to hold a big job fair. He promoted the fair and encouraged companies and veterans to attend. And of course, he also talked about posting jobs on HirePatriots. It was a huge success. The base held the biggest and best job fair in its history—and the competitor's truck was replaced with our HirePatriots member's truck. It also resulted in 600 jobs getting posted on their HirePatriots site from the residents and businesses that saw their representative on the news.

A retired colonel's business joined us in Colorado. A ranger whose injuries forced him out of the Army got a one-day job off of his site. He helped this wealthy man set up for a big party, and then stayed and served. Later, he cleaned up when the guests left. He earned $300 for that night's work. But it gets better!

Once all of the work was done, the colonel had a cup of coffee with this ranger. He had watched him work all day and night and was impressed. He asked the veteran questions and was even more impressed. When that soldier left for home, he was that man's new operations director for the company he owned, at a starting salary of $65,000.

HirePatriots' Vision

I am driven by this mission: to create a nationwide employment safety net for veterans and their spouses. I hope the readers of this book will embrace this dream as their own and participate in making it happen. What if every US region had their own HirePatriots job board? Then every willing and able US veteran would be able to work and earn money every day. I believe that they have earned it and that they deserve it. And I am sure you agree.

About the Author

Mark and Tori Baird are devoted to helping US veterans and their families in every way within their means. As of 2013, they are trying to obtain a donated RV with which to spend their lives traversing the USA and spreading HirePatriots into every region, county and town. If you have a good RV to donate, or if you want to become a HirePatriots Leader, please contact them.

About HirePatriots

The other programs are the Vet-Entrepreneur Program, Military Job Fairs, Welcome Home Parties, Military Marriage Enrichment Retreats, Veteran Job Placement, Job Training. Veteran Job Placement, Job Training, Transitional Training, and Financial Wellness Seminars. And now we have created this book that provides important advice for US veterans, employers, and the U.S. citizens who honor them.

If you want to read a few comments from the people who use our website, visit www.hirepatriots.com/news-and-blogs/entry/what-people-say-about-hirepatriots-job-program.

And if you are a business that is interested in becoming a HirePatriots Leader in your location, here are our simple Ten Steps to Success: www.hirepatriots.com/news-and-blogs/entry/hirepatriots-steps-to-success-in-business.

Mark Baird
CEO, HirePatriots.com
Chairman, Patriotic Hearts
760-730-3734
mark@hirepatriots.com

People Magazine's Heroes Among Us
Past Chairman: CA Economic Council
Past Secretary: United Veteran Council

From President Bush: The Congressional Medal of Merit
From President Obama: President's Volunteer Service Medal

From San Diego: The Visionary Award for Creating Economic Development
From the Chamber of Commerce: The Extra Mile Award
From ABC TV: The Leadership Award

2: Building Your Corporate Military Recruiting Program

CRYSTAL D. DYER

The Why

Many people have asked me how I came to work in the field of US veteran employment. They ask why advocating for civilian job opportunities for every man and woman who has served in our nation's armed forces is my focus. Some have even been so bold as to ask whether or not the business model I created to achieve my mission has "staying power." I usually render them speechless by saying, "I sure hope not!"

They tend to stare at me, wondering if I am simple-minded and really committed to living the blonde stereotype. At that point, I'll usually laugh and say, "When my business model is no longer necessary, then I will have achieved my goal. The day that every willing and able US citizen who has worn the military uniform of our country and served with honor and distinction has a job, then I'll gladly find a new line of work!"

You see, my answer to all of those who ask me why I do what I do is quite simple. I am a veteran. I am a military spouse. My father and mother are veterans. It's not just a passion—I'm passionate about golf and great literature. This is about more than passion. It's personal!

I joined the U.S. Army Reserve right out of high school. Many people will tell you that joining the military service saved their life for one reason or another. I say it in the absolute most literal sense. As a "perfectly healthy" 18-year-old athlete heading off to college as a reservist, I had to undergo the standard physical for military service. That exam detected three tumors that led me to undergo surgery and treatment that I would otherwise never have sought. So the first thing the Army gave me was my future.

As a college student and reservist, I never considered volunteering for active duty service. I knew exactly where I wanted to go in life, and that journey ended with a law degree from Harvard. That was my plan until the morning of September 11, 2001, when I watched two planes crash into the Twin Towers, another fly into the Pentagon, and a fourth crash in a Pennsylvania field. It seemed impossible. The images on television were thousands of miles away on the East Coast. When my phone rang to inform me that my unit was being called up, it suddenly became real.

But the next phone call made this moment even more poignant. My high school coach called to let me know that my friend, a cross-country teammate, and one of the smartest, most generous people I'd ever known, needed help. The young man he was referring to was my first love. The coach told me my friend's father had been aboard one of the planes flown into the World Trade Center.

The images on the screen weren't unbelievable any longer. And I discovered something about myself that I didn't know before: the desire to help people in their time of need became paramount. The desire to protect my country from people who would seek to harm her changed my dreams of attending Harvard Law into something else entirely.

I enlisted for active duty service and spent the next chapter of my life serving in the Army's Chaplain Corps, not as a minister, but as an enlisted chaplain's assistant. The mission of the Chaplain Corps has always been to nurture the living, care for the wounded, and honor the dead. My desire to help others was completely fulfilled.

I derived great joy from ministry, and providing support and resources for soldiers and their families. Mentoring those soldiers was a privilege. And while serving at my first duty station, I met another chaplain's assistant who became my ultimate "battle buddy," my best friend and husband. We've been married nearly a decade. He has become the most incredible father and role model to our three little boys. So the second thing the Army gave me was a family: my dear husband and our beloved sons.

During my time on active duty, I was blessed to have worked with several incredible chaplains who taught me how to counsel and to develop the ability to really listen to others. They encouraged me to be an advocate for our soldiers, and they taught me how motivating it can be when someone empowers you to excel.

One chaplain in particular, with whom I was privileged to work for twice in my career, gave me the greatest gift imaginable. Aside from placing his faith in me, he gave me purpose. He introduced me to psychological tools, assessments and inventories that made it easier for one person to understand another. He encouraged me to become certified to teach using the same tools he did. He helped me find my voice as a speaker and as an instructor.

When the time came for me to decide on an advanced educational course of study, his encouragement led me right to Organizational Development. Years later, when I was wrestling with the decision to stay in or get out, it was that same chaplain who gave me a swift metaphorical kick on my backside by telling me that "the Army isn't going anywhere." So I took my education, my experience, and every last bit of courage I could muster and I took a leap of faith to become an entrepreneur. The third thing the Army gave me was a solid foundation of skills and the confidence to believe in myself.

Not long afterward, my first consulting client hired me to teach a very standard organizational development, team building and leadership workshop for his mid-level and executive managers. About halfway through the day, I was transitioning the group into building a team agreement when it became clear that they were having trouble deciding which course of action to take for each scenario. Without giving it a second thought, I grabbed a dry erase marker, drew a chart, and asked them what the possible courses of action were. I had them delineate the possible outcomes of each course of action and briefly give the perks and drawbacks of each choice. I placed all of the information into a "Ben Franklin" chart. By comparing the positives and negatives side by side, the most effective course of action became obvious. It worked like a charm. I put the group on a quick break and was taken by surprise when some of the workshop attendees began taking pictures of the chart with their phones.

The managing executive who hired me, along with a handful of his senior directors, approached and asked where I'd learned such a technique. I answered, simply and truthfully, "In the Army. It's just a simple version of the MDMP: Military Decision Making Process." Then the senior executive looked at me directly and said, "This is the first time I've ever seen this group agree on anything in less than three hours, so if that's what the Army teaches people, I need more people like that!"

I asked him why he didn't hire US veterans. The answer he gave me rocked me. "We don't know how or where to begin. Do you?"

So much for teaching leadership and team-building workshops! I immediately set to work assisting him in accomplishing his goal of hiring as many veterans as possible for his open positions. If there was a vacancy, my mission was to put a veteran or military spouse in it. If they weren't qualified, we found a way to get them the training they needed to be qualified later. It was such an incredible feeling.

In the blink of an eye I was doing what I loved best: taking care of soldiers and their spouses, and helping them to find a rewarding career. The only difference was the civilian work attire. From a military uniform to a business suit, my passion had discovered its purpose. Professional Coaching Consultants had a defined mission. We've been going ever since.

The How for Businesses

The first thing you need to know about building your corporate military recruiting program is that it is more than the "right thing" to do.

The purpose of each and every HR or talent acquisition department is to bring in the best talent available for the organization they serve. Corporate America is crying out for loyal and dedicated employees. Right now, companies are experiencing the highest turnover rates and replacement costs in our nation's history.

Some of my fellow organizational development consultants specialize in the field of employee retention and they will tell you all of the tips and tricks to finagle stronger commitments from your employees. They advocate for higher wages, better benefits, and even things like flex time. And don't get me wrong, these are all great things to offer your employees.

But consider this: The military doesn't offer any of the things these experts recommend. They offer a modest income, basic benefits, and there is no such thing as flex time. You're certainly not going to get rich while wearing the uniform and the military doesn't know the meaning of the word "overtime." Anytime is more appropriate. And with deployments to combat, you must consider the extended time away from family and friends and the stress one must overcome to function.

Plus, the US military has engaged in two wars since the attacks on September 11. Most service members are required to deploy on multiple rotations to combat zones, sometimes back-to-back. The US Armed Forces have managed to do this with an all-volunteer force. In 2012 alone, the Army met its recruiting goals by the end of the first quarter.

So with those glowing facts, why does the US military maintain such a high retention rate? The answer is twofold: *engagement and dedication.*

US military members are actively engaged in the accomplishment of their daily mission. No-one is without responsibilities, and no-one goes without leadership who maintain accountability. Each man and woman knows their job and does it daily, no questions asked. This level of engagement and leadership is seriously lacking in most corporate environments.

Service members are incredibly dedicated individuals. They were dedicated enough to surrender their personal freedoms to serve their country. They were trained to be focused on the mission at hand. They are dedicated to the man or woman on their left or right. A US veteran that has hung up the uniform of his or her branch of service, no matter whom they work for, are engaged and dedicated.

Recently, the Society for Human Resource Management (SHRM) conducted a study on the retention of veterans in civilian employment post-service. They concluded that veterans maintain a 90 percent retention rate at two years, nearly 30 percent higher than their nonveteran counterparts. They are also more likely to be engaged and invested in the organization's success. Just ask the CEO of Allied Barton Security. He has stated publicly that he'll hire a veteran every chance he gets. He says, "They show up early, go home late, and take care of their team without fail."

Along with these two vital qualities comes a list of attributes that make veterans (and military spouses) an obvious win for any employer. I agree that hiring veterans is the right thing to do, and I applaud any citizen or organization that acts on that motive alone. But let's be clear: Hiring US veterans is also an incredibly intelligent and business-savvy thing to do.

So what are the lessons we've learned by helping organizations all around the world hire our nation's veterans? Most of them are so simple they seem trivial to me. But my mind always drifts back to that training room where a group of executives were wowed by a simple chart plotting various courses of action. Yes, they are simple, but they are also simply necessary.

Lesson One: Pay Attention to Your People

I'm sure that every company out there that has a dedicated HR department will tell you that they pay attention to their people. How many employees do we have? How many diversity candidates are put forward for management opportunities? How many employees have suffered a work-related injury in the last twelve months? I guarantee that the head of HR could produce an answer to any one of these questions within 24 hours with very little room for error in their figures. Yet, when I asked a room full of 230-plus HR directors how many veterans and military spouses they have in their organizations, only one could give me a ballpark figure. The question was even met with multiple objections citing that to require employees to identify their veteran status could violate federal, state, and company privacy laws and regulations. The truth is that companies do not have to require their employees to identify themselves as veterans, because there are much better methods that promote voluntary participation. Here are just two that work brilliantly:

Tip #1: Write a Veterans Day Thank-You Letter.

All employees in any organization like to know that the "Big Kahuna" appreciates their time and talent. The next time Veterans Day rolls around, have your CEO, director, or a managing partner draft a letter that thanks every veteran and actively serving military member in the organization for their service to our country, the sacrifices they have made in the name of freedom, and just how proud they are to have such great Americans belong to the Company XYZ Family. Send it out via email to everyone, but keep a hard copy for every recipient.

I assure you that two things will happen very quickly. First, morale among your veteran employees will skyrocket. Everyone likes a pat on the back, especially one they aren't expecting. And second, the HR department is going to be flooded with veterans asking where their letter is. Be prepared to amend your records, because your veteran population is about to identify themselves of their own free will. The next year send it out again. Lather. Rinse. Repeat.

If you really want to knock this one out of the park in a big way, invest in something simple that allows your veterans to identify their service to you and to each other. BNSF Railroad does this with incredible success. Each year their Veterans Day letter is delivered with a lapel pin that has the BNSF flag on one side and the US flag one the other. Veterans can walk down the hallway or pass in the train yard and make introductions based on their mutual military service experiences. Get ready though, because the "veteran underground" is about to emerge. (Get that strategic plan in place now to put them to good use!)

Tip #2: Get the Voluntary Disclosure Paperwork Put into Your New Hire Packets and Train Your People.

There is a wealth of benefits to hiring veterans these days, but what most companies fail to do is twofold: They fail to incorporate the required documentation into their HR new hire packets, and they forget to train their first-level leaders to help people complete it in a timely fashion. Most federal and state incentives have a very short window for executing these documents (usually less than 30 days from the date of hire) and many clients simply miss out because the process hasn't been properly trained to the user group required to do it. So what is the financial impact of this seemingly tiresome paper drill? No paperwork, no tax breaks. In some states, companies stand to gain *significant* federal and state benefits, and they miss out frequently.

Here's just one example: A Fortune 1000 client used our internal veteran polling to determine that they had hired over 2,400 veterans the previous fiscal year. The company stood to gain over six million dollars in tax incentives if the paper drill had been perfected. Because they failed to do so, they captured a tiny fraction of that amount. (Thankfully we'd been retained by their executive leadership and not by the HR Department, because I'm fairly certain the person responsible for tracking these initiatives had a rather unpleasant office call after our findings were presented to management.) Let's just say that with our help, this company completely restructured its onboarding process and has been putting veterans to work and reaping the benefits ever since.

Don't miss out on the benefits that Uncle Sam and our state legislators are putting on the table to encourage you to hire these phenomenal candidates. The amount of money you will save in taxes alone will offset any institutional investment in starting your own veteran recruiting initiative. Our veterans pay for themselves in more ways than one.

Lesson Two: Put a Face to Your Program

If I were a job seeker wanting to know more about your company and how someone like me fares as an employee, I might reach out to your equal opportunity / diversity group looking for more information. It would stand to reason that a woman would lead your women's group. Your other diversity groups would be reflective of the same train of thought.

So why is it that people frequently ask me whether their veteran recruiting program should be led by a veteran? I'm certain that you have highly qualified civilian talent acquisition managers or diversity recruiters, and I don't doubt their dedication to helping the military community succeed at your organization, but that is not the question at hand.

Tip #3: Put a Veteran to Work Putting Veterans to Work.

The principal reasons that your military recruiting program should be led by a veteran are these: the credibility of your organization and the trust shared by the military community are two critical things you simply must have.

If your organization states that it is dedicated to hiring veterans but can't point to a veteran leading the charge, every veteran that is introduced to your program is going to wonder at that disparity. I'm not saying they can't be successful, but if you expect a nonveteran— especially someone with no link to the military community—to mesh with the candidate pool you're trying to recruit, you're going to be let down. The differences among the branches of service alone are enough to make a recruiter's head spin, but veterans can make sense of the acronyms, translate the fluff from the facts, and have instant credibility with the candidate they are conversing with. If you haven't worn the uniform, or lived with it daily in the case of a military spouse, you just don't cut the mustard.

I can't walk into the local police station and have instant credibility with the men and women that protect our communities. I wouldn't have a faintest idea what their codes and jargon meant. I could stand behind a recruiting desk all day trying to convince a former cop that my company was a "great next step", but without some insight into their experiences, training, and lifestyle I would probably come off as a pompous jerk pretending to know something I know nothing about. I wouldn't be authentic.

Your program can't afford to lack authenticity. If you've already taken action on Lesson #1, then you have a wealth of current employees to pick from when selecting the face of your program. If your company has the ability to draw that person into your HR / talent acquisition / talent attraction team, that's a win for everyone. You would be able to develop a program that resembles the incredible work that companies like Microsoft have built (Joe Wallis' www.westillserve.com). Amazon has a dedicated military recruiting team with branding that appeals to the military community. Any of these companies will attest to the value they've found in having a dedicated recruiting team pointed at the military community.

But what if your organization faces challenges in having a dedicated recruiting team for this population? Perhaps your HR team is too small to support such a luxury, or perhaps your organization is so large that having specialists for every business vertical would be impossible. Fear not. There are proven solutions for your companies, too!

If your firm is too small, you have a two solid options available to you: outsource the recruiting function for this population, or allow a consultant to advocate for you. There are a number of reputable firms that specialize in finding military candidates for corporate entities. Some specialize in what we refer to as JMOs (Junior Military Officers) and charge fees based upon the candidate's first year salary. Other firms recruit across the rank structures, finding candidates for vacancies all across the globe. They have varying track records of success in different markets, so if you need help picking a vendor, give us a call. We'll help you sort the wheat from the chaff. The final option for outsourcing, and one I would urge you to consider strongly, is to utilize small but nimble veteran-owned firms that act as your face to this population and recruit candidates as if they were recruiting for themselves. They have a high success rate and typically are less expensive than your larger staff augmentation firms. Again, if you need referrals, just ask.

Another creative solution for large firms that may have varying internal verticals that require specialized knowledge to adequately recruit talent (where a central team built internally wouldn't be effective) is to have a "referral hub" in place. Identify the veterans already in your employ, and so long as they are willing to help others from the military community transition into your firm, you can proceed with publicizing their contact information and making them the "face" of your program. This approach works particularly well for global organizations. Take the example of AT&T. Chris Norton, their self-titled "Military Guy," didn't begin his journey assisting veterans from the HR department. He began with AT&T in other roles ranging from customer care and operations to quality assurance and planning. In every role, Chris was approached by fellow veterans looking for more information on AT&T, a litmus test on the culture of the organization, help with a resume, or assistance locating the "right" point of contact with whom to discuss employment opportunities. He wasn't in talent acquisition, but he found himself making connections for veterans anyway. Today he leads what they refer to as their Military Talent Attraction program, but he's been helping veterans much longer than it's been implied in his job title.

Lesson Three: Find Where Veterans Fit

Every job has a description that typically showcases the requisite skills and experience necessary to attain the job. What it usually doesn't have is a translator for military skills. This creates two problems for recruiting initiatives:

1. Job seekers will submit their resumes into your "technology tool" (i.e., candidate tracking tool) and they will never reach a recruiter because of the need for keyword filtering. Let's face it: your HR people don't speak military and your job descriptions

will therefore not accommodate military skill sets. For example, civilians look for "curriculum development and training professionals," but the military would simply refer to them as "platform instructors."

2.   Not all jobs in the military have a direct civilian counterpart. And as much as Allied Barton would love to hire every transitioning infantryman and Marine to work security projects for their firm, the truth remains that not every combat-oriented "transitioner" wants to stay in that field. They have gained functional skills in a number of other areas (logistics, training, operations, supply chain management, etc.) that they would prefer to leverage in their new career. At first glance, most HR professionals immediately look at the "job" the service member held (i.e., Military Occupational Specialty or branch equivalent) to determine if they have the skills needed for the job. Very rarely will they seek further information about "additional duties" that these candidates might have had, and by not knowing how valuable those answers are, they can easily overlook great talent.

For instance, a client of ours published a job description for a group training facilitator on all of the major job boards, intentionally seeking a veteran candidate. After the keyword searching eliminated over 80 percent of the veteran candidates we submitted for testing purposes, fewer than 10 percent were referred to a hiring manager by an internal recruiter for consideration. All of the candidates had served as drill sergeants with great success, and none of them made it through the internal "system" for hiring consideration. Talk about losing the war for talent! (Let's just say they were keen to make some adjustments to their approach.)

Tip #4: Identify the obvious and not-so-obvious opportunities.
Microsoft should be commended for developing their own tool to translate jobs at their firm directly to military job codes. They definitely decided to use their core competencies to assist their efforts, and so as

a technology company they created a system to connect the dots. The translator can be found on their www.westillserve.com site, under Military Decoder. (Keep in mind that unless you want to work at Microsoft, there are plenty of opportunities that it won't deliver.) Trust me: if you're a veteran and a job seeker, they built that system hoping you would come. It is first class talent attraction at its finest. They let you see where you fit, and you apply right then and there.

As a first step in identifying vacancies for veterans, you can take a look around your firm and see where you need help the most. Ask a veteran on staff (or hire a consultant!) to draw correlations between that skill set and the military service. You'd be shocked at the similarities they'll map out whereby your recruiting team can intentionally pursue candidates that weren't previously being considered.

The point is to be intentional. Create a strategy and pursue this talent pool. Not only will you satisfy the increased Department of Labor (DOL) and Office of Federal Contract Compliance Program (OFCCP) oversight and inspection, you'll end up with some of the best talent this country has to offer. (If you haven't reviewed the newest implications for companies under OFCCP with respect to veteran hiring, you might want to ask your HR department to get you an executive summary post haste.)

After you've figured out where veterans can fit in your organizational structure and you've begun recruiting them intentionally, it's also wise to ensure that your internal recruiters and HR team have the appropriate knowledge to screen and effectively promote a veteran candidate to your hiring managers. This seems silly, but it greatly increases the number of veterans who are offered interviews. Without the interview, they can't get the job!

Lesson Four: Connecting to the Candidate Pool

So you've identified your internal veterans, put a face to your program, and mapped out where veterans can succeed at your firm. Now what? Now it's time to determine the implementation plan. Where are you going to find the most talented veterans for your job vacancies? How can you appeal to them? These are all common questions.

Here are just a few high-level suggestions for you to consider:

1. There exists a wealth of job boards. You already use Career Builder and the MonsterMilitary.com portal, and I'm certain most companies know about the Hero2Hired.org online portal at this point in time, mostly thanks to the incredible press the White House has been so gracious to put behind the veteran employment initiative. But where else can you go?

   - HirePatriots.com: Every US citizen and any company can post opportunities on this website, where military job seekers can find long-term careers and quick cash-producing day jobs for those looking to close the financial gap. This twofold approach addresses the daily concerns of both the transitioned and the unemployed, the military spouse and even our wounded warriors. I can't recommend it enough.

2. Call the local military bases and introduce yourself to the Army Career and Alumni Program (ACAP; pronounced "ā-cap") or Transition Assistance Program (TAP) office. Talk with a career counselor and let them know the type of skills you're looking for. They will be thrilled to inundate you with resumes of people they have previously vetted and worked with. Read that again: *previously vetted.* They screen them for you. Talk about a win- win!

3. Call your local VA office and repeat the process above. You'll want to ask to speak with their employment representatives, Disabled Veterans Outreach Program (DVOPs) and Local Veterans Employment Representatives (LVERs) who work one-on-one with veterans seeking new career opportunities. They want your vacancies so they can fill them!

4. Call the National Guard headquarters for your state and ask to speak with their Job Connection Education Program (JCEP) coordinator and Employer Support of the Guard and Reserve (ESGR) representative. I've found these folks to be some of the most helpful resources in the business.

5. Don't forget your local workforce offices. Some states have exceptionally robust programs, like California and Texas (e.g., TexVet). Let them go to work for you too.

- These things are easy to do and will pay big dividends. Keeping in mind that most of the people serving in the jobs above are veterans themselves, this is yet another area where having a veteran lead your charge is going to be highly beneficial. Veterans help other veterans—that's just the reality of it. Take one veteran internally and apply all of these resources, and what do you get? Talent. Lots of talent.

Lesson Five: Advanced Concepts

Once you've managed to gain competency at getting veterans to apply (and be considered) for vacancies within your organization, there are a few advanced concepts you should consider implementing.

Advanced Concept #1: *Build Your Own Transition & Training Program.*

For candidates who apply but don't meet the minimum requirements for the job, you always have the ability to create a talent feeder program by developing your own approved training or certification program for your organization. How would that work? Very easily. The Army trains and loses hundreds of network administrators every year and the number is only increasing. They have two, three, or ten or more years of experience in the exact field most companies require, but they lack a civilian certification. To remedy this problem, we've helped companies to refer those candidates to their own approved training program. There they use their earned education benefits to attain the "rubber stamp" the company needs to hire them. Once they graduate, they go to work. It costs the company a small amount of time, and saves them thousands of dollars per hire.

Tip #5: Explore Both Traditional Certification Opportunities and On-the-Job Training Options.

There are pros and cons to each, but it's worth comparing the long-term value of each approach before deciding which to pursue in your organization's best interests.

Advanced Concept #2: *Build a Veteran Employee Resource / Networking Group.*

For companies that really want to go the extra mile to embrace and support their veteran employees, there is one must-do. I encourage you to construct an employee network / affinity / support / resource group so they can connect to one another. Allow them to create and support an informal or formal mentoring program. Give them ways to get involved in the big picture of employee support.

Here's just a snapshot of companies that you can look to when it comes to well-developed (and internally supported) Employee Network Groups (ENGs): JPMorgan Chase, AT&T, Dell, Goldman Sachs, and Northrop Grumman.

Advanced Concept #3: *Get outside your organization and into the community.*

Once you've built an ENG (even a fledgling one), you're ready for what I refer to as Employee Engagement 3.0: Community Outreach. Get the members of your Employee Network Group (ENG) to partner up with a reputable local nonprofit that supports the military community. These veteran service organizations (VSOs) are incredible resources for you in referring more candidates for employment and they also give your employees a way to give back. This "cause marketing" helps your firm to build a more veteran-friendly brand.

Picture this: You have 55 veterans on staff and hire 35 more veterans in the first year. They create an ENG and develop a mentoring program. They decide to partner with a great VSO for a community service project and wear their company t-shirts to volunteer in. The people they are meeting are veterans looking for jobs. They get to know one another and your employees begin referring qualified candidates back to your recruiting team for consideration. You've just found several good things in one fell swoop: a place to push charitable donations for local support that reinforces your commitment to your veteran employees, a way to keep your own people engaged, and 90 new recruiters without incurring another expense or additional training burden. I highly suggest you get to know the following organizations: The Mission Continues; Tragedy Assistance Program for Survivors (TAPS); the Warrior and Family Support Center (WFSC) at Brook Army Medical Center; Project Homefront (a Scott & White Hospital charitable program); Reboot; and

Student Veterans of America, just to name a few. They offer incredible services for our veterans, spouses, and gold star family members, but they need your help—your time and your philanthropy dollars. You'll be so pleased by the results your organization receives by getting involved, you'll wonder why you didn't do it sooner.

Advanced Concept #4: *Get educated and push the envelope by sharing best practices.*

No matter which stage of development your military recruiting and retention efforts are currently in, you need to know about Warriors to the Workforce (W2). If you want to learn how to do all of the things I've mentioned in this chapter, or are just wanting to begin preliminary inquiries into developing your very own military recruiting (and/or retention) program, I'd suggest that you go visit www.warriorstotheworkforce.com and sign up to attend one of our NO-COST educational (and experiential) Best Practices Summits held at military installations all across the country. It's a one day immersion event that allows corporate leaders and hiring managers an opportunity to interact with our nation's military, see the caliber of the men and women in uniform, and learn best practices from our experts and lessons learned from current and former clients. All attending companies have the option to sponsor a table at the follow-on W2 Hiring Event on day two, where all donations benefit veteran service organizations doing great work for the military community.

The transition team at Warriors to the Workforce, in collaboration with the American Freedom Foundation and Career Builder, has an impressive offer whereby they will recruit candidates for you to interview on the day of the hiring event and schedule the day's sessions on your behalf. Forget resume collection; show up and hire people that very day. It's not your average career fair, and coupled with the W2 Summit the day prior, it's the most powerful combination of information and assistance out there. You can visit the website for more details, but it's definitely a must-do for any company serious about hiring veterans the right way and for the long term. Contact the W2 team with any questions you might have and they'll be glad to assist you. For companies, email info@w2summit.com; for job-seeking veterans, military spouses, and gold star family members, email jobs@warriorstotheworkforce.com.

About Professional Coaching Consultants

As the #1 boutique consulting firm in the United States for veteran recruiting and training initiatives—founded by veterans of the Armed Forces, one of whom created the Army Career and Alumni Program (ACAP)—it is the mission of Professional Coaching Consultants (PCC) to bring the values and experience ingrained in our nation's military to the business community at large. With multi-industry and defense experience, they provide the unique perspective to assist organizations in developing and rapidly implementing a military recruiting, training and retention strategy. By providing strategic guidance to corporate leaders, training for HR professionals and functional managers, coaching support for executives that are managing military veterans in their new corporate roles, and veterans now serving as leaders in a non-military capacity, they have assisted many of their clients in becoming recognized as industry- leading, military-friendly employers.

For more information, visit www.professionalcc.com or call (800) 931-9309.

About the Author

President of Professional Coaching Consultants, Crystal is an organizational development consultant and an active advocate for the military community in many ways. She's a veteran of the Army's Chaplain Corps, a proud military spouse, the mother of three boys, an entrepreneur, professional speaker, author and philanthropist who uses every resource in her arsenal to make a positive impact on those who serve this country and those who serve beside them. As a board member of several nonprofit organizations, Crystal provides strategic guidance so that much-needed services are always available to support veterans, spouses, and gold star family members. Her goal in life is to work herself out of a job by eliminating veteran unemployment and military spouse underemployment one client at a time.

For more information, visit www.crystaldyer.com.

3: For US Vets and Companies Wanting to Hire Them

From Battlefield to Boardroom—A Marine's Story of War, Recovery, and Reintegration.

JOSH GALLE

With every generation there is a turning point, a day in history that is remembered. We can look back on that specific day and point in time and know exactly where we were, what we were doing, who we were with and how we felt. We can vividly recall minute details of what would have otherwise been a normal, forgettable day. As Americans, these memories usually center on a tragic moment when our lives and our world changed forever. For my grandparents' generation, it was December 7, 1941, and the Second World War. For my parents' generation, it was when they learned that JFK was assassinated. For me and my generation, that day was September 11, 2001.

On that tragic and fateful day, I was a freshman at Pensacola Christian College, Florida. I was earning a degree in Religious Studies and Political Science. It was a Tuesday morning that started just like any other. I heard the news about the attack on our nation as I sat in my World History class. I still vividly recall the pain and anger I felt when I saw the footage of the planes smashing into the Towers of the World Trade Center. I wanted to react immediately and take the fight to our enemies, even though at the time I didn't realize the complexity of all that had happened.

September 11 was a turning point in my life, not only because it shook the foundation of security that I'd always felt as an American, but also because it ignited a passion inside me to serve in a way that I had never felt

before. On that day I knew that part of my purpose in life was to serve in the United States military and protect American citizens from harm.

I had quite a few friends who had enlisted directly out of high school. Many I knew had been injured and a few were killed. They inspired me, too. They had given their all for our country. I felt an overwhelming sense of pride and commitment to them. I also felt the obligation to do my part, to serve my country in the military and defend it from terrorists. So there I was, with a burning desire to serve and a catalyst to motivate me actually to enlist.

I didn't make that decision to join the US Marines Corps until I was 21 and coming toward the end of my degree program. The recruiter told me that because I was in peak physical condition and scored so highly on all the aptitude tests, I had an opportunity to be promoted quickly into leadership. He told me that I should enter on the enlisted side, learn the basics, and then move to the commissioned ranks. "It would be a good career move for you," he said. This career path, referred to as a "Mustang," was definitely not the easiest one, but if I was going to become a good leader I would need a well-rounded view.

Basic training was tough. It was demanding physically, mentally, and emotionally. I learned quickly that the military is not about the individual. All self-serving behaviors are abandoned in favor of a team mentality. They break you down as an individual in order to build you up as part of an elite team, a cohesive unit. I no longer saw through the lens of me or mine. My eyes were opened to the concept of team collaboration. This makes no mission too big of a challenge for a team of Marines to overcome.

The phrase "Adapt and Overcome" was often touted by my leaders. I adopted this saying as a motto and mantra for my life. Today, "Adapt and Overcome" is applied to everything I do in my personal and professional affairs.

From 2004 to 2008 I served on active duty. My first duty station was RSS Duluth. I served on recruiting detail. And whenever I had leave (time off) it was spent with my fiancée Jessica. (We have been married for nearly eight years now and are blessed with two beautiful children: a son and a daughter).

Infantry and Advanced Infantry School came next, where I learned all the techniques and skills of a Marine infantryman. From there, I was stationed with a new combat battalion: 1st Battalion, 9th Marines (known as the "Walking Dead"). It was during these first few months that I suffered nerve damage and neurological issues from a close quarters combat scenario that was quite realistic and went a bit too far. My injuries and the side effects from this training exercise were so severe that I was convinced I would be medically discharged or retired and never get to deploy as a Marine.

Again, the mindset of "adapt and overcome" set in. I was more determined than ever to continue my service in the Marines. I took a desk job in the battalion's S-1 Administration Office, performing most of the unit's administrative tasks. It was great on-the-job-training that led to my commanding officer awarding me with a secondary job title: Military Occupation Specialist (MOS) in Personnel and Legal Administration. Now I was more of an asset to the Marine Corps and could still serve despite some of my injuries.

Once I had received that secondary MOS in Administration, I knew I was going to wear a dual hat for the rest of my time in service. This was often a negative for me while in service; I took a lot of grief from my infantry brothers, who like to refer to non-infantry Marines as POG's: "Person Other than Grunt." That was okay with me, because in my head I was a "Grunt-plus." Not only could I hook and jab with the best of them, but I could also assist our leadership in ensuring pay, leave, benefits, discipline, and awards were properly administered. These skills have directly translated to my successful transition into the civilian workforce.

I was never officially removed from the infantry and would later serve again as an infantryman and even as a team lead and squad leader. I led Marines in Iraq on combat patrols and security of prisons and checkpoints. My tours in Iraq placed me in the Al Anbar Province, particularly in Fallujah, which had already seen some of the heaviest fighting in Iraq. Our patrols and convoys were often attacked or ambushed, and we always faced the danger of improvised explosive device (IED) attacks. I was face to face with insurgents and jihadists bent on killing me or any other American service member many times.

But it is important that I share this: Not all Iraqis wanted to hurt the US. In fact, an overwhelming majority supported our presence and were happy with the stability we were bringing. Seeing all the images and reminders of an oppressive leader who had ruled this nation through terrorism removed, the people were less fearful of us and more fearful of retaliation by loyalists to the old regime. What I know is that more than one million US military members like me did our part to defend our nation against would-be threats. We removed a dictator, and we gave Iraq, an oppressed nation, a fighting chance at democracy and a taste of the freedoms and way of life we love here in the US.

Due to injuries sustained in service I was not able to reenlist; ergo I also forfeited my career dreams to later serve as a commissioned officer. In retrospect, I would gladly go back and serve all over again. I often miss the camaraderie and *esprit de corps* that I lived each day. I am and forever will be a United States Marine. I had the honor to serve with the Few, the Proud, and the Best.

My transition back to civilian life was difficult. My young wife delivered our first child days after I was officially off active duty, and I immediately faced the challenge of relocation and finding civilian employment. Thankfully, my college background, coupled with some brief work experience before the military and the leadership and human resources skills I had polished while in the Marines, gave me an advantage.

I took my first position back in corporate America with a small firm that assisted transitioning military and matched them with employers seeking to hire top talent. This would be a very brief transition position. I assisted companies in recruiting and marketing to attract veterans, and I interviewed veterans and introduced them to employers seeking their particular qualifications and talents. As short a time as that job lasted, it taught me some tangible skills: networking, sales, and marketing; and it further developed my communication and leadership skills. The knowledge and confidence I gained at this first civilian job after the military gave me a renewed sense of pride. I was fearlessly ready to take on new challenges in a new environment.

The challenges I faced in this first job were different, yet in some ways just as real and challenging as those I had faced while serving in the Marines and in Iraq. I had to adjust to learning new things, despite a traumatic brain injury. Basically, I had to reengineer the way I read and processed information that was given to me. Navigating corporate hierarchy was another challenge. It was far less structured than in the Corps, and often people's titles had nothing to do with their function or role.

I have held several positions and had a myriad of experiences in my post-military career. I have held a few entry-level positions as an account executive that barely paid enough to keep a roof over my family's heads. And I became an entrepreneur. I was instrumental in getting some startups launched, and I am banking as a sweat-equity partner on their future profitability. Ultimately, though, my career path has brought me to where I am today. I am honored to be leading and managing a nationwide military hiring initiative program for a Fortune 100 company. My work today continues to allow me to combine my knowledge, experience, and passions to help my fellow military veterans and their spouses land their own careers and complete a successful transition.

The resources I will share from this point are from two perspectives. One is for those setting out on that transition from military to civilian sector. The other is from the lens of a human resources or business leader that needs to hire top talent, but is not sure how to consider or place military veterans and their spouses successfully into their organization. I encourage each reader to focus on the information and tips provided in this chapter and the pages of this book that relate to your specific situation. I salute each of my fellow veterans who will read this book as they embark on their own transitions. I also thank the human resources and business leaders who will read this and use it as a guide to support their hiring efforts. You have my sincere gratitude as a military veteran and HR professional for any and all of your efforts to support my fellow veterans in completing a smooth and successful transition. You won't be disappointed with your hiring decisions; you are hiring "The Best of the Best."

Tip for Military and Veterans

Take advantage of government transition preparedness programs. Current military requirements are making transition programs mandatory. It's important to approach them with an open mind. Be prepared to ask questions. Speak directly with the presenters or facilitators of each session to get the most information and advice as possible.

Here are some of the common transition programs and services:

- Transition Assistance Program (TAP)
- Army Career Alumni Program (ACAP)
- Department of Veteran Affairs Vet Success
- Local Veteran Employment Reps (LVER)
- Disabled Veteran Outreach Programs (DVOP)

Spend time brushing up your resume and translating your military experience to the civilian world.

One of the most crucial steps to landing an interview is to brush up your resume. Be sure to translate your military experience into civilian experience, focusing on your transferable skills and competencies and removing military acronyms and jargon. Spell out military titles. Do not use military acronyms, and when possible substitute with a corporate title (i.e. squad leader can be displayed as security supervisor or manager). When thinking about roles you may apply for, don't just try to look for that direct translation from military career. Think about the job description and make your experience match the work. Don't limit yourself, but rather broaden your scope. Market your personal brand and determine your transferable skills. Use specific examples from your military career in your resume and in interviews, focusing on those skills.

Consider working with a military headhunter. Some veterans have found success leveraging the services of military headhunters. These below are just a few recruiting firms with which I have worked. Each provides good resources to junior military officers (JMO) and non-commissioned (NCO) and senior non-commissioned officers (SNCO). These firms hammer on interviewing skills, prepare guides on what types of questions are asked in an interview, coach candidates on the exact type of attire to wear, and make sure candidates are as prepared as possible for the interview.

- Bradley Morris
- Cameron Brooks
- Lucas Group
- Orion

Network, Network, Network

Building relationships throughout your career is important. Keep continually networking at all points in your transition and career. It will help you to make connections that can lead to promising career opportunities. Start networking early, even before you plan to make your transition, in order to build the connections and relationships that will serve you well down the road. Plan well ahead, just like you would train for a mission or deployment.

- Network with other veterans that have already had a successful transition. Connect with fellow comrades by leveraging your personal and social network. Ask them about their transition, their current employer, if they are hiring, and tips they have for making the transition. Often they will share strategies and insights that can help you on your journey.

- Connect and network with industry professionals and leaders that are subject-matter experts in their respective fields of discipline. For example, if you are seeking a career in healthcare, then create networks with doctors, nurses, marketing directors, healthcare recruiters and other HR professionals in that industry. If there is a specific company you are interested in, seek out contacts and network with others who are currently employed there.

- Network with professionals both at a peer level and at the senior level. These are critical connections to landing your future role. It is crucial to make a good impression on individuals in leadership and management roles. These professionals will be making hiring decisions for the company, or they may already have a connection or influence that will land you your next job.

- Leverage your LinkedIn profile. A strong LinkedIn profile is a must-have in your transition toolbox. A well-built profile is one that details your past education, work history, military experience, and has written referrals from those you've worked for in the past. Having a strong profile will help you build an online network of colleagues, and it will help make you more visible to recruiters and companies looking to hire. While crafting your profile, be cognizant of your personal brand. Use professional writing and have someone proofread your work. LinkedIn is growing, and many HR and hiring experts agree this site will continue to serve hiring leaders and job seekers well in coming years.

Get creative and think outside of the Monster/CareerBuilder job hunt box. Although traditional job boards are still essential, get creative with use of other sites and strategies to increase your chances of success. For instance, try Google to search for job positions. Due to search engine optimization and online job aggregators such as Indeed & Dice, many companies' job postings will show up in search results. Here are a few other go-to sites:

- Vetjobs.com
- H2H.jobs (Hero 2 Hired)
- esgr.mil (Employer Support of the Guard and Reserve)
- JoiningForces.gov

Remember that you are in transition mode. It is time to think and act like your civilian counterparts. You must adapt and overcome to a new culture and arm yourself with the appropriate tools to be successful.

Resources for Employers

Goal: Provide a framework and information for employers who want to start a US veterans hiring program within their organization. Address common myths. Show realistic recruiting strategies. Share the benefits of hiring a veteran.

Why You Should Hire a US Veteran

All service members today are a volunteer force. They signed up to fight this nation's battles and protect the freedoms that we hold dear. This is only one of the qualities that make military veterans a must-have human capital asset that your company should be attracting. In corporate America we are all aware that we are facing a talent war. There is a shortage of qualified, skilled professionals. In most cases, military veterans can fill in this talent gap. Below are some additional top skills and qualities you will find in the majority of the military veterans with whom you interact.

1. **Leadership:** The military trains people to accept and discharge responsibility.

2. **Team Member and Team Leader:** Essential to the military experience is the ability to work as a member of a team. Many military personnel also serve as team leaders, where they analyze situations and options, make appropriate decisions, give directions, follow through with a viable plan, and accept responsibility for the outcome.

3. **Get Along with All Types of People:** In the Armed Services, military personnel work for and with people of all types of backgrounds, attitudes and characteristics. Appreciation for diversity in race, gender, economic status, thought, age, religion, attitude, intelligence, or physical conditions is common in everyday military life. This experience has prepared service members and their families to work with all types of people.

4. **Work Under Pressure and Meet Deadlines:** One definite characteristic of military service is that service members must perform their job and do it right—and it must be done in a timely manner. They are continuously setting priorities, meeting schedules and accomplishing their missions. Pressure and stress are built into this, but US veterans are taught how to deal with all these factors in a positive and effective manner.

5. **Flexibility and Adaptability:** All US veterans have learned to be flexible and adaptable to meet the constantly changing needs of any situation and mission. Last minute changes are common in the military. Service members are trained to adapt and overcome immediately. You can count on them when your company has urgent demands.

Building a Corporate Military/Veteran Recruiting Strategy

Build a Team

You may be a small organization that needs only one staff member to manage this effort, or you may be a Fortune 100 company that needs a dedicated team to manage the program and process. The best approach is to have a US veteran lead your team. Who better to manage your outreach to the active-duty military and US veteran community? Of course, you need a veteran that is a human resources professional. Here are my recommendations on what to look for when sourcing someone to fill this role:

- HR generalist with 2–5 years of progressive HR exposure in both corporate and military segments.
  - Needs to have hands-on knowledge and exposure to compensation, benefits, standard policies, training and development techniques, and state and federal regulations, e.g., Uniformed Services Employment and Reemployment Rights Act (USSERA).
  - Must also be able to consult with other HR professionals and leaders on proper execution and adherence to such policies and regulations as required.
- Full life cycle recruiting
  - Utilizes standard applicant tracking systems (ATS).
  - Follows standard processes: sourcing, screening, evaluating, interviewing, offering, and retaining candidates.
- Marketing/branding
  - Understands fundamentals of how to market and advertise

such an initiative or program publicly in accordance with company guidelines and/or in partnership with marketing/ PR team.

- Have strategic partnerships and relations with military/ veteran-centric marketing and advertising agencies to ensure your company has the appropriate level of presence and is getting recognized on a local, state or national level, as appropriate to your tailored needs.
- Communications expert
  - Must have highly professional communications skills and ability to communicate at all levels of an organization.
  - Ability to provide context and gain support and enthusiasm for this type of program or initiative from appropriate levels and discern when and where to disseminate such communications to best support the effort.

Online Marketing and Branding

Focus on US veteran and military-oriented websites.

Your goal is to have an online presence and establish your company brand in the web locations that military members and veterans frequently visit: Vetjobs.com, H2H.jobs, Hiring our Heroes, HirePatriots.com, and so on.

- Your online ads should have artwork showing veteran personnel who still have the military look and edge.
- Use patriotic or military colors and themes if they are consistent with your brand.
- A well-crafted online presence and brand will help ensure you stick out on the web. US veterans are spending a significant time searching and applying online.

Print Marketing and Collateral

Focus on US veteran images and themes.

- The messaging and vocabulary of your print ads, brochures and printed collateral should not be too industry-specific. The military veteran will have as difficult of a time understanding what an insurance actuary is as a recruiter would have understanding what a Marine infantryman does.

- We ask candidates to write a good resume; should we not, then, write a well-written job ad or employment brochure that is easy to read and not confusing?
- Consider niche advertising media such as Recruit Military's Search & Employ, GI Jobs, or MilSpouse.

Veteran-Centric Career Fairs and Events

Focus in areas with a high population of veteran job seekers.

- The Department of Labor or your local/state employment offices can provide answers and advice.
- US Chamber of Commerce: They sponsor "Hiring our Heroes" and put on the most military job fairs across the nation, ensuring they are well attended and that they amplify your recruiting efforts.
- Sponsor your own hiring events. Invite other employers to attend, thereby increasing the events' value, attendance and marketing potential.
- Army Career & Alumni Program: This is the transition office on Army and National Guard posts. They put on career events and look for employers to participate and recruit.
- Military event planners: There is no shortage today of agencies and companies that put on job fairs centered on military talent. Some will provide the entire planning and hosting for you; others are a shared commitment to execute the event.

Aligning and Leveraging Resources

Direct communication and partnerships with local, state, and federal agencies:

- Joining Forces www.whitehouse.gov/joiningforces
  or http://joiningforces.uso.org
- Hiring our Heroes www.hireheroesusa.org
  or www.uschamber.com/hiringourheroes
- Army Career Alumni Program (ACAP) www.acap.army.mil

- Local Veteran Employment Reps (LVER)
  www.dol.gov/vets/aboutvets/contacts/map.htm
  www.benefits.gov/benefits/benefit-details/108
- Disabled Veteran Outreach Programs (DVOP)
  www.dol.gov/vets/programs/fact/Employment_Services_fs01.
  htm
  or www.benefits.gov/benefits/benefit-details/106
- Department of Veterans Affairs Vet Success
  www.vetsuccess.gov

What We've Done at Humana

In August of 2011, President Obama challenged U.S. companies to hire 100,000 military veterans and veterans' spouses over a three-year period. In support of this initiative, Humana pledged to hire 1,000 former servicemen and servicewomen or their spouses by late 2014.

We have met our goal far in advance of our initial commitment. Since the announcement, Humana has hired over 1,000 veterans or their spouses in a wide variety of fields, from nursing to information technology to pharmacy and data analytics.

We hired these outstanding men and women through an intensive, multi-faceted recruiting effort. In addition to outreach through traditional employment websites and networks, Humana participates in dozens of military career fairs and similar events. However, the one critical component to our success came as a result of our 42,000 associates who embraced and contributed to this companywide initiative by referring qualified veterans and veterans' spouses.

In our experience, military veterans and their spouses are extremely capable, highly motivated and make an immediate impact when they come to work at Humana. Each brings valuable experience and a unique story.

As we know, the transition from the military to a corporate work environment can be challenging. In concert with our hiring initiative, I'm proud that Humana is taking steps to help prepare veterans to reenter the civilian workplace and support them once they get there. We're contributing to their successful transition by doing a number of things such as donating $1 million to the Entrepreneurship Boot Camp for Veterans with Disabilities (apps.whitman.syr.edu/ebv), a national program that offers cutting-edge training in entrepreneurship and small-business management at no cost to post-9/11 veterans.

We also have created the Veterans Network Resource Group, which connects veterans and veterans' spouses with each other, provides leadership development and education programs, and opens opportunities to volunteer for community events supporting veterans.

As a result of our efforts, we were recognized as a Freedom Award Finalist through Employee Support of Guard and Reserve (ESGR); we were ranked #34 for GI Jobs Top 100 Military Friendly Employers, and also ranked #14 for GI Jobs Top 25 Military Spouse Friendly Employers. *Military Times* magazine also named Humana Military Healthcare Services, our military division, as one of the top 25 "Best for Vets" employers.

Our veterans and their spouses have sacrificed much in the defense of our nation and our individual liberties. We are proud to be able to give them opportunities to continue their career at Humana, where they can serve another noble purpose: improving US healthcare while helping people attain lifelong wellbeing.

Although we have fulfilled our commitment, we will not stop there. Under Bruce Broussard's leadership, we will continue to recruit, hire and train veterans because of the positive difference they make in our organization.

About the Author

Josh Galle is an Operation Iraqi Freedom (OIF) Combat Veteran, served 2 combat tours in Iraq with the United States Marine Corps as a Noncommissioned Officer. He was honorably discharged from active duty in the Marines in 2008 and completed his service in 2012. Prior to his military service, he double-majored in religious studies and political science at Bob Jones University. He continued his education through the Marine Corps Institute where he studied military science and leadership.

Since leaving the military, he has been active in the human resources and business development field and has both managed and directed these functions for startups and Fortune 100 companies. His key niche is recruiting strategy capitalizing on the military and veteran talent pool. Since 2008 he has successfully recruited and hired more than 2,000 military veterans and their spouses. He is a frequent speaker and advocate for veterans' issues, and brings an honest, personal, and current perspective to these discussions. Serving his fellow military/veteran community through employment is a key passion and assisting business leaders to realize the value of talent this group brings to the workforce is a career objective.

4: Veteran Leaders

Resilient Professionals for Turbulent Times

MONA SINGLETON

It's probably not news to anyone that we are in the midst of turbulent times. The rapid acceleration of change and uncertainty is a clear indication that it's time to bring in the boldest, the brightest and the best to step up and lead in America.

Volatility, while disconcerting to some, stimulates others to action. It brings opportunity. It calls for fresh solutions and the people than can bring them to fruition. Enter US veterans!

Why hire veterans? America is starving for leaders. The 21st Century has ushered in a new degree of change and challenge. Businesses, like the military and other organizations, need people that are ready, willing and able to meet unprecedented challenge. Veterans have accomplished more in their early years than most people have accomplished in a lifetime. They have demonstrated they have the right stuff.

How so? Veterans possess a matchless blend of skill, expertise and ability. They have gone places where few Americans have ever gone. They have unique expertise and rare life experience.

United States veterans are well poised to step up and fill critical leadership roles left unfilled in America. Strong and effective leaders are in short supply for a variety of reasons. Business owners, corporations, and nonprofit organizations have to compete much harder to attract, hire, and retain good leaders and staff members as baby boomers retire with fewer qualified candidates to replace them.

Today's workplace is becoming more intense and unpredictable. Each day brings with it new challenges. Leaders at all levels must be prepared to lead well and guide carefully if an organization is to prosper and succeed.

Next-generation leaders need a strong strategic mindset and a lot of new know-how. They must be quick to think, engage, and follow through without the luxury of fully staffed organizations and favorable environmental conditions.

Specifically, veterans from across the US Armed Services have passed many grueling tests. Some have served honorably in the officers' ranks, and some as enlisted members. Some are graduates of military academies, Officer Candidate schools, specialized schools, and basic training "boot camps." The military wastes little time qualifying their candidates. Those that are not up to par are sorted out early in the process. Each member of the Armed Forces has to meet minimum standards of conduct and performance. They either meet them or they don't.

American companies need leaders with the right balance of will and skill to deal with complexity and ambiguity. It's not enough to be knowledgeable. It requires tested leaders who can actively engage and mobilize people. Veterans have proven they are up to the task.

While many veterans are relevantly young, they are often more mature than their non-veteran peers. That gives them an edge and a strong head start at meeting the increasing workplace demands of this century. Employers would indeed be wise to give veterans serious consideration as a means to help build and maintain strong, resilient American businesses.

Who are the next-generation leaders and where do you find them? The next-generation leader is not necessarily limited to the younger generations. Many people elect to begin new careers after serving many years in a variety of roles and positions. Wise organizations look for seasoned high performers who have the potential to do the job and do it well. Some of the best leaders emerge when you least expect them to and when you most need them to!

This is not to suggest that veterans are always better contenders than non-veterans. Every person brings something to the table no-one else can bring. Each has a different style and personality. Each has a role to play and each has different gifts. Veterans have life skills and experience that only come from serving in the uniformed services. They bring a very different perspective to the workplace.

It's the character of a leader that makes him or her great at leading. It's not rank or status. It's not a title. It is who people are and the principals they stand for. The best leaders don't waver and won't abandon their values. In challenging situations, it takes the right person at the helm. In many, many cases, veterans are well suited for the task.

Why is leadership, or the lack thereof, so often on the radar? Billions of dollars are spent on the business of educating and growing leaders. Reliable leaders are vital to the survival of business. The most successful institutions know that. It's getting the right people in the right roles at the right time.

There are some things you can't outsource. Technology and automation are often overrated. Processes, procedures, tools, and technologies, while important, mean little without skillful people who can use them to accomplish the desired results. Even great ideas are just ideas without people who can and will bring them to life. Competent people are needed because only capable people can think and act to make things happen. Across the branches, military members are great at implementation.

All organizations have problems. That's a good thing. Problems are part of what makes an organization necessary in the first place. Unless your business is solving real-life problems and providing real good solutions, there is little use for it. When businesses cease to be relevant or fail to serve the customer's needs, they lose purpose and value. Then they fail. The customer goes elsewhere. America needs leaders who understand this and can keep the company viable and useful. Business owners and organizational leaders need good problem solvers who can deliver great solutions to the customer.

While business problems and challenges create opportunity, unplanned and unexpected calamities can be deadly and destructive. Crisis management and emergency preparedness is becoming a necessity in many of today's business organizations. America needs a new breed of leader, one that can effectively prepare for the unimaginable. Crisis situations, natural and man-made, are a reality. Failure to prepare and be ready to respond can result in severe consequences. Military leaders are no strangers to mounting obstacles and crisis situations. They are familiar with operating in the realm of ambiguity and complexity.

The elite members are able to simultaneously adapt to changing situations and forge ahead to complete their mission.

Uncommon leaders surround themselves with the best. They seek out people who are eager to contribute. These leaders are discerning and careful to select the best people they can find for their team. They don't settle for mediocrity, nor are they threatened by working with equally capable subordinates. They aren't interested in inviting yes-men and yes-women to the team. They find people that are loyal, trustworthy, and respectful. They surround themselves with people that will step up and lead when it's necessary. They bring in people with the right stuff and are candidates clearly capable to advance to the next level of leadership when the time comes.

Leaders don't last forever. When will your leaders leave? It's inevitable that they will, whether it's sudden or eventual. Wise businesses leaders know that a smooth transition is essential for continuity of operations. Part of a leader's job is to train replacement leaders and ensure a good exit strategy that will prevent things from falling apart when they leave.

Great leaders are what Jim Collins, author of the book *From Good to Great*, calls "Level 5 leaders." In his book, the author describes several levels of leaders. Level 5 is the best. According to Mr. Collins, "Level 5 leaders channel their ego needs away from themselves and into the larger goal of building a great company. It's not that Level 5 leaders have no ego or self-interest. Indeed, they are incredibly ambitious—but their ambition is first and foremost for the institution, not themselves." Mr. Collins goes on to say, "Level 4 leaders are often effective and charismatic; yet the company falls apart after they leave, since Level 4 leaders put their personal success and egos ahead of institutional success." There are many level 5 leaders in the US military.

Some might be more familiar with the term "servant leader." Who are servant leaders? Servant leaders are leaders who willingly choose to be of service to others. They fit the description of Level 5 leader. Servant leaders serve a purpose greater than themselves. Millions would point to Jesus as the crowning example of the ultimate servant leader. Like Jesus, true servant leaders transcend the test of time. They are people who can change the course of history, or serve less visibly but no less valiantly behind the scenes. Many veterans have a servant's heart and soul. They are fearless and humble. Many don't serve in the limelight; they are unsung heroes who serve in silence. They stand head and shoulders above the crowd.

True servant leaders inspire others to thrive, not just survive. They don't leave people to sink or swim. They don't leave people behind. The great leaders do what's right for the greater good, not their own personal interests. They know how to inspire others to willingly contribute their best. They protect their people and their people know they have their back. In turn, the leader earns the loyalty of their followers. Many veterans can rightly be characterized as servant leaders.

What about followers? Well managed businesses have to attract and keep balanced, self-disciplined individuals that are both moral leaders and sensible followers. Leadership and followership roles are iterative and intrinsically linked. They go hand in hand. They are like two sides of the same coin. Leaders cannot lead without followers, followers cannot follow without leaders. One role simply can't exist without the other.

What's the big deal with followers? A fundamental quality of being an elite leader is that they were first earnest followers. A seasoned leader is also a seasoned follower. People that have learned to lead well learned it by following well. They had stellar examples to learn from in the military. Wise and prudent followers make great leaders because they follow great leaders. No-one is born qualified and prepared. No-one parachutes into a top position without proper training and groundwork.

What are the characteristics of a great leader? The answer is, it depends. It depends on the organization and the context. Leaders wear many hats and play a variety of roles based on the need, situation and environment. They are required to know and do many things.

Character and credibility are critical. First and foremost, competent, capable leaders know who they are and who they aren't. They know their role. They know the vision. They are clear and comfortable with their style, temperament, strengths, weaknesses, and values. Folks like these are rare and hard to find. It's what makes them so valuable in business. They have a strong sense of identity.

Smart businesspeople, as well as military officials, pay attention to aptitude. While assessment and instruments are available to help select people suitable for a job, it definitely helps to consider people who naturally know who they are and how they can best contribute.

Don't most veterans have skills that are military specific? Yes and no. They have specialist and core skills. It's not unusual for some hiring officials to focus on the military-specific skills and miss their other great attributes. Think about what a veteran could bring to the table. In what areas of your organization could you use someone who has great decision-making skills, loyalty, respect for self and for others, self-motivation, courage, and values?

What about all the negative stereotypes in print and on television? It's best not to believe everything you read or watch on television. Veterans are a diverse subset of Americans and as such, they are as imperfect as everyone else. Like civilians, they are human beings that have their own special blends of strengths and weaknesses. There are no clones. Some veterans are high achievers, some not so much. At the end of the day, Armed Forces members are as unique and complex as everyone else. Preconceived notions and stereotypical labels have little value. They tend to exaggerate flaws and ignore a person's virtues.

In reality, there are few slackers in the military. Loose cannons don't stay in the service for long. Military organizations simply can't afford to jeopardize critical missions by taking undue risks with the wrong people for the job.

Rather than buy into the stereotypes, ask the veterans about their values. Be curious as to what prompted them to volunteer for the service. They certainly weren't drafted. They chose to join. Some will say they wanted to contribute. Perhaps they wanted to play a part in protecting the freedom and safety of Americans and allies. Some may have elected to prove themselves in tough and critical situations. They may be people who value significance and experience. Some may value learning. They may have joined to earn money and benefits for college and were willing to jeopardize their safety and the comfort of home to earn their way to college. There are many reasons people volunteer to serve in situations few others would even think about. Intentions are telling. Ask why they joined.

As a final consideration, how successful do you want your business to be? Fast forward to one year from now: Who do you need on your team that will help you achieve the success you envision? If you want reliable people who have a proven track record, consider a veteran.

It has truly been an honor to serve in the United States Coast Guard. I honor and salute all those who now serve and those that have served before them. America needs more good men and women who will boldly step up and lead when we so truly need resilient professionals. Thank you for your service.

Semper Paratus.

About the Author

Mona Singleton is a United States Coast Guard veteran. She served a four year tour of duty as a Radioman 2nd class. She is an author, certified corporate business coach, and project management professional. Mona is an excellent leader, coach and mentor and is best known for her energy and enthusiasm. Her new book *Lead With Your Gifts, Why Who You Are, Not a Label Defines You as a Leader* is due for publication in summer 2013. Ms. Singleton has served as a two-term president of a 501(c)(3) nonprofit organization and has worked for many years in public service. Mona lives in Point of Rocks, Maryland. For more information about Ms. Singleton visit www.monasingleton.com.

5: How a General Helped Prepare the Army for Transition

The Army Career Alumni Program

LT. GEN. DONALD JONES

Before I specifically address the issue of properly preparing our US veterans for a successful transition into the civilian world, I will give you a brief summary of my military career. Every member of our nation's Armed Forces serves every American citizen. It has been an honor to lead such stellar men and women.

I entered the Army in March 1957 as a young enlisted soldier from Campbellsville, Kentucky. I had attended a one-room country school for eight years before entering high school. I entered active duty without a college degree. During my time on active duty, I was able to obtain both an undergraduate and graduate degree while maintaining a full-time job in the military.

I took basic training at Fort Knox, Kentucky. After completing basic training, I was assigned to an air defense unit in Arlington Heights, Illinois. The mission of the organization was to protect Chicago, Illinois from hostile air attack. After several months on the job, I was accepted for Field Artillery Officer Candidate School at Fort Sill, Oklahoma. In November 1958, I was commissioned a second lieutenant in the Field Artillery Branch.

I served numerous tours in artillery units including assignments in Korea, Vietnam and Turkey. In Vietnam I had the opportunity to work with Major Colin Powell, who was a great mentor and went on to be Chairman of the Joint Chiefs of Staff, National Security Council Advisor and Secretary of State.

After I was promoted to colonel, I began to receive assignments in the personnel field. These included assignments as Corps G-1, Commander of the U.S. Army Personnel Command and as Deputy Assistant Secretary of Defense for Military Manpower and Personnel Policy. In that position, I was responsible for all personnel policy for the Army, Navy, Air Force and Marine Corps. I was also responsible for pay, commissaries, post exchanges, recruiting and many other personnel issues. In these positions, I felt that I had an opportunity and an obligation to do all that I could do to help all service members realize a successful career in the military.

My rise from Private E-1 (the first enlisted rank) to Lieutenant General was a result of working for and with good leaders. They were responsible for instilling in me a strong desire to assume greater and more demanding assignments. I personally felt that I was a representative of every service member who was serving this nation. I had an obligation to assist them in any way I could.

When I retired from the military in 1991, I took a job as the Vice President of Disaster Services for the American Red Cross. I had the privilege of working for Elizabeth Dole. This job allowed me to serve those who were affected by disasters. Upon retirement, I felt that I had an obligation to give something back to the men and women that are serving this nation. I served on the board of directors of the Armed Services YMCA for 23 years, the American Red Cross for 12 years, and Military Child Education Coalition for 12 years. I have raised funds to support Wounded Warriors programs and programs that assist gold star family survivors, plus programs to help all veterans find meaningful employment opportunities.

Shortly after assuming command of the United States Army Military Personnel Command during the summer of 1987, it became readily apparent that the soldiers separating from active service and returning to civilian life were not adequately prepared to find meaningful employment. Most had given little if any attention to the next phase of their life. Unfortunately, many of the separating service members believed that their time in military service and the skills they had acquired would qualify them for any job in the civilian sector. When they returned to their home of record they soon realized that this was not the case.

The total force consisting of all ranks was cut from approximately 1.4 million active duty personnel. Very few members of Congress had served in the military and most had little interest in maintaining a strong defense. The Democratic Party was also looking for money to spend on social programs. Many veterans were very upset that they were being involuntarily separated after they had done what their service had asked them to do. Some had expected to serve a full career in the military service. At that time, I realized that most veterans did not know how to translate the skills they had acquired in their military service into terms that the business world used and understood. Additionally, they had little knowledge of how to interview for a job. Realizing this challenge, I instituted a new program to help correct this condition. The new program was called the Army Career Alumni Program (ACAP). Its purpose is to assist soldiers with their transition to civilian life.

The program was designed to assist them in preparing a meaningful resume that would enhance their chances of finding a job for their skill sets. They were also given guidance on how to interview effectively. This included information such as how to dress, what they needed to know about the history and culture of the organization with which they were interviewing, and proper interviewing techniques. Too many soldiers were not knowledgeable about how to network effectively. They were not requesting assistance from those with whom they had served. They were not asking for letters of recommendation for inclusion with their job application. Nor were they using their former co-workers as references on their resume.

When ACAP was initially implemented it included contact information related to job opportunities by state, as well as the Department of Labor information. It was anticipated that service members would check to see if there were job opportunities in the location in which they wanted to settle before making a final decision. Initially, it was optional for them to use these services when they separated. But after seeing that many were not, the Secretary of the Army made it mandatory that all soldiers use these services. When they leave the service they are required to have a resume in hand or an acceptance letter from a university agreeing to accept them as a student. This directive from the Secretary of the

Army designated ACAP as a 'Commanders Program,' meaning that all commanders were required to get involved in helping separating service members find meaningful employment.

When soldiers return from combat zones, the foremost thing on their mind is to return to their families. Rarely do they give much thought as to what they are going to do to earn a living. Before I created ACAP, the military only required returning service members to go through a three-day orientation on how to reintegrate back into civilian life. They received no guidance or counsel related to the actions they would need to take to find a meaningful job. The guidance that they did receive was primarily focused on how to reintegrate into their family and how to drive safely.

However, several years after implementing the ACAP Program, it became apparent that it was not achieving the desired outcome. Too many separating members of the Armed Forces were not getting job interviews with potential employers. It was clear that the employers did not know how to access a veteran candidate. Most organizations are not familiar with the culture of the military service or how to access veteran candidates. The only companies that have some knowledge of the military culture are those that have acquired defense contracts. Since there has been no mandatory draft for decades, many of the leaders of major companies have never served in the military and do not understand its protocol, nor do they appreciate the value of US military training and service.

Then, as it often is today, there was concern about hiring service members that may have post-traumatic stress disorder (PTSD) or traumatic brain injury (TBI). The employers were concerned that they would not know how to respond to soldiers that exhibited PTSD or TBI symptoms. The key to overcoming that obstacle was to educate potential employers on the proper methods to access veteran candidates:

- To assist them in writing an internal plan to hire this category of potential employees

- To help them prepare a job description that targets former service members with the requisite skills for their companies

- To brief their hiring managers and recruiters on how best to promote a veteran candidate

- To spend some time with the veterans that they are being asked to hire

When potential employers are invited to military installations to interact with the separating service members, they should send representatives that can make a decision to hire these outstanding candidates.

This time spent with the veteran candidates helps the potential employers realize that these veterans possess the requisite skills and integrity to be outstanding employees. They are also able to realize that most are self-starters and highly motivated.

One of the greatest challenges we face in finding meaningful employment opportunities for separating service members is determining the number that are actually leaving active duty. This is a challenge due to the uncertainty of possible budget cuts affecting potential employers. There is also the fact that additional service members will be involuntarily separated due to sequestration. An additional challenge is the lack of collaboration between organizations that are trying to assist separating service members in their search for employment. Consequently, there is a lot of duplication of effort. We need to understand how best to maximize our efforts.

The National Guard and Reserve soldiers (NG&R) have a more difficult time finding employment opportunities. Due to their geographical separation throughout the states, they may not have ready access to the programs that are found on active duty posts. Another challenge is that separating soldiers fail to begin their separation process early, to research and identify training assistance that is available to them, and to help prepare them for the job search. They often attend job fairs without having a quality resume. Consequently, they often return to their home of record and realize that there are no employment opportunities in their hometown. That is due to the failure to do adequate research and to determine if there are employment opportunities in that location. All of these challenges must be addressed if veterans are going to be successful in securing sustainable employment.

At one job fair I was attending, I asked a young non-commissioned officer what kind of job was he was seeking. His response was, and I quote, "I want one that pays me." Needless to say, he did not find an employment opportunity at that specific job fair.

The number one thing that we all need to do if we are going to be successful is to educate the potential employers and allow them to have access to potential veteran candidates. Many potential employers believe that all they have to do to reach a veteran candidate is to post a job on their job board. This approach by itself will never be successful.

The Judge Advocate General of all military organizations provides the legal counsel to the commanders and renders a decision as to whether an activity is legal and authorized by policy and law. Many of the Judge Advocate General personnel believe that they are violating a joint ethic regulation if potential employers are allowed to come on US military bases and to interact with separating service members. If this condition is not rectified, most hiring programs will fail. It will also require greater involvement by the leadership at each installation. Also, the fact that ACAP has been designated a Commanders Program doesn't mean that every commander will support the effort. Some form of federal legislation may need to be passed to override the Judge Advocate General's concerns.

To be effective, there needs to be some method of measurement to determine how well the commanders are fulfilling their duties related to this program. If they fail, the overall program will fail, and the separating service members will not find meaningful employment opportunities. If we are going to be successful in finding employment opportunities for separating service members the government must take a more active role in the program and devote the resources to make the hiring program a success. Failure to do so will leave many young men and women that have sacrificed so much without a means to earn a living.

Therefore, failure is not an option. We all need to step up and do our part to ensure that we assist all separating service members in finding meaningful employment. If we fail to do this, our country has failed those that sacrificed the most. To rectify this situation will require action by the federal government, the leadership of the military services, the commitment of employers to hire veterans, and better collaboration between all organizations that are involved in finding employment opportunities for separating service members.

Donald W. Jones

Lt. Gen. US Army (ret.)

About the Author

Lieutenant General Donald Jones was born in 1935 in Hudgins, Kentucky. He holds a Bachelor of Science degree in Business Administration from St. Benedict's College and a Master's Degree in Business Management from Central Michigan University. He was commissioned a second lieutenant in field artillery upon graduation from Officer Candidate School at Fort Sill, Oklahoma in 1958. His other military education includes completion of the Field Artillery Basic and Advanced Officer Courses, the U.S. Army Command and General Staff College and the Army War College.

Over his military career, Lt. Gen. Jones held a wide variety of troop leadership positions as well as staff assignments. He was the Deputy Assistant Secretary of Defense for Military Manpower and Personnel Policy, Office of the Secretary of Defense. His other key assignments were as the assistant Deputy Chief of Staff for Personnel, Headquarters, United States Army and as the Commanding General, Military Personnel Command. He was also Assistant Division Commander of the 1st Cavalry Division at Fort Hood, Texas, from 1983–1985. His overseas assignments include Korea, Vietnam, and Turkey. He served in the United States Army for 35 years and retired with the permanent rank of Lieutenant General.

Lt. Gen. Jones' awards and decorations include the Defense Distinguished Service Medal, The Army Distinguished Service Medal, the Legend of Merit, the Bronze Star Medal, the Meritorious Service Medal and the Army Commendation Medal.

Upon retiring from the Army he was asked to serve in the American Red Cross under the direction of Elizabeth Dole. He joined the organization in 1991 and was there until March 2000.

Lt. Gen. Jones has served on the National Board of the Armed Services YMCA for the past 21 years and on the Board of the Military Child Education Coalition for the past 8 years.

He is married to the former Betty Karnes and they have two children, Lori and Donald.

6: Transformation

LT. COL. JOHN PHILLIPS

*"What you get by achieving your goals is not as important
as what you become by achieving your goals."*
Zig Ziglar
(1926-2012)

Trans·for·ma·tion: a complete or major change in someone's or
something's appearance, form or being.

Now it is time to learn about transformation: a process of rebranding
yourself. There's no doubt that the transition process will require a great
deal of work. There also will be hurdles, challenges and sometimes
frustrations. You should also keep in mind that despite the challenges and
sometimes broken promises along the way, the United States of America
is still a beautiful place to call home!

Regardless of when you make the decision to leave the military, the
transition and transformation process often begin simultaneously. Almost
as soon as you decide to exit the military the process of transforming
from a service member to a veteran begins.

Your first priority is to prepare for the job search. Your second
priority is to manage the move from the military culture to the civilian
culture effectively. This is called transformation. The intensity of the
process differs depending upon your circumstances. For example, how
much planning took place before you exited the military? What goals
were established during the exit strategy?

If you have already taken some of the necessary steps to transition before you left the military, you may encounter solid opportunities
waiting outside the gate. This is not an impossible situation. In fact,
with time, proper planning and transitioning, some of you will walk out
of your boots and into your loafers or pumps very quickly. But even

for those of you fortunate enough to experience a quick, easy transition, the transformation process is still important. My transition process began while I was still in boots, yet I still encountered a few interesting turns in the road about five years after retiring and moving into the private sector.

One such event: I remember a conversation with a manager I had when I was a finance manager in marketing. He had received feedback from some of my peers. Basically, he told me I needed to consider rebranding myself because my peers viewed me as hard, inflexible and difficult to communicate with. What he was really saying was that John Phillips was still "The Colonel," with a direct communication style and approach that was not always received well. While my manager validated that I was definitely performing well in my job, he also said that I would perform even better once I figured out how to reinvent myself. I knew exactly what my manager was saying. The simple truth was I was no longer in the military and I was slipping back to how you communicate while you're in boots. No nonsense and direct, and that made my peers very uncomfortable. Of course, in my heart I know I will always be a soldier. But if I was going to succeed in this role, I had to take a long hard look inside myself and develop a plan and make some changes. I did just that. Now, eight years later, I have been very successful in the company.

Rebranding or reinventing yourself is the basis of transformation and starts with the obvious: military language and communication style, home-life events and activities, and of course, the career. For all practical purposes, you are rebranding yourself to live, work and play in a new way; from commissaries to Walmart, from field artillery to finance, and from softball with the guys and gals in uniform to coaching T-ball at the local YMCA.

The change begins and it is a wild ride.

What is Rebranding?

"Either you deal with what is the reality or you can be sure that the reality is going to deal with you." —Alex Haley

A quick personal story on rebranding going back to Day One of becoming a soldier:

When I graduated from high school, I enlisted in the US Army. The minute the bus door opened and my drill sergeant came on board at Fort Jackson, South Carolina, I knew I was about to undergo a significant change very quickly. What I didn't know was that I was about to learn how to "rebrand" myself from an immature teenager to a soldier. Although my early years had been spent on Army bases around the world as my family moved from one military tour to another, those indirect experiences did not completely prepare me for the rebranding process I was about to undertake. By the time I got off that bus (very quickly, I might add), I realized that I would soon learn an entirely new way of life I knew nothing about, despite spending my entire life in and around the military. Several components of change immediately became apparent: communication style, culture, attitude, life choices and decisions, and much more. Those first moments of awareness of what rebranding is all about were lessons that would be played out again some twenty years later as I entered the private sector.

Your rebranding route is the natural process of shedding your military lifestyle and donning the ways and behaviors of civilian life. Rebranding does not require you to compromise core values; instead, you must reinvent yourself and apply those values in a completely different environment. You should view the rebranding process as a fresh start with a chance to seize new opportunities, to implement lessons learned from mistakes, and to capitalize on years of experience while in uniform, making them an advantage in the civilian world. The necessary adjustments differ for each person, so you must do your homework, be adaptable, remain flexible and use your training to watch, listen and transform. This move into the civilian world requires adjustments to specific aspects of your life; status, position, communication style, work life, and home life to name a few.

Communication: From Military Language to Civilian Equivalent

First and foremost, communicating in the military is most often direct and to the point. Misunderstanding a communication can have dire consequences. The military environment, sometimes marked by unpredictable and violent situations, dictates the need for quick, concise and very direct communication with fellow service members. This method of communication is rarely found in the private sector. Former service members can find the private sector's more relaxed style of communication confusing. Consequently, you may feel isolated and anxious. If you find yourself in this situation, reach out. A fellow veteran or a close coworker may be able to give you advice on how to communicate more effectively. Social occasions with friends and family can also provide a safe opportunity to learn more about how civilians communicate.

Service members also speak at least one foreign language. If not French, German, Japanese, or any of the more than 6,000 distinct languages on this planet, it's military lingo. In fact, military language is unique and generally only understood by those serving in the military. It's often filled with military jargon, acronyms, service branches, rank structures, and much more. This is not to say you have to throw away the language you learned in the military; rather, you have to find the civilian equivalents for many words and phrases in order to communicate effectively outside the gate.

Look at communication as the vehicle that will take you from your previous role and life to your new one. With that in mind, you will need to discard military language and learn private-sector terminology. You'll need to exercise patience and pay particular attention to your surroundings and how others communicate, both verbally and nonverbally. You also have to know that most nonveterans do not understand the military experience, its unique language or its culture. Struggling with change and varying methods of communications is a normal experience when you move into the private sector.

This particular aspect of your transition and transformation is extremely important to your success outside the gate. Take time to watch, observe, and learn, just like you were trained to do.

Status and Position

One of the first changes you will make pertains to status and position. The military is a culture of order, structure, and a clearly defined hierarchy. For many career military members, especially those who have held positions of rank, moving into the private sector is a reality check.

Their military positions and ranks have earned them prestige and respect. Their subordinates followed their orders to the letter without question and snapped to attention when they entered a room. Even today, I still find myself jumping to my feet when my manager or a company officer comes to see me in my office. It is in my DNA. Their position in the civilian world may not come with the same level of responsibilities and authority, and even if it does, response to that authority is significantly different. Rank in the civilian world is measured by job titles, pay levels and, for some, material possessions and perks. In the business world, military medals for bravery and gallantry in action are replaced by bonuses, stock options and other rewards and incentives.

Some veterans may welcome this change and lack of responsibility while others may view it as a demotion. If you prefer to manage others, to make decisions and to direct processes and functions, you need to seek employment that immediately allows you to lead. Exercising authority in the private sector when your job does not give you that responsibility can result in resentment from co-workers, reprimands from managers, and questions from others about your future.

In order to effectively transform yourself and succeed in the private sector, this is one of the key aspects a veteran will need to get past. If a coworker or manager doesn't show you the respect you most certainly deserve, take the time to educate them on the service you did for the country. It is not a sign of disrespect when your co-workers simply don't understand the military. That is why we are the other one percenters.

Private Sector Work Life

Learning to manage the numerous differences or professional nuances encountered in your new workplace is an important part of your successful transformation. Many adjustments you will face in your new career depend upon the cultural aspects of the company and, in some cases, the industry where you choose to work. Your rucksack (backpack) should contain the following points for future reference:

- Your attention to detail likely is more intense than that of your civilian counterparts because of your military training and combat experiences. This trait gives you a distinct advantage in the workplace; however, the absence of it in your co-workers can be a source of irritation and frustration. Your natural impulse to create order out of chaos may run afoul of the private sector culture. You need to use your skill for tolerating and managing ambiguity to your advantage.

- Managing private-sector employees is very different from directing service members. Barking orders and expecting them to be carried out to the letter without question is not the way it works in the private sector. Expect a conversation and taking into account the feelings of your co-workers and associates. Unlike civilian employees, service members do not have the luxury of disagreeing with their commanders, questioning authority and walking off the job when disgruntled. Since as a service member you have not been accustomed to these freedoms, you must adjust your leadership and communications style to the new workplace

- The military requires payment from service members to attend social events and other sponsored occasions. Not so in the private sector. Companies that host similar events either pay in advance for employees to attend or they reimburse them through expense accounts.

- Key soft skills you bring to the workplace are punctuality, excellent attendance, and superior work ethic, traits that are valued by private sector managers. You may notice that some of your civilian co-workers do not share these characteristics, so you may use these to your advantage.

- Job duties must be performed at the highest level to meet or exceed the expectations of managers. One of the worst mistakes you can make is to "let your hair down" once you are out of uniform. Likely a primary reason you were hired was not only your leadership capabilities and technical knowledge, but also your soft skills. Therefore, your continued proficiency in these areas is paramount to your success.

- The private sector does not have "lockdowns" or red, yellow and green training cycles. Depending upon the job that you get, you may be on call 24 hours a day, 7 days a week and be required to carry a company-paid cell phone. Typically, salaried management employees are paid to be available 24 hours a day, 7 days a week, 365 days a year, the same time required when the employee was "in boots."

- A code of business conduct and ethics still exists, even though you are no longer in uniform. Whether off the job, on a business trip or on vacation, you represent your company. You must not jeopardize a job by exhibiting inappropriate behavior.

- Your personal life for the most part is just that, personal. Although you are free to share personal information with co-workers, peers and managers, you should first consider your comfort level with these individuals. Some people just don't like sharing this type of information. A good manager takes an interest in the employee, his family and his outside interests because, quite often, what you do outside the workplace reflects the type of employee you are at work. Common ground with co-workers builds relationships and valuable friendships, which contribute to a more satisfying work environment.

Home Life

Marriages and family relationships are often impacted by the stresses of a military career. Absence during deployment, training and special assignments can place an emotional and financial strain on the service member and his family. Preparing your finances long before separation from the military may alleviate some of this stress. For example, saving a portion of pay to build a transition fund is critical to defray the financial burdens incurred by a protracted job search, relocation expenses, housing and day-to-day living expenses during your transition.

Once you exchange your boots for loafers or pumps you will have more time at home with your family: a change that can bring a new set of challenges for you, your spouse and family. This is what most service members have dreamed about and yearned for during their military careers, a life outside the gate that allows them to appreciate and build the relationships they have missed. Whether inside or outside the gate, establishing open and honest communication between the members of your household is critical to keep families close and committed. At times, all the key components of transformation will play an important role in your personal and home life.

When you were deployed in the military, the strong family network that exists in every unit on military bases provided a strong support for your family. These support groups may not exist outside the gate. Once you exit the military, you and your family must build a new support network with family members, new and old friends in the civilian world and members of your new world. Churches, veterans' groups and other support groups are available, but you have to reach out to them. Take advantage of any work and life balance programs offered by your company or community that will enhance both your work and home life experiences.

Stereotypes and Diversity

Although veterans represent one of the smallest minority groups, they are perhaps one of the most diverse groups. The military represents a cross section of all segments of society; its members are white, black, Asian, Hispanic, Protestant, Catholic, Jewish, Muslim, handicapped, gay, lesbian, and more.

Companies that employ veterans not only access the unique skills that veterans bring to an organization, but they also benefit by adding individuals to their ranks who have excelled as a single unit, regardless of their preconceived labels. Service members have learned to use each other's talents, skills, teamwork and training to survive in dangerous environments without prejudice. The meaning of teamwork is defined by the veteran. This is an exceptional character trait to bring to an organization.

Business professionals who want to grow their workforce talent by hiring veterans will benefit from reading *Boots to Loafers*. Potential employers tend to stereotype veterans as a result of misinformation and media biases; therefore, many members of private sector companies must undergo their own transformations to discover the true benefits of bringing this small population on board. Subsequently, rather than placing the usual labels upon veterans, they will then recognize them for their service, sacrifices and talents. Companies that value a veteran's qualities have become aware of the unique and powerful contributions they can make and have changed their hiring, on-boarding (organizational socialization), and training processes for them.

Boots to Loafers wishes to educate those leaders who have been reluctant to hire veterans due to the stereotyping of their combat experiences. Company leaders and hiring managers must also remember that not all veterans have been deployed into war zones. A veteran is much more than what he has seen or experienced; he is a person who has served his country and is now able to use his skills, training and talents to help a company prosper. Whether he is inside the gate or out, what matters most is how he uses his capabilities to accomplish great things. It is important for all people, military and civilian, to remain in pursuit of Martin Luther King, Jr.'s dream for people to judge each other by the content of one's character.

Work and Life Balance

I would go so far as to say I am a pretty good example of a soldier who has experienced a successful military career, transitioned through the gate, transformed into a successful businessman and achieved balance between my work, family, and friends. *Boots to Loafers* represents my journey. Work and life balance is extremely important to me, and as a director in a Fortune 100 company leading associates, I try to instill in them an appreciation for establishing a grounded approach to balancing work and life. My thoughts and feelings in striking this balance are spelled out below.

A large part of any soldier's transformation is reaching a balance between work, family and life. Chasing this balance is sometimes elusive; many tend to prioritize the wrong things in life. Exercising control over my work and personal life is the fun stuff for me; simply put, I work so I can play. For me, this is one of the most important aspects of my life outside boots. As soldiers, we lived a life in uniform and were subject to be called to any part of the world when diplomacy failed. The next logical step was to insert the military to take care of the nation's business. I loved the military, but those days ended in late 1999, and my love for the service member continues through this book. Today, I cherish my time off and planning trips with my family and friends. Time spent with my longtime friends Jim and Jerry is very important to me. We grew up trying to kill each other on the football field for a starting position on the team, and we have managed to remain connected for more than four decades, despite life's leading us down different paths. My relationship and time spent with my brother Steve and his sons are also special and a bright spot in my life. Another important passion for me was creating a bucket list of things to achieve: traveling to exotic places with my wife, taking hiking trips around the United States, sailing in the Caribbean, rafting or canoeing with my brother and best friends out west, fly fishing in the western and southeastern United States, and golfing with all the guys on our spring and fall golf trips.

Every veteran will find his passions as well. For some, new careers will become priorities. For others, the freedom to reconnect and spend quality time with family and friends will take precedence. Once out of boots and into loafers, all will be able to do the things that have been neglected because of deployments or other tours of duty. Creating one's own bucket list and accomplishing things that are important will enrich your life outside the gate. Becoming involved with network groups, veterans' groups, churches or charities, civic organizations, and professional associations can help others make the transition by paying it forward. Now that you are out of boots, do yourself and your family a favor and take the time to do those things that you put off for years because of the deployments. They deserve to have you around, you'll not regret it!

Summary

This journey through the transformation phase depends upon one's circumstances, exit plan and personal goals. Much of the transformation will depend upon attitude, support network, and the realization that you will not make this journey alone.

The one percent who served their country possess the training, skills, and experiences learned during their military careers to embrace this life-changing process. The strengths of veterans—loyalty, values, leadership, discipline, adaptability, diverse experience, and the ability to bring order to chaos—will serve you well in this next phase of your life. In the rebranding/transforming process, holding tight to these traits will certainly result in a successful move from boots to loafers.

About the Author

John W. Phillips has had a distinguished career in both military and civilian service. John is a retired US Army Field Artillery officer and Comptroller with 20+ years of service in corps artillery, division artillery, and the Army Headquarters and Forces Command, (the largest command and the generating force provider for combatant commanders at home and abroad). He has served in Europe, throughout the Middle East and the United States. He has been awarded the Legion of Merit, Meritorious Service Medal, and the Air Assault Badge.

John has worked in finance, program and project management, and sales roles for The Coca-Cola Company located in Atlanta, Georgia. In his spare time, John spends his time in either the mountains of north Georgia fly fishing, in the British Virgin Islands sailing, or out west camping, rafting or canoeing. John holds a BS in Finance from University of Central Florida and an MBA from Syracuse University. John lives in the Atlanta area with his wife.

7: Recruiting Veterans: A Calling Found

CARL VICKERS,
SR. MILITARY RECRUITER

Every veteran is different. The civilian population makes the mistake of branding all veterans the same. However, you will find that they are as diverse as you and me. They all have different personalities. The only true similarity is that they have all been through a very similar training process in the US military. This is a process that has been honed to perfection when it comes to reshaping lives.

The point I want to make to companies and their civilian executives and hiring managers is that you need to better understand and appreciate the value of US veterans. This will greatly enhance your company and your position within it.

The point I want to make to fellow US veterans is that we each will take a different path, strategy and method to come to the same objective: to retain fulfilling employment that sustains ourselves and our families. And if you have not yet reached that peaceful plateau, take courage. There are good companies with earnest US veteran military recruiters like myself who will help you get there.

My own search began when I left the service in 2005. I had attended an exhausting three day Transition Assistance Program (TAP) class designed to help us to walk back into the civilian world and pick out a high-paying job at our leisure. It turns out that the US Armed Forces had decided that all of us in the TAP office should undergo a personality and career guide test to see in what career we would most likely succeed. We were to find a career on which to structure our resume and on which to focus all of our energy. We were assured that when we returned to our "home of record" whatever career we had decided upon at TAP would be hiring in droves upon our return. However, we all know this is not the case.

When I returned to my home of record, I took some time to visit my local unemployment office and pay a visit to the veterans' representative. I explained to him what I was looking for based on my background and experience. I was quickly told that I would need to look outside of my home of record due to the lack of opportunity in the state.

To make a long story short, I finally came home to Indiana and found employment. I began work at a steel fabrication facility. I worked third shift as a maintenance technician. I worked very long hours and in a very unsafe environment. This lasted for a few years. I gradually worked my way into a higher level position on the day shift. A few years later, I was brought into a management level position. But I was still unhappy with the way my career was headed.

But then, my employer decided to step up their military hiring initiative! A focus group was formed of US veterans currently employed by the company. The idea and prospect was for me to grow into a position within the company that I was extremely excited about. For years I had dreamed of being in a position where I could help others, especially my fellow veterans, as a military recruiter.

My family and I had relocated to Greenville, South Carolina, to take advantage of this big break for me. I had no formal training to be a military recruiter, but what I did have was a growing thirst for knowledge and passion for being a great military recruiter. I read article after article. I searched the ends of the Internet to learn from others. I asked questions. I LISTENED to my fellow veterans as they were transitioning. I attended job fairs, TAP classes; you name it, I was involved in it. I gave advice. I took advice. I truly loved what I was doing and what I do now.

The more involved I became, and the more I learned, I grew more and more concerned about the true plight of US veterans leaving the military service and coming to the civilian world. My experience of being "exiled" from my home state by a Veterans Administration (VA) representative who should have been there to help me increased my desire to help other veterans avoid the same thing.

I started being my company's military recruiter in November, 2011. In January, 2012, my wife and I found out that we were being blessed with twin girls to go along with our 5-year-old boy and 1-year-old girl. We were so excited. I had my dream job, and my family was growing. But just two weeks before the twins were born I received a totally unexpected phone call. Someone from my company called to say that my "position was being eliminated due to an overall reduction in force" and that I should begin another job search. My job as a military recruiter for this company lasted just 12 months. I was shocked and angry. But the company I worked for needed someone at one of their other facilities to fill a different position outside of recruiting, and since I was the closest soon-to-be-unemployed member of the team, they asked me if I wanted the job. But my family and I would have to relocate. It was in a very high crime area and I did not want to put my family in that situation. More importantly, I wanted to get back to what I had been doing and what I had finally found to be my calling: recruiting and assisting veterans with employment and other needs. So I turned down their offer. With a growing family, that was a risky decision.

I prayed for an opportunity to be allowed to do more than I had been able to do at my former company. In my past role, I could only recruit for a specific skill set and for specific locations, and I had to beg and implore the hiring manager to take a strong look at US veterans. It had not taken me long to realize that I was working for a company that only stated they wanted to hire veterans. In reality they only wanted one in a thousand. They turned away so many skilled veterans that it made me feel sick. They never learned that for a company to be successful at recruiting veterans they have to be willing to make the initial investment in training those veterans. This investment will pay for itself ten times over in the long term through reduced retention costs.

My life changed when I received a call from PeopleScout. This is a company that has the knowledge and experience to be the leader in their industry. God answered my prayers. I was hired as their military recruiter. This was the opportunity about which I had dreamed: To have the ability to place many veterans from many skill sets into roles across the United States.

Their culture and streamlined processes that allow for innovation from within is inspirational. Their drive for excellent customer service is second to none, both for their clients and for the employees that work for them. I am blessed and honored to be a part of the PeopleScout team and be their senior military recruiter.

We all have heard the same things repeated time and again about how valuable our veterans are and how much of an asset they are to the corporate world. That is why I ask: Why do we have so many unemployed veterans? Is it lack of job opportunities? Is it because their skill sets are not needed in their hometown, as was my case?

It is very easy for soldiers that have had one mission on their minds for so long to forget what civilian life is like. They drive to work each day and pay bills and get their vehicle serviced when it needs to be just like everyone else. The difference is that they had job security in the military for anywhere from four to thirty years. Some may have never had a civilian job. To join the military does not require you to go through a traditional job interview process. This may be hard for a lifelong civilian to understand. Furthermore, those that are transitioning out of the service may have forgotten what inner skills they truly have in order to market themselves to an employer. It is a difficult situation: an employer and an employee who do not recognize the skills that translate for them to their mutual benefit.

Here is an illustration: Go into a restaurant and tell the cook you would like something to eat because you are very hungry. But there are only certain things you are willing to eat; and, you can't tell him what they are. Likewise, the cook only knows how to cook certain things, and he isn't sure you will like the meal enough for him to waste his time cooking it. So he says, "You may as well leave, because I do not know what you can eat and I am probably not able to cook it anyway."

I have been to numerous job fairs and Transition Assistance Program events across the United States. I feel that job fairs and being part of employer panels is one of the most helpful things a corporation can invest in. These events assist veterans in understanding what corporate America is looking for. They also help them to see the many questions that are generated by being in front of a recruiter, but in a casual setting, without actually being interviewed.

I hope that more companies dedicate a few days a year to visiting US military installations. That is how they will become part of the solution, instead of just one of the town criers telling the world how bad the veterans have it. US veterans do not want you to feel sorry for them. They just want someone to see them for what they have inside, to bring them on board and have sincere gratitude and appreciation for their military trained value.

One of the biggest rewards I receive is when a US veteran is happy to have a human answer the phone when they call to ask a question about getting employed by our company. We in the HR industry are ambassadors for the clients we serve and for the candidates we work with. It is important for us to take time to listen to what job seekers say and to dig into their skills. Sometimes they do not have a full grasp of what they are capable of doing.

I once met a young lady at a TAP class in Norfolk, VA. She stood up and asked me a very important question. She said, "I am a parachute rigger. What type of job could I apply for with your company?" I asked her what she did on a day-to-day basis and what some of her collateral duties were. And as it turned out she had experience and training for planning and scheduling maintenance activities for all of the equipment they use in her department. She thought she could only find a position as a seamstress!

Uniformity is a crucial part of life in the military, from the first day of basic training until the day we separate or retire. This in itself is an invaluable tool all veterans possess and all companies require: the ability to maintain procedures and processes in accordance with the rules and regulations given in any employee handbook. We also have the confidence and empowerment to make quick decisions outside the box should such a situation arise.

Where Is the Real Issue Between Military Members Exiting the Military and the Available Jobs?

One of the most interesting things I have noticed is the attitude of exaggerated worth. There appear to be many who feel they are worth much more than the position they are looking for pays, whereas too many veterans sell themselves short. This is an extremely tough situation for both the possible employee and the employer. The real issue starts with lack of communication and misinformation. TAP/ACAP facilitators give separating members the false impression that they should add their base pay, Basic Allowance for Housing (BAH), Basic Allowance for Substance (BAS), and any other additional pay together in order to come up with their minimum salary requirements. This, however, is not the case and leads to nothing but frustration for the veteran. At the same time, there is a group of individuals teaching them to be more realistic. Standardization would solve this issue; the TAP/ACAP is a mandatory step in all veterans' out-processing. This is a government-run program that should be working to remove these barriers.

Another solution that may be feasible is to create an online training software package that puts the basics together. Of course there will still need to be ongoing counseling and a facilitator for questions. In addition, this program will allow for a more realistic approach to wage assumption that could be directly linked to the Department of Labor and the Department of Labor Statistics' websites. This would provide more real-time information for estimating salaries based on job interest and location. Gone will be the tattered and yellow pages of wage charts based on your rank. Say goodbye to the out-of-date hiring-trend spreadsheets and bring real time and realism to our real growing problems. We are in a mobile age; everything we do is in real time. The solution is simple: take the guesswork out of transition, and use the technology that we already possess to create streamlined training that is the same no matter what base you are leaving or which state you are transferring to.

Since I have been a recruiter for a company that was not sincerely making an effort to recruit US veterans, and because I now work for a company that is doing all that they can to recruit veterans, it was very interesting to see the differences in how the recruiting department of the company I worked for in the past operated. It was scary. They processed so many candidates that they would filter out candidates based solely on the salary expectation they put down on the application. This technique might be more acceptable when dealing with civilians in a specific industry that should have a clear idea of what their time, knowledge and experience level pays. However, an exiting military member does not have a clue in regard to salary. They can only research and make an educated guess.

I once had a situation in which I was dealing with a retired member of the United States Air Force (USAF). He was a perfect fit for the position, but he had been rejected in the applicant tracking system due to the minimum salary requirement he had put in his profile. I called the recruiter who was filling the position to find out why he had been rejected and she stated that his requirement was too much and so she went onto the next candidate. I asked if she had contacted him, since he did have the skills, and she replied no. So I called and spoke to him and he was very happy to take less. And the military was willing to relocate him there, as it was his home of record. To make a long story short, he was offered and accepted the position and is well respected in the organization.

How many times has this happened, not only in my experience, but in many recruiting departments? This will continue until we find a way to bridge the gap between these virtual guessing games. We can avoid this by eliminating the minimum salary requirement in a company's applicant tracking system if the applicant has checked the field "Yes," indicating that they are a US veteran. Another possible solution is to allow for a salary range to be indicated, so that would allow for a search based on requirements.

Persistence Pays Off

My family and I are home in Indiana, around family. We have been truly blessed. I am able to continue my passion for assisting veterans with their employment search. I had spent much of my life trying to pinpoint what I was called to do in this world. I went through many ups and downs, trials and tribulations, but I persevered and tirelessly followed my dream. And now I am at a point in my life I can truly say gives me fulfillment and purpose.

The ability to help others and truly enjoy and love what you do is invaluable. You may not know all the answers, but the passion you hold inside will drive you to continue to learn and better yourself. If you choose, you can leave this world a little better than you found it. That is really my goal.

About the Author

I enlisted in the USAF after September 11 and became an AGE (Aerospace Ground Equipment Technician) serving in the United Kingdom. I truly enjoyed my job and my fellow airmen with whom I was stationed. My wife ran an FCC-licensed daycare from our base housing unit that was supported by Royal Air Force (RAF) Lakenheath. My wife's name is Lisa Marie Vickers. Our children are Carl (5), Ava Marie (2), and Milly (a few weeks old).

PeopleScout is a world class Regional Planning Organization (RPO) dedicated to unparalleled customer service. It was ranked #1 Worldwide RPO Provider of 2012 by HRO Today's Baker's Dozen, and has been ranked as a Top Provider seven years straight! I am proud to say that I am a member of a team that truly believes in doing the right thing, empowering their employees to be innovators in their fields and promoting the passions that drive the day-to-day success of being an outstanding group of human resource professionals.

We enjoy outdoor activities when the weather allows and traveling. We also have a 75-pound Golden Retriever named Piper who has been my constant companion since I returned from overseas, and he supports our troops as well.

8: The Path to Finding a Career

DOUG BEABOUT,

The "Career Talk Guy"

On a very cold day at Wright-Patterson Air Force Base in January 1978, I walked out of the United States Air Force (USAF) personnel administration offices as a civilian. I had nearly seven years of experience doing very important and challenging things. I also had the advice of a noncommissioned officer (NCO) at the USAF discharge office who told me that to find a job, "just look at the classified ads and send resumes." He assured me that this was all I needed to do to start my career as a civilian. I was certain that the world was waiting for me and now I could pick the job I really wanted. After all, I said to myself, I just served my country and I deserve the opportunity I want.

I left active duty as a highly trained and skilled person with a very clear knowledge of my responsibilities and the specific steps I must take to carry out my missions. I recall feeling unprepared upon entering civilian life, although I was not lacking the courage or convictions that had served me in my military duties. I was ready to jump into the fray and not stop until I had acquired the job I wanted. Just the same, I often felt like one does in that common dream where you find yourself in front of a class wearing only a smile.

It took hundreds of resumes and weeks of discouraging lack of results before I realized that the world did not see me as being as valuable as I came to believe from my military service to our great nation. I tried going to the phone book and looking up every employer in my area. I sent them resumes with no particular position in mind. When I went to employment agencies, I was asked if I could type, or if I would I be willing to load cement bags for minimum wage, while they "looked hard" for the job I really wanted.

By then, I was really wondering if I should have left active duty. I was told to try an outplacement firm that for the nominal fee of $4,000 would show me how to place myself. In spite of the fact that they professed belief in me and insisted that they held veterans in the highest regard, my senses told me something wasn't right. It turned out that my gut instincts, honed by my military experiences, were on target. When I asked questions of the outplacement representatives about how they would assist me in gaining this 'assured success,' I was given a lot of optimistic encouragement and many compliments about my background, but never a concrete or persuasive answer. They went on to tell me about the thousands they had helped before me. I asked for references. They avoided providing them by telling me that they were "confidential'. So I passed up their offer to help me.

Finally, after several months of do-or-die effort and a rapidly thinning bank account, I sat down at a recruiting firm in response to an ad they ran for a management trainee. The recruiter tasked with interviewing me spent a great deal of time asking me questions, learning about my desires and career plans. At this point, I had receded from being the person anyone ought to hire to having little more than a burning need for a paycheck.

The recruiter sent me on three interviews at three large companies. I received an offer from each employer. I turned them all down. I was offered management training jobs, production supervision jobs and a job as a pharmaceutical sales representative. All paid less than what I had earned on active duty, which wasn't much. But under the umbrella of the military economy, I was provided housing, healthcare and access to very inexpensive living goods. So their offers were just not as much as I felt I deserved. My ego as an aviator and my confidence as a veteran probably played a big factor. Nonetheless, I felt I was worth more and really didn't like the jobs offered. I just could not adopt the "beggars can't be choosers" adage as applicable. I knew that surrender was not an option.

In the course of decades in recruiting, I have been fortunate to see the employment process from the inside. Mastering the management of candidates and developing excellent interviewing skills is requisite to being successful in recruiting. It seems ironic now, but in order to succeed in recruiting, I had to master how a person seeks, pursues and wins an offer of employment.

On active duty, most people need to be tough and of strong character. That does not end when you walk out of the discharge office. It takes courage to pick up the phone and call someone you have not met and who has no clue about what you bring to the table. It takes no particular strength to click on a computer mouse and send a resume to anyone. Finding employment is and always has been a contact sport, literally.

You are now about to take on the most important mission yet. You are now in charge of your future and career. We will take this one step at a time and put you on the pathway to a victorious outcome: Gaining employment with the employer you seek and who offers the opportunity you deserve.

Five reasons why it is necessary to continue reading this chapter:

1. 23 million Americans seeking work
2. New class of college graduates
3. Millions of under-employed Americans seeking higher positions
4. New federal taxes combined with the National Healthcare Plan will force many employers to reduce their number of full-time employees
5. As baby boomers continue to retire, employers must replace critically needed people

Here is a practical, actionable, systematic process that puts the seeker of employment in an empowering and results-based approach to find civilian employment.

What always has been the standard practice for doing a job search? Create a resume, send a resume, and then hope for a positive response. Period. This simple technique worked for the vast majority of job seekers until the late 1990s. Companies selected qualified employees almost entirely by the information presented on candidates' resumes.

Since 1978, I have had countless conversations with job seekers. Nearly every person felt their resume fell far short of illustrating their total ability to contribute to an employer. This is especially true when attempting to illustrate the value and experience forged in the crucible of military experience.

Job seekers have to discover why the position is open. It is not to serve the job seeker. It is to serve the employer. Therefore, the job seeker has to come to the realization that they must present themselves as a solution to the employer's problem. The problem is the employer's need to identify a great candidate who can fill the qualifications of the open position. By understanding this, the job seeker can proceed by finding out what an employer really needs. Then they can write a letter or seek an interview to discover what the employer is specifically seeking. Then they can present themselves as the solution to his need.

Job seekers and employers both make poor assumptions. The job seeker assumes that a potential employer can determine from their resume that they are qualified enough to be pursued and employed. Employers assume that job seekers are able to describe their skills, abilities, education and accomplishments sufficiently so that they can readily identify from their resumes which candidate is qualified for their open position.

Many employers are not very good at writing a job description, including exactly what is required for a position. So it is necessary to ask them the right questions in order to properly comprehend what is sought for a particular position.

For example: One very common question that has to be asked is, "When you hire the right person for this position, what will be the specific challenges of that job?" The follow up question is, "What qualifications, skills and abilities will that person possess that will allow them to succeed in meeting those challenges?"

These are two seemingly simple questions. But from speaking with hiring managers daily, I know that many have not thought through these two questions thoroughly. Sometimes, the job description was simply dusted off from the last time it was used. The hiring manager's assumption is that everything is complete and there is no need to change it. Many times the hiring manager thinks in terms of day-to-day activities. They do not consider a person's hidden skills like patience and perseverance, or how well that person will interact as part of the team tasked with accomplishing the defined objectives and goals. The solution for the job seeker is to be well prepared and to learn all about the company, position, culture, etc. Untangle all the vagueness in a job posting and get to the information required to present yourself effectively.

Most companies are not skilled at attracting qualified talent. Employers tend to be slow to change, regardless of how much it will serve them or cost them if they do not. Therefore, it is up to the job seeker to take charge of deciphering what the hiring manager needs and providing that information. Both parties benefit greatly from taking that approach.

Many of today's jobs require some form of training. Even labor jobs have been widely replaced by ever advancing technologies. Downsizing in most companies has eliminated many people and their responsibilities. Their duties have been absorbed by those who remained. These "morphed" job descriptions are problematic for both the job seeker and employers.

It is erroneously believed that the current rate of unemployment provides a massive pool of college-educated employees. Actually, fewer are available. U.S. Bureau of Labor Statistics reports that unemployment rates among individuals with 4 years of college or more, 25 years of age and older, is less than 4%.

However, employers that once insisted on candidates possessing four year BS or BA degrees have begun to realize that people with Associate's degrees or certifications can just as effectively perform many roles, particularly in the field of technology. This is great news for today's job seeker. Both institutions of higher learning and technology schools offer many online or "virtual" college courses. Adding technology certification to your accomplishments makes you far more competitive, particularly when combined with prior military experience.

Recently I spoke to a community college professor who had a long corporate career prior to joining the academic world. He conducted a great deal of training for corporations at all levels. He stated that his contacts in many companies were telling him they no longer insist that people have degrees. He was told if people had the specific certifications they needed, they would hire as many as his school could then turn out.

Many companies have learned that due to the frenetic pace of technological advancement, waiting for individuals to get a degree takes too long, and they are often behind the latest technology when they graduate. They prefer someone who has the latest certifications and can show that they can learn more technology as the need arises. Military training and experience is sometimes accepted in lieu of certification, but it is wiser to get a certificate that is accepted in the civilian world. Veterans' benefits often cover the cost of much of this education and training.

Let us take an X-ray of a position. Positions are defined in three dimensions:

- The position duties and required skills
- The projects, challenges and issues to be managed by the individual in that position
- The employer workplace culture

Discovering the particular facts, in all three dimensions defined above, is a prerequisite task to succeeding at finding a job that fits you best. You are the only person who can accept responsibility to capture the job you desire. You must actively approach employers, engage in dialogues with hiring managers, and learn about the employers' needs. There are obvious and not-so-obvious questions that need to be asked. As they are asked and responses are provided, other questions beg to be asked. Steps to take in this process are detailed in this chapter.

Approaching numerous employers and asking if they are hiring is not as effective as research and precision. Hard work and a "gung ho" attitude is a common characteristic of military veterans, but applying this approach to resume distribution is comparable to carpet bombing. A sniper approach is more productive. In other words, when brute force is ineffective, sound strategies and tactics that lend precision will create the desired result. If all you are seeking is interviews then remember: "Coming close only works with hand grenades and nuclear weapons." I will bet you heard that one before. A strategy that puts the job seeker in charge of their success is essential to gaining the best opportunity.

This raises the question, "How does technology help or hurt the job search?"

Consider the following: Technology insulates both sides from the insights to match the best qualified person accurately to the position requiring the skills and experience in all three dimensions defined above. While it is true that you can send countless resumes to potential employers with just the click of your computer mouse, a personal interview is always far better.

A great way to begin your job search is with a group of veteran peers and honest friends. Sit down and take a detailed inventory of what talents, abilities, achievements, training and education you bring to the table. Getting together in the same physical location may be difficult or impossible. The Internet offers very accessible means of group meetings via tools such as AOL AIM, Windows Messenger, Skype, GoToMeeting and FreeConferenceCall, to name a few. Those who lack Internet access or a computer can usually gain it at local libraries and adult education facilities.

Hold a Group Discussion of the Following Questions
- What areas of expertise do you bring from your military experiences?
- List technical skills and systems applications where you have demonstrated application and skill
- What did you achieve? Describe your military leadership experience and responsibilities, but in civilian wording.

Military service offers many opportunities to achieve great results with minimal resources. In the civilian world, the demand for individuals with proven abilities is at an all-time high. Today's multitasking positions require people who can overcome, innovate and persevere. Employers rarely see that in those lacking military experience, whereas US veterans have developed the core strengths and confidence needed in today's workplace. You must strive to present comparative evidence of these unique professional assets in order to illustrate your value as an employee.

I was in aviation, so before I took off on a mission, I always made certain my gear was in hand and my parachute was properly packed. I gave my plane and my crew a preflight check. I am suggesting you now do the same.

Create Presentation Materials

Armed with your inventory of assets, compile a detailed list of accomplishments such as:

- Did you achieve milestones? What were they?
- Did you exceed the expectations and output of your role? By what measure?
- Did you cut time wasted? How and why was it of benefit to the organization?
- Did you save money by being more efficient and using fewer resources? Try to be specific in this assessment.

Develop references. List the individuals who observed your performance and achievements. Contact them in any manner possible, preferably by telephone.

Fill them in on your goals. Request that they provide both written and oral references that attest to your accomplishments and value as an employee and team member. Relate each reference to your achievements, so you can provide the most appropriate references.

Research the industries that you know. This may seem a tall task if you have had only military experience, but it can be done quite well.

- What equipment did you use?
- What systems did you utilize?
- Many of the above tools, processes and systems have civilian counterparts or similar "cousins" in the public and private sectors of our economy. Refer to them when possible.
- "Spinoff" technologies from military development and deployment can be easily researched.

Research the industries that hire people with your qualifications. Targeted industries should fall into four categories:

1. Those where you can offer immediately applicable skills.
2. Those for which you have training and/or a keen interest.
3. Industries for which you plan to gain post-military education.

4. Those that arise opportunistically in your job search or because of your contacts' recommendations.

Take advantage of the research resources freely available in public libraries or Vet Centers across America. Develop lists of employer organizations and export them to a usable form such as a spreadsheet or database file. You can also simply print them out: One employer per page, so as you make contact you have space for notes. Once the full list of potential employers is developed, it can be utilized effectively from a computer.

Your research cannot be limited to developing a list of potential employers. You must study the industries of choice before you engage with contacts within them. Seek answers to these questions:

- What are the current conditions and how are they affecting that industry?
- What are the near-term prospects and potential within each industry?
- What particular challenges must be overcome?
- What is the long-term and near-term outlook?

The Beige Book is the Summary of *Commentary on Current Economic Conditions*. It is a report published by the United States Federal Reserve Board eight times a year. The book is a resource to discover the answers to the questions above. It is provided freely by your former employer, the Government!

This missive is compiled from hundreds of conversations conducted by industry analysts located at the twelve Federal Reserve Bank regional offices across the U.S. with industry leaders. These "movers and shakers" are selected for their insider perspectives and their industry's operations, initiatives and challenges. Their collaboration with the Federal Reserve Bank's industry analysts provide real-time insight and allow for accurate projections for those industry sectors. Stay on top of these reports as you conduct your search for employment. The "talking points" you can reap from these reports affords you the very attractive asset of being aware of what is hot when engaging in conversations with key people within an employer organization.

As you approach hiring decision makers (described in-depth later), these insights give you facts and talking points that you can weave into a conversation with them. This often creates the positive impression. It shows that not only have you done your homework, but you complete your due diligence before taking on any challenge. This knowledge also gives you the chance to converse with people about what they do, something nearly everyone embraces. More than a "foot in the door," it shows your sincere interest in an opportunity within their industry. It also compels people to respond with questions about you. This opens the opportunity to put your skills and strengths on the table.

I have seen very positive reactions to insightful questions I asked based on the intelligence I reaped from the Beige Book reports. Showing the caller you have done your homework truly separates you from your fellow job seekers in a very positive light.

Create a script for initial contacts. We are not going for an Oscar here. However, the most celebrated actors seem natural in the roles they play. It is the result of drills and repetition, much like those skills you mastered on active duty. The script should be questions you ask, rather than just answers to anticipated questions. The script you develop will help prepare you to be more relaxed and effective in an interview.

A huge difference between the old and broken approach to gaining employment and the one we want you to master is that it begins with you asking the questions. Your initial mission is to make the person with whom you speak feel understood, so asking questions just makes sense.

A sample opener for these conversations is: "Hello, my name is _____. I am calling to gain more information about your position (name job opening as listed). I am keenly interested in learning more about your company and listening to your insights about that industry. And I have a few questions."

When you encounter a response like, "I am very busy now," respond like this: "I will not take any more than twenty minutes. When is the best time for me to call you again?" Never ask a question where they can say "No."

Rehearse or role-play with an honest friend who will give constructive advice so you can fine-tune your words, tone and the impression you make. Do not expect or strive to be perfect at this. Coming off as real and sincere is your objective. I cannot overemphasize this point. Many people want it to be letter perfect, which often results in sounding insincere and self-serving to the listener.

Develop responses to objections. The hiring managers you reach are widely understaffed today. As a result, they are very busy. You should expect objections. Do not avoid or ignore them. An objection is actually a request for more information. They offer you an opportunity to engage in a dialog. In these calls, the recipient of your approach will commonly be seeking a reason to give you some of their time and to stay on the phone.

Common Objections

- How did you get my name?
- What do you want from me?
- What are you selling?
- I am too busy!
- You should talk to human resources.
- I am not the best person with whom to speak.

Answers to objections are friendly, sincere and helpful. Responses are best presented in a brief answer, followed by a question about the core of the objection.

Example: "I am too busy right now," followed by your response: "I know that you are a very busy person. I really value your input. What would be a better time to call?"

Or, an alternative to consider is, "I knew you might be busy. When would be the best time for me to call back and speak to you about why I am reaching out to you?"

You may get, "You should be contacting our human resources department." If so, reply "Of course! I certainly will. But would you mind if I asked you a few questions about your company first? I could really use your help." (This sincere closing comment is very effective at opening doors.)

You are less likely to gain a conversation by leaving a voice message. So try to reach them again early in the morning, during their lunchtime, or late in the day when hiring managers are not as besieged by issues and problems and more likely to allow for a dialog with a caller.

If you do feel compelled to leave a voice message, make it very brief, Example: "My name is ___. I was referred to you as the most knowledgeable person in the ___ area. Please call me back at (your call-back number). I am confident that there will be a mutual benefit in our conversing. Thank you."

When you receive any unrecognized phone call during your job search, always answer: "Hello, This is _____. How may I help you?"

Record a formal, friendly and professional voice mail response for callers such as: "This is ___ and you have reached my voice mail. Your call is very important to me. Please leave your name, number and a convenient time to return your call. Thank you for calling."

Track your call performance plan. Simply stack them up in front of you with the telephone in hand and start calling them without pause or delay between calls. After each conversation or failed attempt, keep a note of it. You must maximize your exposure to potential employers to accelerate your search and to acquire employment sooner than later.

Set Up Three In-boxes on Your Workspace and Label Them A, B and Z

- A= High potential of results with a given employer
- B= Possible potential for employment but not high probability due to timing or a cold reception
- Z= Zilch, No go (not to be called again)

After continued calls and dialogue with hiring managers, you will see the lists of employers change. "A" employers may devolve into "B" or "Z" classifications, based upon the way your dialog takes you. "B" employers may evolve into "A" employers.

If you fail to connect with anyone at a company, simply put that page at the bottom of your stack of leads. You will work your way to them again. Continue calling until you reach the last page of leads. If needed, go back to your employer research resource and expand to include more employers.

Send a follow-up email to those individuals with whom you have a positive dialog.

- Be brief
- Thank them for the opportunity to engage in a dialog and for sharing with you
- Be sure to include a fact or item they shared
- State your continued interest and reiterate the date and time of the next call.

Once you make an initial contact with a hiring manager, always set a date and time for a follow-up call, no matter how brief the first call was. An individual's willingness to accept a follow-up call is an indication of a positive direction. If the first call is a dud, try another hiring manager within that same company. You may be directed to the human resources department. Be sure that you ask for the name and title of the HR person you should approach.

If using Microsoft Outlook or any contact manager, when you get an appointment, set the date and time in your calendar. Then send them a reminder from the toolbar: "Invite attendees."

The old saying is true, "It's who you know." But now it is up to you make yourself known and to know those people within organizations, particularly hiring managers.

You are a valuable and important individual with a great deal to offer any employer who seeks your potential and abilities. You sacrificed an easier existence to be of service to your country. You faced dangers and perils that few civilians ever see or understand. I thank you for your service, but the battle is not over. You must face the challenge of gaining meaningful employment. You know you deserve this. Now it is up to you to charge ahead and make your way to your objective. The process is there, but you must put your "skin in the game" again. Follow this process and you will land where you truly belong.

Persistence pays in your search for employment. Do not allow the process to defeat you. Objections to your efforts are a natural part of this process. Strive to overcome them. Walk away from losing battles and seek an employer that appreciates the special advantages and value your experience brings to them.

About the Author

My background has been forged in the crucibles of military service in Strategic Air Command aboard B-52 bombers in the Vietnam War, and over thirty-five years as a recruiting firm owner and trainer. I have started and sold five successful recruiting businesses while helping over five hundred people start their own personnel services business. For over twenty years, I have trained thousands of recruiters and corporate human resources professionals in best practices. My partner, Kevin Sutton, and I have combined experience of over fifty years in the placement and career improvement of thousands of people from minimum wage to executive level. I speak to groups in my industry, employers and associations across the globe. Our combined knowledge helped us to serve thousands in these challenging economic times. No-one knows what really works best in finding the best opportunity than recruiters whose livelihood depends on razor sharp skills and practical insights. CareerTalkGuys.com is our newest enterprise, created to focus on providing skills and practices that guide job seekers to the opportunities they seek. Our exposure to the errors and misguided actions of both job seekers and employers has allowed us to create a very practical and proven job-seeking process.

9: A Virtual Solution to Helping Veterans Find Employment

KEVIN O'BRIEN

So you are ready to start sourcing jobs now that you have left the military. But where do you go to find them? The job search process has evolved quite a bit over the years, for better and for worse. Remember the days of reading the newspaper to find a job, perhaps circling the job, and then calling or walking in? How about finding a job in the paper and then faxing your resume? Of course, we can't forget about the job boards which made it easier to search for available jobs, based on location or job title.

Now we have sites like LinkedIn that allow us to connect with peers even if we do not have a personal relationship with them. Perhaps you went to the same school, or belong to the same group, or have a mutual contact. Regardless of if you know them or not, professionals are using LinkedIn to connect, network, and most importantly source jobs on a more personal level. There is no substitute for a referral into a job opportunity, because hiring managers value the opinion of a qualified third party. The process has become a little more efficient, but along the way it also made it less likely that you would actually interact with a real human being through this initial process.

The same evolution has not occurred for the career fair. Career fairs are conducted today much like they were decades past. It used to be that you could attend a career fair in your best business suit or dress, have resumes in hand and meet with the staff working the career fair for an employer. Many job seekers left these events with an interview or a job offer in hand. Unfortunately, that is no longer the case for a variety of reasons, which has resulted in the traditional career fair really being not much more than a branding opportunity for the employer and an information session for the job seeker. It is not that employers wouldn't like to be in a position to make offers on the spot, or at least to set up interviews. But there are several things preventing them from doing so, including:

- Background checks   ·
- Employment verification
- Criminal checks
- Education checks
- Reference checks
- Credit checks

Today, the many regulations and policies that ensure all employers are giving fair and equal access to all candidates have greatly reduced the time companies have to qualify and hire job seekers applying for their open positions. This often results in a job seeker feeling as if the employer is ignoring them. In most cases, that is not the truth.

In recent years, the virtual career fair has made it possible for employers and veterans to connect and interact in real time from anywhere in the world. The virtual career fair allows the employer to recruit worldwide in one day. They save time on travel, table setup and marketing expense for booth giveaways. Plus, recruiters from all over the world can participate in real time without leaving their offices.

Virtual job fairs allow employment seekers to build a profile that includes their resume, picture, fields of interest, and desired location. They can research employers by visiting the virtual booths even before the virtual career fair begins. Our US veterans may view and apply for the employers' open positions, chat live with recruiters during the virtual career fair, and network with fellow veterans and military spouses in real time.

Unfortunately, it is far too common for a service member to wait until they have left the military before they really start their civilian employment search. Statistics show that when that is the case, it is often too late. However, through virtual career fairs they can explore employment opportunities with many of America's leading employers, regardless of where they are stationed. Soldiers in Kuwait, Afghanistan, Korea, Germany, Australia, and several other countries participate in virtual career fairs. One soldier wrote and thanked us for hosting an event in 2011 in which he participated from a submarine. He wrote, "Thank you for hosting such a great event. Through the virtual career fair, I was able to connect with Amazon, who is based in my hometown, and I will be connecting with them as soon as I get back."

The virtual career fair also gives equal access to the veteran or military spouse who might have difficulty traveling to and from a physical location. They may not have the luxury of affording child care on the day a traditional career fair is being hosted.

Through the virtual career fairs that my firm has managed over the last two years, more than 15,000 veterans and military spouses have been hired by employers such as Aetna, Amazon, American Express, AOC Solutions, Arise Virtual Solutions, Camping World, CBRE, CHSi Middle East, Citi, Coach USA, Convergys, DaVita, Dish Network, Dr. Pepper Snapple Group, General Motors, Graybar, Intercontinental Hotels Group, IM Flash Technologies, Level 3 Communications Inc., Lowe's, NCO Financial, Northwestern Mutual Life, Penske, PepsiCo, Pfizer, Philips, Progressive, Sears Holdings, State Street Corporation, the SI Organization, Travelers, TSA, the U.S Department of the Treasury, the U.S Office of Personnel Management, Union Pacific, Waste Management, Xerox Business Services, and more than three hundred other Fortune 1000 employers. Virtual job fairs are a legitimate and a relied-upon option.

Many who hear the term "virtual career fair" automatically think they need to be tech savvy to participate, but that is not the case. If you can type an email or visit a website, you have enough skill to participate. There are some things you can do to ensure your virtual career fair experience is both productive and pleasurable:

1. **Treat the virtual career fair as you would a traditional career fair (sans suit and tie of course):** Just because the career fair is online, that does not mean you should not be putting your best foot forward. You only get one chance to make that first impression, regardless if it is virtual or in person.

2. **Do your homework before attending:** Too many times, we see veterans or military spouses attend our virtual career fairs who have clearly not taken the time to do any research prior to attending. This becomes apparent very quickly to the employers who are participating. Take a few hours to visit the virtual career fair prior to the live day. Research which employers are participating and what they have to offer. Browse all available jobs. View and apply for jobs that interest you. Then, and only then, engage the recruiters about specific jobs in which you have an interest. This is your time to shine. Asking generic questions that you could have and should have answered for yourself prior to speaking to a recruiter will result in you coming across as irresponsible and unprepared.

3. **Watch your comments and chats:** Most virtual career fairs will have a public chat room in addition to private chat areas in the employer booths. What you post here can be seen by all. It can easily result in an employer getting a bad impression of you.

4. **Ask for contact information of every recruiter with whom you come in contact:** Send them a follow-up thank-you for connecting with you in the virtual career fair. This will show that you are serious about your job search, helping you stand out from many of the other attendees.

5. **You will get out of your virtual career fair what you have put in:** If you show up unprepared, with a lax attitude, you are probably wasting your time waiting for the phone to ring. But if you do the preparation, treat the event as if you were face to face, and do the follow-up, you stand a much better chance of securing interviews.

The tips and advice above apply to the veteran or military spouse, but there are also things an employer must do and understand to ensure they are also getting the most out of their virtual career fair experience. Just because the career fair is online does not mean it is as simple as showing up and waiting for every attendee to visit your booth. On the contrary, you are in an even more competitive environment because the virtual booths are so easily accessible. With the proper preparation, design, and attention, you can be sure to attract the best talent to fill your open positions.

1. **Are you sending the proper message to veterans and spouses?** This does not mean having a picture of a soldier on your website or throwing up the military friendly flag at various events. It goes much further than that. Do you have a veterans group at your company? If not, you should start one soon. You will be surprised at how many veterans work for companies that never knew about the merits of hiring veterans. Veterans groups are a great support system; they provide services ranging from support when a loved one is deployed to volunteer activities in your community on the company's behalf. Find a veteran in your organization and ask them to lead the effort.

2. **Do you have a dedicated place on your company career page that speaks to veterans specifically?** Many getting out of military service do not know exactly where they will fit into the civilian job world. It is in your best interest to help them understand. Plus there are skills translators such as the one found at www.veteranrecruiting.jobs.

Whether the career or job fair is in a traditional or online environment, it is paramount that you have realistic expectations before attending. The chance of you attending any career fair and coming away with a job the same day is quite slim. The more preparation you can do before attending, the more educated, qualified, and desirable you will appear to be to the recruiters in attendance.

The career fair is really just an opportunity for you to see what is available with the employers attending, and an opportunity for you to demonstrate why you would make the ideal hire for the respective positions available. When chatting with the recruiters, ask them what their hiring process is and what you can expect with regard to communication.

As with any job search activity, follow-up is the key. If you were interested in a job while talking to a recruiter at the job fair, follow up accordingly by sending each contact a personal thank-you along with another copy of your resume. And be sure to ask for their card. On the back of it, jot down a line or two that will help you in calling their attention to your conversation at the career fair. Boilerplate responses are a dime a dozen when following up, so be sure to make your correspondence as personal as you possibly can.

If you are active duty, Guard, reservist, veteran, or a military spouse, Veteran Recruiting would be honored to assist you in your search for meaningful employment. In addition to the virtual career fair days we host throughout the year, we also keep our site open all year to allow you the opportunity to research employers prior to connecting with them in the virtual career fairs. Visit www.veteranrecruiting.com to sign up.

About the Author

Kevin O'Brien is the managing partner of Veteran Recruiting Services and a pioneer in the virtual career fair space. O'Brien has been instrumental in bringing together hundreds of industry leading employers with more than 200,000 active duty, guard/reservists, veterans, and military spouses in less than two years.

In 2008 O'Brien developed Milicruit and Unicruit, aimed at bringing industry leading employers and job seekers together in a fully interactive, virtual environment. O'Brien joined forces with UBM Studios in 2010 to bring his virtual career fair vision to a much wider audience. Milicruit helped more than 15,000 veterans find employment with industry leading employers in two years.

In 2001 O'Brien joined Genesys Conferencing and led the company's sales efforts in North America. Genesys was ultimately acquired by West Corporation in 2008.

10: Putting Your Best Foot Forward

Wisdom from a Military Wife

KRISTINA SAUL

My name is Kristina Saul. I am a military spouse (retired) after 23 years of my husband's 27 years of service, and I learned what it was like to live the ups and downs of the uncertain life of a military family member. The life of a military spouse is not easy, but it is what makes us unique! We have adapted to moving every two to four years; living months or years without our spouses' presence; and being both mother and father. We find and work at a job wherever the military sends us. At the same time, we help other military families that are having problems while their warrior is away, trying to make it through a deployment and return. We tend to take on a lot without asking for much in return. I guess that is why the military spouse tends to be called "Semper Gumby" (always flexible) and the "Hero at Home."

For the last ten years my background has been in military employment initiatives and recruiting. I currently manage the Milicruit Online virtual career fairs. I have been able to watch and learn a lot along the way. Actually, during the writing of this book I am going through yet another career change and hope to share some of what I am going through with you.

I hear the frustrations in people's voices when job seekers chat online during our virtual career fairs. They complain of not being able to find a job. I understand those frustrations. I always put myself in the job seeker's position when I help them. As a job seeker you must remember that you are not alone; others are going through it with you. Remember to stay strong and put your best foot forward, whether in person or virtually.

There are many ways to get your name out there, and you need to use them all. I am going to list a few for you that will get you on the road to getting your resume out in the market.

LinkedIn – Get a profile set up and start networking. Remember that this is a professional social network, not a place to complain about not being able to get a job. LinkedIn also has some great articles on the best ways to use the site as well as on how to build your resume and how to handle interviews. There is also a job board and recruiters who post job listings daily. Connect with recruiters and make sure that you have a complete profile. Reach out to prior co-workers and prior supervisors and ask them to endorse your work. This is a daily must-use site.

Virtual (Online) Career Fairs – These are popping up as the new way to go to a career fair. Please remember you're not going to get a job in one day by going to one of these. But you will get connected to a recruiter, and all the information you need to know about a company is in one place. Your feet won't hurt from standing in line, you won't have to drive in traffic, and you can upload your resume right then to the company website.

There has been great success, but like any other company your resume has to fit the job description. Remember to touch each booth. For instance, banks are not just looking for tellers, they need IT folks and administrators as well. The same for hospitals; they need lawyers and HVAC engineers to run the facilities. Keep the umbrella open. The important part of these types of fairs is that all the information is in one place. So make sure you are researching the companies before asking questions to the recruiters. Don't embarrass yourself by asking if there is a job in Oregon when that information is already there for you to find. What type of impression does that leave in the recruiter's mind for what kind of job you would do for that company?

Live (Traditional) Career Fairs – Make sure you do not go into these career fairs with a feeling that you will hand the recruiter a resume and then get a job or an interview. A lot of the time the actual recruiter or hiring manager is not there, and you cannot even be evaluated without your resume being in their applicant tracking system.

Tips on how to go to a live event:

- Research the companies that will be there.

- Apply to the companies and positions you qualify for

- Take a copy of your resume and post a note with the company name and include the requirements for the job you applied to on that resume

- Once at the career fair, go to that company's booth. Meet with the representative. Let them know you applied to that position. Before you leave each booth, get the hiring manager's information or at least the senior recruiter's contact information. Most companies now have military recruiters, so ask for that contact as well

- Ask any additional questions you may have

Follow up in two days. Tell them that you were at **X** career fair, you applied to **Y** position, and spoke to **Z** representative at the career fair.

Online Job agents: There are multiple agents out there. Look for your veteran friendly ones first, like HirePatriots.com. Then branch out to the larger ones like Indeed and Monster. (See the Resources list in the back of this book for examples.)

The Importance of Training Certificates & Licenses

There are many modes of service (MOS) in the US military. So after 20 years in the service it is time to retire and you are in the middle of your job search. You've spent two tours in Afghanistan patching up solders; now you are applying to positions with hospitals, but you can't get a job because you're not certified. There was no time to get this done while you were in the service. Now it is too late and you need a job because you're getting out soon.

You discover that in the civilian world you cannot even legally put a bandage on anyone. They have been working on laws to change this, so check the latest information online. Make sure first, before you begin work on your license and certification. I called the military medical schools and they highly recommend that you do this while in the military, but most military members do not. They do not keep up on the licenses and certifications. But it is vitally important that you keep your certifications up to date. Do this for your future. Once you're out and not licensed it is hard to get your foot in the door without starting over.

On September 21, 2012, a very important bill was passed: **The Veteran Emergency Medical Technician Support Act, H.R. 4124.** It provides demonstration grants to states with a shortage of emergency medical technicians (EMTs) to streamline state licensing requirements for military veteran EMTs. The National Association of Emergency Medical Technicians explains that the legislation "has the potential to help veterans return to work upon their completion of military duty and reduce unemployment among veterans." H.R. 4124 was approved by voice vote: energycommerce.house.gov/sites/republicans.energy-commerce.house.gov/files/letters/hr4124/20120404NAEMT.pdf.

This is great news to those of you who have worked hard at what you do and have hit so many roadblocks. I have worked with Daniel Nichols, who was a principal architect in getting this bill passed. He is a prior Navy chaplain and now a reservist with the US Coast Guard. He spent a lot of time in the field and has been right there listening to your stories. If your military spouse is in the healthcare field, they have made advancements for them too. They are permitted to transition medical licenses from state to state as they move from duty station to duty station. Twenty-three states now have signed an agreement to join the military Spouse License Portability Program: www.whitehouse. gov/blog/2012/06/26/23-states-have-now-passed-pro-military-spouse-license-portability-measures

After the Transition Assistance Class (TAP)

There are many hurdles our military run across as they transition from active duty to civilian life. Going through TAP class and trying to remember all the information packed into four days is just one of them. You go into all that with your mind already full with, "I need to find a job before I get out," and "How are we going to move?" Just think of it as another set of orders and handle it then.

What I find is that everyone is trying to take shortcuts. But think of your job search as your job and it will pay off. The more time and effort you put into your search, the more success you will have. One suggestion I have: bring in your spouse to help you. They will be your best partner in helping to network your resume. After all, they are the one that has had to move around and make new friends and find a new job at each new duty station. They are great at this and will be a lot of help.

As military spouses we learn to adapt as our military member gets moved around from duty station to duty station, so we always need to look for jobs. One thing people forget is that the military spouse's unemployment rate is three times that of the veteran. Military spouses tend to not seek employment because we always get asked, "How long are you going to be here?"

When I met my husband way back when, I was in retail and eventually moved up into management. Years later, I went into finance and had retail to fall back on as we moved. I learned you always want a fallback career. These two careers led me into what I do today. It all broke down to customer service, regardless of the job or industry.

As I mentioned earlier, I am in search of a new career myself. Over the last ten years I have helped many people find jobs, so I am using the tricks I tell you today. Do you have a fallback? Consider jobs that you have done and base one of your resumes on that job to create a military to civilian resume.

As I apply for these positions for which I know I am qualified and get declined, I try to think what was it in my resume that I may not have hit on or that I should have left out. It is hard to put so much of our life and what we do into one or two small pages. Do not load your resume down with impertinent information unrelated to the specific job for which you are applying.

Keywords are also important. The online technological application systems are set to pick up keywords. There are online systems like Turbo Tap that give you these keywords for your specialty. Or just pull the specific keywords out of the job description so you know your resume will be picked up. The goal here is just don't give up. Stay positive. No-one is out to get you. You are competing against probably many others and you need to stand out, so take time with your resume.

You may need to move, or you may need to take some time away from the family to go and get started in a job away from home just to keep things afloat. One does what one must do.

When my husband was retiring from the service in 2011, we were stuck between a rock and a hard place. We were a Category 5 Exceptional Family Program member. This meant the family needed to be near a large medical facility, but the military member could still be moved around. Well, as every military family does, one day we had to make the decision for the family to stay in Georgia while my husband moved with his command. This lasted for five years.

When you're in the military, you don't think about all the benefits that come out of a civilian paycheck and that you become responsible for. When we retired we really noticed the loss of our tax-free Basic Allowance for Housing (BAH) and the addition of the copays for medical. We noticed the price of medication went up dramatically. State and county benefits of paying reduced property and excise taxes no longer applied, since these only applied to active duty service members, not veterans (this varies from state to state). There were a lot of little discounts to active duty that we no longer received, 10% here, half off there, etc. It makes a big difference when you add it up.

The addition of civilian life insurance was a shock. As the military covered him throughout his career at a low rate for a large amount, the same amount of coverage in civilian life can easily be double or triple that cost, and it often has to be renewed yearly!

Unless you are fully covered by your employer, medical insurance will now come out of your paycheck as well. Whereas Tricare took a relatively small chunk of money out of your paycheck, it is not uncommon for civilian medical insurance to be ten times that amount. A family of four can pay almost $10,000 a year between health insurance and copays in the civilian sector. In comparison, Tricare runs about $500 a year for that same medical coverage for that same family. You will also need to balance the difference in costs if you are retiring or just leaving the military. You will have certain benefits like the commissary and exchange that you can still use if you are retired, but you can't if you leave the service.

When my husband finally retired, he set up a LinkedIn account. He put his resume out everywhere. He had at least 15 different versions, as well as a great general version that would get at least a company interested in him. I sent his resume out to people I knew and asked them to send it out to people they knew. He contacted three headhunters and finally he was going on interviews. This required close to 40 hours a week of networking and reading career books like you're doing today. It paid off with two very good employment offers.

Like any good military family, we sat down around the kitchen table and between the two job offers in two different states, we chose the best one. Then we had a garage sale, put the house up for rent, and moved just like we had gotten orders. We now live in New Mexico and he is doing something he never thought he would be doing: He is in the manufacturing field.

My last marketing piece for our December 2012 newsletter went out with this title: "The Best Time to Find a Job is During the Holidays!" I received many comments and some nasty-grams back telling me that they had not found that to be true. I wrote every one of those folks back and said that I would love to review their resumes. I reviewed the resumes of everyone that sent me one. They were all either too long or did not give enough information. They were just really bad resumes. So I gave them some pointers on how to rewrite them, and now I think they will land a job.

So I want to leave you with this: Make sure you are always putting your best foot forward in all parts of your resume. Tell your next employer what you did and how you did it. Let them know how successful you were at it. Did you save the company any money? How many people did you train? How many were you in charge of?

Be positive! It will spread like good news and soon you will reap the benefits. You will see how easily resumes flow out of you and those connections start coming through.

It is important to sell your military experience and accomplishments in your resume. Numbers are important! Sell yourself! There is plenty of help on the web; just search resume writing and you will see many examples. See page 285 for a great general resume to get you started.

Wishing you good luck,
Thank you for all you do!
Kristina Saul

About the Author

Kristina Saul is a proud Navy spouse, married to Brett Saul, who retired as a senior chief petty officer after 27 years in the Navy.

Kristina is a "jack-of-all-trades" regarding military initiatives, information, and referral of military resources, employment strategies and networking. With 23 years as a military spouse, countless household moves, and the mother of two wonderful children, one which is Autistic/Bipolar. She is also a two-time cancer survivor.

Her previous work history includes being a three-time certified Navy family ombudsman, cofounding a military spouse employment initiative, recruiter entrepreneur, retail management, general banking, mortgage lending, consumer finance, virtual events producer and now a webinar producer.

Kristina's website picks:

Military Connection- www.militaryconnection.com
Hero 2 Hired - h2h.jobs
Warrior Gateway - www.warriorgateway.org
Military Spouse Employment Partnership Program - (MSEP)
msepjobs.militaryonesource.mil
Military.com - www.military.com
American Corporate Partners - www.acp-usa.org
GI Jobs - www.gijobs.com
Turbo Tap - www.turbotap.org/register.tpp

National Military Family Association (NMFA) -
www.militaryfamily.org
TAOnline-www.taonline.com
Indeed - www.indeed.com/military

11: Transition: Where Do You Start?

CESAR NADER, U.S. MARINE, RET.

It takes months to train regular civilians to become "basic" military professionals in the U.S. Armed Forces. The selection, processing and training is costly and requires a heavy manpower effort on the part of our military leaders. In contrast, when it is time to transition out of the military, the mandatory requirement is only one week to complete a Transition Assistance Program (TAP) and to complete DD form 2648, the Pre-Separation Counseling Checklist.

While the efforts and improvements of the TAP program have begun to address the need for a more effective and targeted transition plan for our heroes, the fundamental problem is not lack of effort. The issue is a lack of effective and relevant transition training that addresses the skills and abilities of each veteran. Then they need to be matched with the right career path, at the right time, and in the right place.

When I joined the Marine Corps on 14 November of 1990, I had no idea what I was getting into. I also never expected to stay in almost 21 years. I just wanted to serve my country, travel the world, play with guns and have a good time. Seriously, that is what I thought I would be doing each and every day. I never thought I would have to leave the Corps unless, as I foolishly prayed, I met a glorious death in battle.

I joined the Corps when Desert Storm began. I had just returned from living in Ecuador for ten years. You see, I was born an American citizen in Los Angeles, California, at St. Anne's Hospital. But much of my early years are a blur due to my later combat experiences in Somalia. I lived in the city of Guayaquil until I was 18 and then decided I would become a doctor and make my mother proud. I found out that as an American citizen I would have to pay a higher tuition because I was a foreign student. Given my household's economic situation, I knew that would not be possible. But as the oldest of five children and without a father in the home, my mother relied heavily on my ability to make something of myself to support the little ones coming after me.

Not knowing what else to do, I went to see my grandfather. I asked him if he would let me borrow enough money to go back to the United States so I could get a job and send money back to Ecuador for my family. He replied "If you can save enough for a ticket, I will give you money to get you started." Given my entrepreneurial spirit, I was ready for the challenge. I spoke to all of my relatives and asked them to pitch in and help me get my ticket. My grandmother and my mother somehow made it happen and within a few days, I went back to my grandfather and he put $200 cash in my hand. This was the first time I had seen this rare currency everyone coveted. The mighty dollar was a symbol of success and prosperity in Ecuador. If you could flash even one dollar, you were somebody. I now had 200 of those green bills in my hand and it was my time to make good on my promise to support my family.

On 18 March, 1990, I took flight and landed at my aunt's small apartment in Palm Springs. Within a week or two I was able to land that job at Alpha Beta, and just a few days later I started working at Arby's. I was happy and felt successful. I was helping my aunt with the bills and sending money to Ecuador to my mother. I even had enough money left over to buy a few things I had always wanted. Life was great, but this "lavish" lifestyle would not last for long. When Desert Storm began, something in me called me to duty. Naturally, I answered that call.

On the advice of my aunt, I went to visit the recruiting center in Palm Springs. I remember walking into the recruiter's office unsure of what to say. I stood there and waited to hear what the Marine recruiter had to offer. He had me sit down and watch a video on boot camp. He asked me a few questions. And then I was told to get up on the pull-up bars. I could barely get myself up to meet the bar with my forehead, much less clear it with my chin. I tried to do sit-ups but cramped after 15 of them. He looked disappointed, but he must have had hope, because he asked me to take a preliminary test to see if I was smart enough to compensate for my weak physical state.

When I was done, I knew it was not good. But he seemed to have enough trust in me and decided I would do the processing at the San Diego Military Entrance Processing Station (MEPS). We drove all day and got there late at night. I remember taking an aptitude test and undergoing intense and very detailed physical exams. It was amazing to me to see how elaborate and organized this whole process was and how everyone seemed to know where to go and what to do. It took two days to get through this portion of my enlistment, and to be quite honest, I barely passed it.

When I finished the entire two-day event, I was taken to another Marine who sat me down and reviewed the paperwork with me. He told me that I had barely passed the aptitude test (ASVAB) and that they could not offer anything other than an open contract. I asked what that meant. He responded that the Corps would decide for me what I would become, depending on the needs of the war and what was available at the time I completed boot camp. I figured he knew better than me. The Corps was more knowledgeable than a kid who just got back from living overseas for over a decade. So I signed on the dotted line and enlisted as an open contract with a combat arms option.

My entire military career was a very enjoyable and successful series of events that allowed me to become the man I am today. I was selected to gunnery sergeant (Enlisted-7) by the time I had seven years in the Corps. When I was admitted to the Marine Enlisted Commissioning Education Program (MECEP), I took advantage of the opportunity and completed three majors and two minors. I also studied two foreign languages. As an officer I was able to go on to be selected for the Naval Postgraduate School (NPS) and completed two Master's Degree programs.

The advice and counsel of those who came before me was invaluable to my success and my achievements. It is ironic, but I never felt that anything I achieved was the product of my own doing. It was the consequence of the leadership advice I received from so many great Marines. I might not have known what to do, but I could always ask another Marine.

Consequently, when it was time to retire and leave the Corps, I felt I knew what I had to do and whom I could ask for advice. My retirement plan was bit different than most. I started planning for retirement soon after my commission as a second lieutenant on May 5th, 2001. I was concerned about what of one of my leaders had told me: "Sooner or later, we all have to leave the Corps." Before that time, I figured I would be one of those Marines who would simply never leave the Corps and die on the battlefield or of old age while clinging to his uniform and his rifle. I was so naïve. Life was good and simple in the Corps, and with every re-enlistment I was able to reset the clock once again on that pesky issue of transition. I grew up in the Corps and referred to those not in uniforms as "puke civilians." I was not going to become one of them.

As the clock started ticking on my officer time, I realized that I had to figure out what to do and fast. After all, I was now beginning a new career and sooner or later my run in the Corps was going to be over.

When I got to my first command in Iwakuni, Japan, I began looking for ways to learn about transition. I started to look into the transition classes on base. I tried to remember those hip-pocket classes our non-commissioned officers (NCOs) would give us in the field and in garrison about preparing for transition. I actually remember attending one of the TAP classes at Camp Pendleton when one of my fellow Marines was getting out after we returned from Somalia. I did not pay attention to anything they said, but I wish I had. I spent the next ten years refining what I have learned since to create a "transition strategy" for all veterans leaving the service. You can see a sample of these seminars on YouTube by searching for "Military Veteran Transition Seminar (Part 1 of 3)" or going directly www.youtube.com/watch?v=xhjqDpq_jGU. I will describe that strategy here for you to employ in your transition plan.

Transition Strategy

The first thing I tell every veteran I have spoken to about transition is that you should not listen to broke people if you want money advice. I learned this while reading a book on real estate. The author talked about being careful not to listen to advice where that advice is not born of experience. Equally valuable is that you should not take advice from people who have not yet transitioned or who did not transition effectively.

If you are going to make a successful transition, and you feel that TAP and other resources available are not going to provide you with enough tools for you to execute an effective transition strategy, then listen to me. I will tell you how to make sure you make the most of the resources you have, what you should do, and in what order. I am not a professional recruiter, nor do I claim to be a certified coach or public speaker. I don't even claim to be an authority on transition. What I will claim and attest to is the experience and tools I gained along the way, as I have assisted over 100 veterans who have transitioned since I began my journey back in 2002 at my first command. I will tell you what steps to take first and how to ensure you make the right choice. I will do so by sharing a method that is being used by veterans now who have listened to my transition strategy and can personally provide testimony of how that helped them make the right decision. Note that I did not tell them what they should do. I merely gave them the tools and helped them figure it out.

First "Who", Then "What"

Until you know who you are as a professional, you should not venture into the question of what career path you should choose. After being in the military for one or several tours of duty, you are not the same person (a civilian), and you certainly have many more skill sets than when you joined. It is critical that you fully assess what you have in your leadership tool bag and who you have become in order to define the most effective path to a successful transition. You can determine this by consulting with your spouse, significant other, or those leaders and peers who know you best as a professional. You should also consider taking a strength and personality test if you feel you have too many questions about who you are and how to refine that profile. At the end of the day, after all the counsel is in and you have done your due diligence, the decision is yours. Once you can answer this question with a degree of confidence, you can focus on the second step.

Prioritize Your Transition Goals

Too many who transition will tell you that if they could go back, they would do it better the second time around. If they could just do one thing differently, it is usually setting the right priorities early so the decision about what to do becomes clear and focused. This is critical and imperative because the right order of your transitioning goals will set in motion the right path to a successful career transition.

At the end of the day, there are three transitioning goals that most veterans stress over to the point of no sleep. Their decision is clouded because they listen to broke people or they focus on what to do, not on who they are, prior to deciding how to prioritize their transitioning goals. Furthermore, sometimes it is difficult to know how to prioritize if you don't even know what those priorities are. Well, let me tell you what they are: *money, location* and *job satisfaction.*

You can always have one, and if you choose right maybe two, but you may never have all three. That is why they are mutually exclusive and interrelated. Choose right and the rest will fall into place without friction. Choose wrong and you will spend your next few years going from job to job, stressing about every decision and trying to justify each move with another wrong move to cover up your original mistake.

Some people will immediately try to deny that their top priority is money. The truth is that to some, this is their top priority and goal. Whether it is because of debt or financial objectives, making as much money as they can earn is more important than where to live and what job they get. This is often how some end up with jobs overseas, deployed, as if they were on active duty, but now making the money they feel they are worth. If you have such a priority, make sure you understand what you are sacrificing and what you are gaining.

In most cases veterans choose either location or job satisfaction as their top priority, because that is truly where they find the most joy and contentment.

For those who chose location, the question of money or job satisfaction is a second thought. Most important for them is making the choice to live where they know they will be most happy and least stressed. What job they get and how much they make is secondary to their most important priority of living where they always wanted to live. This is also tied to where to start or grow a family, or where to retire and grow old and happy. In other cases they pick a location where their extended family lives; they want to go back to their roots. Either way, those who choose location make the decision knowing full well that their lives will be better if they follow their hearts.

Finally, for those who feel that job satisfaction is extremely important the joy of doing what they love is more important than money or location. One example is Junior Reserve Officer Training Corps (JROTC) instructors. The life they pick for themselves aligns with the satisfaction they get from doing something that gives them a feeling of achievement.

Too often our fellow veterans feel a sense of pressure to show success in their transition. And too often they choose wrongly, because they prioritize satisfying their peers' idea of success over their own desires. This is not something that you learn in TAP, but it is one of the most important topics that should be discussed before actually doing a transition back into civilian life.

Which Path to Choose

Once you have prioritized your transitioning goals, it is time to decide which path to take. There are four paths to choose from as you begin to answer the "what" part of your transition.

1. Education path (traditional college or technical certification)
2. Employment path (get a job, be the job or own the job)
3. Entrepreneur path (investor or business owner)
4. Retirement path

The education path has two branches. One leads to a full college degree completion and other to a technical certification that follows a specific employment path linked to that technical degree or certification.

The employment path is interrelated with the entrepreneur path, which I will discuss later. Before deciding on "getting a job," you must decide the type of job you want. You can choose between private, public or nonprofit sectors. Each of these sectors has its rewards and challenges. For example, working in the nonprofit sector is always more of a calling, as the financial resources are always scarce and there will always be more work than there are people available to do the job. In the private sector, the choices are also different if you choose to work as a government contractor, where the job may be seasonal or temporary depending on contract length and government funding. The other side of the private sector is represented by companies such as FedEx and Amazon, as well as medium and small companies who hire personnel to develop them within the company. Finally, the public sector may include federal, state and local government positions where the lifestyle and rules may be similar to those of the military. These are generally called government employee positions. One note of importance is that to apply to these jobs, the application and the resume required is completely different than for those jobs in the private and nonprofit sectors. Indeed, when applying to government jobs, being a veteran provides a certain level of advantage against other candidates who are not veterans. This is commonly referred to as the veterans' preference.

As I mentioned earlier, the employment and entrepreneur paths are interrelated when the answer to your transition is to "own the job." Franchising and small business ownership is not as glamorous or comfortable as it is sometimes portrayed. It is certainly a great way to be your own boss, do what you love and earn a living doing it, but you must understand how this path will turn out before you embark on this venture. The entrepreneur path offers great reward if your business ventures are successful. The reward is that someday you may hire others to run your small business, especially if your business grows to become a big business. The difference between owning a job (small business) and owning a business (big business) is in what happens when you take a vacation or you are away from your business. If your business must have you there to make money, you own a job. If you can get away from your business, and your business continues to earn you money while you are absent, then you own a business.

The Next Steps

The next steps obviously depend on which path you choose. Each path has a set of steps that must be followed and developed in order to make your transition successful. While many would like to believe that being an entrepreneur is the path they want, it may not be for them. This is why most small businesses fail after only five years of operation. On the other hand, too many veterans are too gun-shy to start a business or become consultants because they don't know how to start one. In my soon to be released book *Transitioning Strategies for Veterans*; I discuss each path in detail with specific tools to use to ensure a successful transition from the military.

What I will do here is discuss the most common path for veterans: the employment path. And I will discuss in general terms what you need to do next to get a job.

How to Get the Job You Want

Let's assume you have decided that you have certain skill sets that allow you to promote yourself to employers who are looking for someone with your professional caliber. You have been exceptional in your military career and received awards everywhere you served. Your evaluations are always ranked among the best and you know there's nothing you can't do if you are given the task and responsibility. How do you translate that into quantifiable actions that employers will value?

Your resume is the tool you use to make a first impression. Generally, as military professionals we have a hard time translating our achievements and our career progression into civilian terms. Often we embellish or state incorrect facts that lead employers to believe that we may not be qualified or prepared for the job they are seeking to fill. An effective resume is as important as your interview. Here's another time where I will invoke the saying, "Don't listen to broke people."

When I provide resume advice to fellow veterans, I get a typical answer: "Why do you tell me to remove (or change) this when this other person told me that I should leave it in?" They become confused about whom to listen to and what will be the right formula for getting that job. I always reply with: "If the person who gave you resume advice is *not* a hiring manager and has *never* hired people or interviewed them for jobs, then you should *not* listen to that advice." After reviewing hundreds of resumes for my company's positions, I have hired six employees so far. I have developed a keen understanding as to what is effective and what is not effective in a resume. I know a winner when I see it, and that does not happen often. Almost every resume needs some polishing.

Here are some effective resume-building tips you should consider:

- Do not put your full address on your resume. City, state and zip code is enough.

- Don't put your military rank after your name, unless you are applying for a military job.

- If you are applying for a government position or government contractor position, put your level of clearance right beneath your name with an expiration date.

- Create an email address solely for employment. Don't use your personal email unless it is a professional name.

- Include a decisive and concise objective. (This should also be used as your 'elevator' pitch.)

- Create a Summary of Qualifications

- Include a Core Competencies section, if different from your qualifications.

- In your Professional Experience section, make sure your titles are not military titles. Examples: *NCOIC of Testing Control, Maintenance Chief, MSG, American Embassy London.*

- When describing your billets or jobs, include a brief description of what that title (position) actually does in the organization. No-one wants to hear that you were "hand selected" to that position. They want to understand what it means and how much responsibility it holds.

- Include no more than three bullets detailing your accomplishments in that position. Be mindful of military terminology and work to make the terms comparable to civilian positions, so the employers can clearly understand your achievements.

- List your education with highest education first.

- If you want to list your certifications and awards, create a section for Awards & Certifications.

- Some veterans like to include their volunteer work. Make it relevant or leave it out.

- Do not exceed two pages. You are advised to put your best information on the first page. Sometimes recruiters and employers do not go to the second page if there's nothing to grab their attention.

The bottom line on resumes is that there's no official format. The key to success when writing a resume is how you present yourself and how effectively you lay out the information. The resume is only an invitation to a phone call or possibly an interview. Make it count, but don't try to fit everything in, hoping something might be the catch of the day.

About the Author

Another effective way to market yourself is by creating a profile on LinkedIn (www.linkedin.com). This is a virtual resume portal that works for you 24/7/365. Before I decided to start my own business, I asked my personal and professional network to share my resume with those seeking professionals like myself. Their efforts combined did not do what LinkedIn did for me. As a disclaimer, I have no ties or business relations with LinkedIn. My statements are born from experience and results. Through LinkedIn I was able to do over 200 phone screenings, 47 job interviews and had 11 job offers on the table prior to retirement.

I was introduced to LinkedIn by a fellow Marine, John Stanton, who helped me get started. I committed discipline and time to this networking resource, and to this day it continues to pay off. There's too much to cover on LinkedIn, so I will simply state that it is imperative that you have a profile on LinkedIn if you are serious about finding a job or being known in your professional circles.

What Happens Next

The most important tools and rules for an effective transition strategy have been laid out before you by someone who has walked a mile on each of the steps I have shared here with you. I put myself through the job-seeking process and the hiring process to learn and evaluate the battlefield. I applied to companies in the nonprofit, private and public sectors. I considered all sources of resumes and tried the principles and advice of all of those who offered their counsel.

I practiced and trained for each stage of the process. Ultimately, I decided to start my own business. I spoke to accomplished leaders such as Francis Hesselbein (CEO and President of the Girl Scouts), and Marshall Goldsmith (executive coach and leadership author). I spoke to CEOs and vice presidents of companies who shared their stories and their secrets to success. I have dedicated individual time and conducted seminars and workshops to help others transition. I am sharing with you the most valuable lessons I learned from those battles, so you can take my lessons learned and improve upon this strategy.

There are five more things I should discuss with you about getting a job, but they are not as critical to your success as the ones I have covered here. Creating a business card, the right attire and reading some relevant books and references will add value to your transition strategy. There is plenty of debate on which is the best way to address these topics. I will let you decide what you feel is appropriate to you. But if you want my advice, feel free to contact me via LinkedIn.

Having a military background is valuable. Learn how to use it to your advantage in the civilian battle space and you will be successful regardless of path.

Cesar Nader, U.S. Marine, Retired

Experience/Background

Cesar Nader is an executive coach with over 15 years of experience coaching and mentoring individuals, couples, teams and organizations to improve and realize their potential with practical and proven methods. Mr. Nader leads from experience and with the understanding that there's no limit to the will of the human spirit.

After living abroad for 11 years, he returned to the United Stated with only $200 in his pocket. In 20 years, he completed an honorable military career with two combat tours, three undergraduate majors, two minors, studies two languages (Chinese and French) and finished two masters programs. Among his other achievements, he started several companies, helping people and organizations attain maximum effectiveness. His background and expertise come from a wealth of leadership positions in the United States Marine Corps. Leaders from all walks of life have used Mr. Nader's expertise and his knowledge of Marine Corps leadership to synergize their productivity and achieve personal and professional growth.

Mr. Nader's corporate background includes a consistent record of starting and growing businesses from the private to the federal sector. In addition, he is the President and CEO of X Corp Solutions, a Language and Culture Immersion Services Company that also specializes in leadership development and professional training. He also serves as the CEO of The Homestead Company, a natural skin-care product company.

As an executive coach, Mr. Nader works with leaders and individuals alike without distinction or segregation. His practical experience from military combat and business development are a perfect blend of fireproof leadership tools for those seeking to experience the ultimate level of coaching in any of the six different core areas of life coaching: personal, spiritual, nutrition, health, financial, and professional.

Clients

Mr. Nader's clients list is confidential and private.

Education

Mr. Nader holds an MBA, a Master's degree in Business Administration and Supply Chain Management.

Contact Information

(831) 917-8581
cesar@cesarnader.com
www.cesarnader.com

PROFILE

Coach Name: Cesar E. Nader
Location: Virginia and DC
Website: www.cesarnader.com
Years of Experience Coaching: 10 years (military and civilian)
Years of Experience in Business: 20+ (First business when I was 9)
Years of Experience as a Leader: 20+ (At different levels)
Highest Degree earned/discipline:

- DUAL MBA: Business Administration; Supply Chain Management.

- B.S. Degree (Triple Major): Computer Information Systems, Business Administration, and Managerial Accounting.

Description of Coaching Approach and Philosophy

- Philosophy. No matter who I meet and when I meet them, they are the most important person in the world while I am with them. I imbed myself in the person I am listening to so I can absorb their true and most deeply covered fear. Touching that fear is the core of my mission.

- Approach:
    - Phase I. Discovery – Expect them to hide the truth or not know what is their true need or fear.
    - Phase II. Q&A – Ask as many questions as you can to validate the initial assessment.
    - Phase III. Detoxification – This is the toughest phase and it includes a true look in the mirror, a validation of all fears and the commitment to stick through it to see the results.
    - Phase IV. Face the Fire – Once it gets hot, people will either quit or face the fire. I challenge them to face the fire.
    - Phase V. Conviction – Once they see the value.

12: My Journey from Ranger to Entrepreneur

JOHN EYNOUF

My name is John Eynouf and I am a veteran of the United States Army. My story isn't typical. The how and why I joined and the almost unbelievable amount of things I experienced during my four short years in service are unique. For me, it all started on September 11, 2001.

I will never forget waking up on my couch at my dad's house and seeing horror play out on television that I never thought possible. Just like many Americans, I will never forget the image of that second plane crashing into the tower and knowing that we were under attack. This was not only a wake-up call for me but an event that would forever shape how I view the world and life in general.

Because of my Christian upbringing, watching people kill other innocent people in the name of their religion or faith was completely perplexing. I had to know why. I had to understand how people could do this. For me, it sparked unprecedented curiosity. My curiosities made me want to be immersed in these countries' cultures and to have the opportunity to experience them firsthand. I started to spend almost all of my free time watching war movies, reading military books, and visiting every military-oriented website I could find in the pursuit of learning more about what was going on and how I could get involved for my country.

While in prayer one night, I asked Jesus to give me a sign and to let me know if joining the military was what I was supposed to do. The next morning, I woke up to a phone call. It was a childhood friend of mine from Oklahoma that I hadn't talked to in about four or five years. He immediately started with, "Your grandmother gave me your number because recently I have been thinking a lot about when we were kids and we said we wanted to go to the military together one day." From the moment he said that, I knew it was my sign and what I was meant to do. Keep in mind that I had a girlfriend I loved, my own apartment, an amazing job, and I was making extremely good money at 20 years old. But it didn't matter. I knew what I had to do. I moved to Florida a few months later, and my childhood friend joined me. We began the recruiting process together.

After we completed Military Entrance Processing Station (MEPS), in Tampa, FL, we were set to ship out as "battle buddies" to infantry basic training at Fort Benning. We were assigned to the 82nd Airborne Division in Fort Bragg, NC. Unfortunately, things didn't go as planned.

While playing basketball one day with some of my friends I severely injured my ankle. It required surgery to correct. Needless to say, this delayed my departure for boot camp, and my friend ended up going ahead before me. At the same time, the doctors were telling me that with the condition of my ankle I would never make it through a week of basic training, let alone airborne school and having a career as a paratrooper. They simply couldn't have been more wrong. They only fueled my fire to prove my commitment and achieve even more than what I was originally going for. After months of rehabilitation, recovery, and waiting, I finally left for boot camp in May of 2003, a month after turning 21 years old.

After completing 16 weeks of grueling training at Fort Benning, I graduated infantry school and moved straight into three weeks of airborne school. I learned that jumping out of planes is actually not all that hard. It is picking yourself up off the ground after landing that is ridiculous!

With airborne school completed, I was off to report to my unit with the 82nd Airborne at Fort Bragg, NC, at the end of October. To say I was a "deer in the headlights" is an understatement. Any confidence I thought I built up in basic training was nothing compared to the environment I stepped into. My unit, Charlie Company, 2-504 parachute infantry regiment (PIR), had just returned a few months prior from a year-long tour in Afghanistan and I quickly learned the value of a CIB (combat infantry badge) and the meaning of the word "cherry," although I was not meant to be one for very long.

In an Airborne unit like mine, you are put on DRB (Drill Readiness for Battle) status, which basically means that you have to be ready to be on the ground anywhere in the world within 18 hours of a call out. Our unit was already on DRB status when I arrived because all the other units in our division were deployed between Iraq and Afghanistan at the time. So when some the guys from my platoon and I were hanging out at Ruby Tuesday one night and saw a CNN ticker saying that 2,500 Airborne troops were unexpectedly being deployed from Fort Bragg, we looked at each other and knew we were going to Iraq. Within two weeks of that day I was in Baghdad. It was January of 2004. I was 21 years old, barely two months out of basic training. Finally, I was right where I had worked so hard to be: in combat.

The initial culture shock was far more than I could have ever imagined. One of my most vivid memories is leaving the main FOB (forward operating base) to go to my platoon's area of operations. It was next to an oil refinery on the other side of the Tigris River from the Green Zone. As soon as we pulled out, both sides of the street were filled with the most trash I have ever seen. It stretched the entire length of the highway. I was bombarded with strange noises and people everywhere. Broken-down cars were in the middle of the highway, and chaos reigned. It was nothing like the everyday order that we are used to in the States. People were staring at us everywhere we went. When we drove by everyone stopped what they were doing and stared at us. Because of my curiosity and need to know as much as possible about this culture, I found myself even more aware than usual, just trying to soak it all in.

It is amazing how quickly training takes over and the culture shock just fades into the background. We took over all combat operations in our area of operation (AO) within 24 hours. During the four months that we were in Baghdad, I felt like we never stopped. I often told people back home that the only way to explain it was like living the movie *Mad Max: Beyond Thunderdome*. We executed countless raids, patrols, recons, escort operations, and responses to other units that were under duress in and outside of our AO. Plus, there were some things that I prefer not to go into detail about. War is ugly and there is a reason why my favorite quote that describes my job and what we did is, "People sleep peaceably in their beds at night only because rough men stand ready to do violence on their behalf." (George Orwell).

When we got back from Iraq I was on cloud nine. Rid of the "cherry" status all new infantrymen go through before combat, I was driven to advance myself in training and never quit. Over the next few months I won Battalion Soldier of the Month as a private, beating out peers that had much more time in service than I did. I was also fortunate during this time to participate in the Expert Infantry Badge Course, which consisted of rigorous physical and mental tests. I not only passed, but went "True Blue," which means I went through the course without a mistake on any part. Completing this course just fueled my desire to test myself, so I decided to go to Ranger School. After months of training with the scouts in my battalion, I was ready to go to the 82nd Pre-Ranger course, which must be passed before you can go to actual Ranger school.

Two weeks before my Pre-Ranger course was set to start, my unit was volunteered to test a new experimental piece of equipment called a Parachute Deployment Bag (PDB). The PDB was an extra 15-pound bag that you put your rucksack (backpack) into. This would be the first and last time we had to jump with the PDB, as it was a catastrophe in terms of safety. We were dropped at only 400 feet, minimum normally was 600-650 feet. Needless to say, it was an absolute disaster. We took 90% causalities, and I was injured too. I hit the ground at probably over 40 mph and immediately heard my back snap. I couldn't feel my legs and was being dragged across the ground by my parachute, unable to detach myself. I was completely freaking out. I thought I was paralyzed. The pain was more than anything I had ever known. But instead of going to sick call and potentially ruining my chances of going to Pre-Ranger school, my squad leader put me on quarters for three days to stay in my barracks room and rest. I toughed it out and left for Pre-Ranger school as planned and successfully completed the two-week course while masking my excruciating pain.

After this course was done, I took leave to come home for Christmas and married my high school sweetheart, Alicia. After a very short two weeks together I was off again to Ranger school at Fort Benning. My experience in Ranger school could be a complete book on its own. It was one of the worst and best experiences in my life. It was 64 days of virtually no food and sleep, pushing your body to the limit while carrying out missions and completing a wide gambit of training exercises. I went straight through the course in the winter, and graduated with the confidence and leadership skills I needed to be able to be a fire team leader back at my unit. When you push yourself past the point of what you ever thought your body can handle and not only survive but complete missions, you prove to yourself that you truly are capable of anything.

With Ranger school completed, I had another two weeks to spend time with my wife and then was shipped out with my unit to complete a year of duty in Afghanistan. It was March of 2005. Within a couple months of the deployment I was finally promoted to E5 sergeant, although I had already been leading my own fire team since the second month in the country. Throughout the year that I was in Afghanistan we covered the entire country. Our time there was completely different than Iraq in more ways than I have the time to explain. We had no clear mission, and our hands were tied behind our backs fighting politics more than doing our job. It broke me and the majority of our unit psychologically. This was compounded when we experienced our first casualty: the death of our medic, Spc. Chris (Katz) Katzenberger, from a double-stacked anti-tank mine.

With the mental breakdown came the inevitable physical breakdown, as I no longer could suffer through the ever-increasing back pain from my previous parachute injury. Crashing Humvees down the sides of mountains certainly didn't help either. I finally sought out help and saw a doctor towards the end of our deployment at the main airbase in Bagram, Afghanistan. I was diagnosed with scoliosis and told to get an MRI as soon as I was back stateside to further investigate my injuries. I returned home on St. Patrick's Day, March 17, 2006. My wife moved up to Fort Bragg with me and we spent the next year fighting to get the medical care I needed. My MRI showed severe herniation in my back and I was deemed unfit for infantry duty. Mentally this was the final straw, even though I had aspirations to continue advancing to Special Forces. My career was over. I was honorably discharged from the Army in April, 2007. I chose not to follow the path of medical retirement; it would have prolonged my time at Fort Bragg, and at that point I just wanted out. I could no longer do what I signed up for.

I started work within two weeks of coming home with the same job I had left four years earlier, sitting behind a desk. It took me a couple of months to realize that it was really over. To this day I still struggle with the fact that I will never be able to be a soldier again. I was detached from my friends and the life I left behind with no-one around me really able to understand. I spent countless days at the VA hospital going through test after test, trying to receive the medical care I needed. It was a nightmare. I was lost, broken down, lacking purpose and with no idea of what I even wanted to do next. Worst of all, somewhere along the way I lost my faith. It's hard to even pinpoint when, but it was gone. I was empty. I stopped exercising, stopped dressing well, and generally stopped taking care of myself.

I was working and providing for my wife. I had a comfortable job with co-workers who loved me. The owners of HBW, Inc. hired me back without even a second thought after my military service was over. They also worked with me and never gave me a hard time about all the work that I missed or the times that I wasn't feeling well. Their confidence in me helped me to slowly piece back that confidence in myself. This period of rebuilding lasted over a year and a half.

During that time, I poured myself into online competitive video gaming. It became a great therapy for me. Gaming kept me from falling into depression, and it distracted me from the constant back pain I experienced. I played Rainbow Six Vegas 2, a first-person shooter title, which was on the Major League Gaming (MLG) circuit. I can't explain how therapeutic it was to learn and advance in a completely new culture and industry, e-sports, and be able to connect with like-minded people. I loved competing and testing my skills. Please understand that it is not the violence of the game or the act of shooting that was helping me. It was the tactical aspects, the competition, and the team building. I was always the team captain. I took the leadership role and motivated my guys and taught them strategy, as well as how to mentally push through adversity

Slowly but surely, I found myself again. More importantly, I returned to my faith in God. My wife and I bought a home and began to settle into life. My passion, eagerness to learn, and my fierce patriotism returned. This led me to become involved in local politics. I joined several different local organizations and volunteered. I led myself to new directions for my future and continued to regain confidence. I felt like I was a leader again and fighting for my country in a new way. I realized my life was not over, but that a new one was starting instead. For me this was my catalyst to taking charge of my future and carving out a path where I could exercise my leadership skills and my fullest potential. So I continued working for HBW. But I also went to school and took additional jobs with other companies.

I stayed active in local politics and my church. Then I started an annual Patriot Camp, where we teach children about the role of faith in the founding of our country and feed the patriotism of the next generation. Through my local political groups I found out that there was also a national initiative for Patriot Camps and joined the Board of Directors for CCF (Constitutional Champions Foundation). I assisted with establishing the national curriculum and helped to raise awareness for the program. My wife and I continue to hold our annual camp at our church every summer. This past year we had our highest attendance yet, with an average of 50 kids a night for the week.

I gained a wealth of knowledge and experience. I also joined several different organizations like my local Chamber of Commerce (SCCC), BNI (a national networking organization), the local Christian Chamber of Commerce, Coffee Club (a local networking organization), and more. I volunteered to give speeches at events and the local technical college. I learned how to network again and engage in conversation with a variety of different people within the business world. This was an invaluable experience, and being a veteran was a huge help in meeting new people. The response in the business world for veterans was phenomenal, and really helped me gain massive amounts of confidence in myself. This really advanced my personal growth as a veteran businessman.

One of the best opportunities that these networking events led me to was getting connected with HirePatriots.com, an effort to create a nationwide safety net for US veterans and their families. I became their local ambassador for Orlando, Florida. Connecting with an organization that truly helps US veterans in a tangible way is an honor for me. It provides a way for me to continue to lead my fellow soldiers to success. I have always had an internal need to serve and help my fellow brothers, and this fulfilled that for me.

A great example of how networking helped me was organizing my first charity golf tournament. Because I sat on the small business committee for SCCC, I was able to volunteer to be a moderator for one of their marketing events. One of the perks of being the moderator is the added publicity after the event. Plus, I worked out a deal to be able to talk about my local HirePatriots chapter for Orlando. One of the fellow chamber members in the audience came up to me after and said, "My name is Ron Lane. My brothers and I own a local printing company called Ranger Printing." Then he explained how his dad was a Ranger and that he wanted to help me in some way. He then said to me, "Let's put on a charity golf tournament this year!" I was flabbergasted because I knew nothing about golf, much less putting on a tournament. I told Ron, "I really have no idea how to or the resources to do something like that". Not to be denied, Ron said, "I know how to set up a golf tournament; I will help you put it together."

Long story short, in 2012, with the help of Ron and his family, we were able to put on HirePatriots.com's first annual Support Our Troops Golf Tournament, with all proceeds going to Patriotic Hearts, the 501(c)(3) of which HirePatriots.com is a program. We were able to get our community involved and put on a great event. Local business owners and a longtime local congressman, John Mica, attended. The focus was on helping veterans get back to work.

I am now creating a program for golf tournaments that can be put on nationally by all HirePatriots ambassadors to help raise money for their local US veterans and spread the word about HirePatriots.com. None of this would have happened had I not gone outside of my comfort zone, volunteered for things like being a moderator, and allowed others to help me.

Helping US veterans get back to work and reestablish their roles in civilian society is very important to me and close to my heart. It took me a while, but I realized that the military actually does train us how to conquer the world outside of combat too. It is just like on that first day of boot camp, when you are terrified and have no idea what is happening, when veterans first return to the civilian world. In the military your training makes one realize that you can do things you never before thought possible. That ability to learn does not leave when military service ends. If veterans approach the civilian world and business in the same way our military training taught us, we will find success.

Most importantly, I know that everything I learned in the military has translated into the civilian and the business world in various ways. I have led men through battle and been responsible for their lives. My military training and experience has given me the assurance that I can learn and train my body and mind to do anything that I set out to do. The Army pushed me to the limits countless times. I know that I am best when I am in front, blazing the trail, and leading people. And I know I was made to be an entrepreneur. In 2012 I officially launched the website for my new company: ReadyUp Gaming (www.facebook.com/ReadyUpGaming). I am excited about continuing to build this company and the challenges I will face and overcome.

Through it all, in the seemingly short but very long 30 years I have been on this earth, I have learned valuable lessons that have helped me to survive and create a future for myself. Ultimately God is in control, not me, and I have learned to roll with life and not get defeated when things don't go as I planned.

Everything we experience in life happens for a reason and there are always lessons to be learned along the way. If I hadn't been injured I wouldn't have gotten out of the military, and who knows where that path might have gone.

I will forever miss being a soldier and I still dream about being able to go back. But now I have new dreams to look forward to that will become realities. I now know I can conquer anything life hands me.

About the Author

Originally from Texas, John Eynouf has lived in Seminole County, Florida since 1996. He joined the United States Army in the spring of 2003 where he served as an Airborne Ranger with the 82nd Airborne for four years. He completed two tours of duty: Iraq 2003–2004 and Afghanistan from 2005–2006. Fortunately John was able to find work after completing his military service, but for many veterans that is not the case. HirePatriots is an important tool to help facilitate veterans in finding their way back into the work force and into society as a civilian. John and his wife have since settled back in Lake Mary where they own their home. John's focus and passion is to help veterans and to educate our youth about the history and founding of our country. John is the founder and CEO of ReadyUp Gaming, Inc.

ReadyUp Gaming, Inc. is comprised of eSports industry (competitive video gaming) enthusiasts and professional video gamers with a vision of uniting the eSports community. Our main goal is to create a hub of information for everything relevant in the eSports community. Ready-UpGaming.com is your go to place to get all the news of the industry and calendar updates with ALL tournaments and events. The possibilities are endless for the eSports industry and ReadyUp Gaming will serve as a catalyst to raise eSports up to the same level as all other mainstream sports in existence today. Millions of people are at home right now playing a game, many in the hopes of becoming a "Professional Gamer." Others are researching leagues and tournaments, or just enjoying watching people compete professionally. ReadyUpGaming.com will serve as a tool to connect all these people on one platform to accelerate the growth and give everyone what they are looking for in one place with new and exciting ways to connect and follow the teams, leagues, or the games you are most interested in.

I am a US Army Veteran!

13: Veteran Women: Launching a Small Business

KARIN ABARBANEL

My small business journey began after I had spent more than ten years in marketing at a global consulting firm. When the firm's marketing division was reorganized, my job and I were axed. My career was at a crossroads: I could hunt for another senior marketing position or become my own boss. My son was one at the time and I wanted more flexibility than a long commute and a corporate job would give me. So I decided to start a home-based business as a marketing consultant.

A retainer from my former employer helped launch my venture. Over the years, I have built up blue-chip clientele as an entrepreneur, designing communications projects for companies like Morgan Stanley, Chase, and Accenture. I love being my own boss, but getting there wasn't easy. Making the transition from employee to 'solopreneur' was more difficult and stressful than I expected—I wasn't just changing jobs or careers, I was changing my identity. But I was not prepared for the emotional ups and downs.

Figuring out how to price my services and find clients was tough. In talking to other women, I found I wasn't alone. Many of them were also struggling to adjust to the realities of leaving traditional jobs and creating new businesses. This led me to interview a wide range of women about "taking the plunge."

Inspired by the Internet and the incredible surge in female entrepreneurship, I recently coauthored a book called *Birthing the Elephant: The woman's go-for-it guide to overcoming the big challenges of launching a business.* Its goal is to create a step-by-step road map to the business launch process, and to offer frontline advice from creative women in a range of fields, the accomplished women who shared their insider secrets and strategies with me.

If you are a female veteran weighing the pros and cons of launching a small business, you have some powerful assets to draw on. Your military training may already have fostered some of the key ingredients required for small business success: Discipline, ingenuity, persistence, and rapid decision making, to name a few. If so, then you're in good company: In a recent survey of 800 female veteran entrepreneurs, 55% said that their military leadership experience motivated them to launch their own businesses.

Beyond these personal assets, there are a growing number of programs designed specifically to support your startup decision. In addition to the Small Business Administration's (SBA)'s Veteran Business Outreach Program, a new government-sponsored initiative called V-WISE (Women Veterans Igniting the Spirit of Entrepreneurship) combines online training and ongoing mentorship. And Capital One Financial Corporation is partnering with a nonprofit called Count Me In to launch the Women Veteran Entrepreneur Corps (WVEC), a mentorship program focused on business startups and expansion.

There are also broad-based groups that offer training and networking opportunities to female entrepreneurs; among the best-established are Ladies Who Launch, the National Association of Women Business Owners (NAWBO), B.I.G., Powerful You, and eWomen Network.

But even with all these resources at your command, launching is daunting. Starting a new business isn't for the fainthearted: within four years, one out of two new businesses will fail. What separates those who survive and thrive from those who do not?

One critical success factor is a proactive, sharply focused startup strategy: One that arms you not only for the economic challenges you'll face, but also for the emotional ups and downs you'll experience during your launch.

As a potential business owner, you may think that finding money for your startup is the biggest hurdle you'll face, but most seasoned entrepreneurs will tell you that it is not. If you really have the drive to launch, then you'll find the dollars to do it, even if you have to start out on a shoestring. In interviews with scores of women entrepreneurs, I've learned that the biggest startup obstacle isn't money. It is motivation: finding the staying power and resilience to handle the failures and setbacks of starting a new business.

Yes, launching a venture is demanding in many ways, more than being an employee with a steady income. But building a business can also be enormously rewarding. After all, when you're the boss, no-one can fire you! Depending on yourself can provide a sense of security that no employer can offer. And while you will invest tremendous amounts of time during your startup, being on your own gives you much more flexibility than a traditional job. With all this in mind, let's look at five business-building, smart startup steps to take and five pitfalls to avoid.

Success Step #1: Commit to a smart startup strategy. Make a decision to find a way to launch a business that works for you, not just financially, but emotionally as well. You're going to have to leave your comfort zone to make the leap into entrepreneurship. But don't push yourself so far and so fast that you feel overwhelmed and at risk right from the start. Build your business at your own pace and on your own terms. Let it grow organically. This means starting small and taking a do-it-yourself approach. It may even mean working for someone else while moonlighting to gain the experience you need, or until you can gather seed money to launch.

Come up with a budget you feel comfortable with and make a decision to work within it. Some of the women interviewed in *Birthing the Elephant* started very modestly. Ann Afshari and Laura Hagler were nurses with no business training. They launched Exclusively RNs with a few hundred dollars. Brenda Newberry, an Air Force veteran, "loaned" herself $1,000 to buy equipment to get started and found consultant work on the side, while she built her high-tech business. Makeup mogul Bobbi Brown began her global empire, Bobbi Brown Cosmetics, with a $5,000 nest egg she and her husband had saved.

Think big, but start small. Focus on one product or service. Keep your eye on delivering exceptional service and quality with that limited offering, and then build on it. Bobbi Brown started her global cosmetics business by creating a single product, a lipstick with a natural look, and used it as her launch platform. Liz Lange, who pioneered in designing stylish maternity clothes, began by designing a simple dress that appealed to young expectant mothers. Ali Brown started a successful Internet information marketing business by writing an online newsletter and sending it to a handful of clients.

Doing your homework is the key to a smart startup strategy. Many new ventures fail because their owners didn't take time to thoroughly investigate whether their business ideas were marketable and profitable enough to merit investment. Your inner momentum has to be fueled by solid research and practical planning. The more you know, the better your chances of success, and the more precisely you can time your launch.

Go beyond basic Internet research on market statistics or competitive offerings. Reach out for a range of resources when you're investigating your idea's market potential. When Ronnie Fliss was looking into starting her organic pet treat business, Fat Murray's Doggy Treats, she supplemented her online research on growth trends in the pet market by talking to trade industry experts and retailers. She also turned to a local community college for marketing support.

Adopting a "figure it out or find it out" mentality can be invaluable during your startup. Hiring other people to do work that you can actually do yourself before you can afford it is a serious cash drain. To launch, you're going to have to get past some of your self-imposed limitations and understand every aspect of running your business, even things you don't enjoy and don't think you're good at, until your net profits or business development needs justify the expenditure of paying other people.

Success Step #2: Substitute brains for bucks. As a female veteran, you may have access to targeted funding sources: the Patriot Express Pilot Initiative, for example, or state-level initiatives like Employ Illinois - Military Reserve Loan. Using www.business.gov you can also identify grants available through the federal government, though resources are limited and competition can be keen. There are also microloan and crowd funding programs like ACCION USA, Kickstarter.com, GoFundMe.com and Indiegogo.com that may be worth exploring. And some funders, notably Key Bank, are especially welcoming to women business owners.

But realistically, many female entrepreneurs find that outside funds are hard to come by. Women business owners generally find it difficult to obtain Small Business Administration (SBA) loans or credit lines when they are starting out; only a small percentage of venture capital dollars go to women-owned startups. This is because women tend to launch in the service sector rather than in the high-tech arena.

As a result, 'bootstrapping' may be the most likely path to success: Like other women entrepreneurs, you may find yourself turning to personal savings or going the F&F route and borrowing from family and friends. Going this route can definitely be a path to success. Women are amazingly adept at a critical startup skill: using creativity, instead of cash. By igniting your ingenuity, you can transform your tight budget from a liability into an asset by using "barter" and provide a strong springboard for growth. Here are a few "brains-for-bucks" examples from *Birthing the Elephant* to inspire you:

- When fitness trainer Lisa Druxman launched Stroller Strides, one of the fastest-growing franchises in America, she traded free workout sessions to a lawyer in return for legal assistance in setting up her company.

- When Sarah Levy launched her chocolate business, she kept her overhead low by using her mother's kitchen to test recipes. She also turned to one of her sister's high school friends to design her first website and created gift baskets for a photography firm's clients in return for eye-catching photos of her products.

- While restoring an old inn, Becky Rohrer recruited her mother as a temporary cook and gave weekend stays to a financial advisor in return for his professional expertise.

- Jennifer Lovitt Riggs turned to her brother-in-law for free expert help in designing her product. She also designed a survey of businesswomen to test market her idea inexpensively and create buzz for her business.

- While launching her home design business, Crystal Johnson saved thousands of dollars by learning how to design and manage her company's website. She also designs her own advertising.

- When she first started Patricia's Yarns, Patricia Scribner took advantage of free advice from retired executives at Service Corp of Retired Executives (SCORE) and free legal counsel from the SBA.

- Ronnie Fliss, the founder of Fat Murray's Doggy Treats, turned to a community college's marketing department at a critical point in building her business. By persuading the instructor to use Fat Murray's as a case study, she received thousands of dollars in market research for free.

Make it a point to talk to seasoned small business owners about their startup days and you're likely to uncover a wealth of money-saving ideas that can help you stretch your own precious startup dollars. Many aspiring entrepreneurs find that the very act of launching unleashes untapped sources of creativity when it comes to financing.

Success Step #3: Make marketing a top priority. Building your new business is important, but without marketing you won't have a business to build. Here's what Ali Brown, a highly successful entrepreneur who coaches female business owners, says about marketing: "Whatever business you think you're in, you're not really in that business, you're in the business of marketing the business you're in." One business owner estimated that she spent about 20 percent of her time developing her business and 80 percent of her time marketing it. Most fledgling business owners would agree that this is on target.

You may be tempted to adopt a "build it and they will come" attitude and focus all your time and energy on developing and fine-tuning your product or service. But a business that doesn't promote what it has to offer will quickly fade away.

Marketing is a critical activity in launching a business, but many people avoid it. Why? They see marketing as "selling" and don't feel comfortable in this role. Successful entrepreneurs have a very different mindset: to them, marketing isn't selling, it's sharing. It's letting potential buyers of your product know about how and why they will benefit from what you have to offer.

When Bobbi Brown developed her first lipsticks, she went to a party and was so excited that she started telling everyone about them. One of the guests happened to be a buyer at a major Manhattan department store who was so impressed with Bobbi's enthusiasm that she gave her a table to sell some of her samples. Later Bobbi looked back on this first big break in building her global cosmetics business and said, "I didn't know anything about marketing at the time, but I guess I was marketing."

She's right! Marketing is really about sharing your passion with a target audience. By building on her enthusiasm for a high quality product, Bobbi gained valuable exposure. She also avoided a major startup trap on the marketing front: buying costly advertising or hiring a professional public relations firm to make a splash in the media. Costly outlays like this are rarely a sound investment for a startup.

So how do you let potential buyers know what you have to offer? The best and most cost-effective strategy is adopting a do-it-yourself approach, often referred to as "guerilla marketing." No-one is better equipped than you are to tell the story of your new business. As a U.S. veteran-turned-entrepreneur, you have a unique dimension to your startup story, one that will interest others and gain their support, especially in your local community.

One of the appealing aspects of marketing is that there are so many tools at your disposal, from writing and distributing press releases to speaking at local businesses or social events to joining networking groups. And of course, promoting yourself and your business via social media can be a highly profitable and low-cost marketing vehicle for many new ventures.

Taking a community-based approach by finding timely and news-worthy "hooks" that appeal to local newspapers and TV stations can be a great way to get valuable exposure. When Lisa Druxman launched her Stroller Stride exercise program for new moms, she was long on passion but short on dollars. So she started contacting local editors and reporters and "pitching" them colorful story ideas. One example: She held a Fa-ther's Day class for new dads and their babies and persuaded a local TV station to film it. Over the years Lisa generated priceless publicity for her business via news tie-ins.

As your launch gains momentum, so will your marketing. Most entrepreneurs freely admit that you have to throw a lot of marketing ideas on the wall for just a few to stick. That's why this has to be a continuing priority. When the two coauthors of the extraordinarily successful *Chicken Soup* series were struggling to get exposure for their startup, they committed to: 1) coming up with seven marketing ideas every day, and 2) putting them into action, no matter what! This single-minded focus led to big results.

Marketing may be a whole new world to you. If so, there are a variety of budget-friendly ways to learn how to wield this powerful tool. SCORE is a great place to start:

Many entrepreneurs gain incredibly useful advice from retired marketing executives through this no-cost resource. There are many affordable how-to guides on do-it-yourself marketing and online sites like Duct Tape Marketing and Copyblogger that offer small business advice. You can also look into marketing courses at local community colleges.

Success Step #4: Call in the troops. As an entrepreneur, you may be in business for yourself, but you don't have to be in business by yourself. To succeed, you're going to need help and lots of it. It's not only the kind of help you hire, but the kind you inspire: people who are going to care about your contributions as a veteran and encourage your dream of being your own boss. Whatever business you plan to launch, finding people who "have your back," both economically and emotionally, is critical.

How do you create a support system for success? Start where you are. Make a list of your personal, professional, and military contacts, anyone and everyone you can think of. Most of us can actually come up with at least 200 names in our personal networks. Make it your mission to reach out to a number of these people every day and let them know about your new venture.

Ask them for advice, for leads, for suppliers, for small business accountants, for media contacts, for whatever you need and whatever they volunteer to provide. Don't just rely on email; even in today's high- tech world, making personal connections by phone or face-to-face is still the most powerful way to build relationships.

Ask. Ask. Ask! And keep on asking until you find the advice and contacts you need. As you reach out, you'll sharpen your mission and your message. You'll also begin to identify a core group of people who consistently offer ideas and practical advice.

Another effective way to begin building a support system is to find mentors. When Ronnie Fliss launched Fat Murray's Doggy Treats, she turned to a business professor she knew for help. The professor gave her startup advice, invited her to events, and shared her network of experts. Ronnie also found a mentor in an unrelated field, the wine industry, who gave her invaluable advice on pricing her products.

Liz Lange had no fashion design, business, or marketing experience when she started her pioneering maternity wear line. She encountered many naysayers who thought her idea for stylish maternity clothes wasn't marketable. To stay motivated and to gather both practical and emotional support, she would meet weekly with two friends who were launching new ventures in entirely different fields at the same time. Over lunch they shared their startup problems and then brainstormed solutions for each other.

Once her information technology firm was up and running, Brenda Newberry built a support system for herself by creating an informal "kitchen cabinet" to guide her firm's growth. Every few months, she would invite a group of advisors in other industry sectors to dinner so she could "test drive" ideas with them and tap their expertise.

Success Step #5: Strengthen your resiliency muscle. As an entrepreneur, you're going to have to regroup and rebound when you hit obstacles—and you will. You'll face tough decisions, cash crunches, sudden market shifts, suppliers who won't come through, and clients who'll unexpectedly cancel orders. How you respond to setbacks like these will be critical to your success. You'll need more than just passion and persistence; you'll also need the ability to bounce back: Adapt to change and approach problems positively.

According to research, small business owners share "resilient personality" and many other positive traits. Successful small business owners don't waste time on negative emotions when they hit a crisis; they consider this counterproductive. Instead they quickly shift into a strategizing mode and focus outwardly on making the right things happen so they don't lose valuable momentum.

Above all, resilient entrepreneurs meet obstacles with optimism. They expect to come up with a workable solution. They also recognize that positive emotions boost problem solving. That's why they ask proactive, forward-looking questions like: What's my new reality here? What needs to be done right now? What's the easiest, most efficient solution? What hidden benefit can I extract from this situation?

We become resilient by acting in steadfast ways, and then reinforcing this behavior. That's why when entrepreneurs hit roadblocks, they respond not by retreating, but by pushing forward. They reach out. They do not entrench; they ask questions, generate ideas, solicit feedback, make decisions, and then push ahead.

One way business owners bounce back quickly from situations that might derail them is by having a brainstorming strategy already in place, one that they can put into action quickly as soon as a major obstacle appears. When you hit a big stumbling block, it can feel very isolating. That's why getting outside input can be so helpful.

When Suzanne Lyons and her partner came up against a big problem, they had a business coach on tap, someone they'd call in for a day to help them lay out issues and map out their solutions. Or you can take a tip from Brenda Newberry and create a "brain trust", a small, supportive team of advisors you can call on when you hit an especially thorny problem or have a major strategic decision to make.

Avoiding burnout is also critical for boosting your resiliency. A relaxed mind is a creative mind, and that's exactly what you need for inspired problem solving when you hit a rough patch. Resiliency flows from feeling strong and centered, so make sure you give yourself time to recharge your batteries physically and emotionally.

Now that we've looked at five success steps for launching, let's briefly explore five missteps—cash-draining business blunders that the dynamic entrepreneurs we interviewed for *Birthing the Elephant* cautioned women in startup mode to avoid.

Mistake #1: Romanticizing about being your own boss. The desire for more control over your time may be one of the major drives behind your decision to start a business of your own. However, you may find that the kind of control you're hoping for eludes you. During your startup, the demands that your business will make on your time are neverending. You can easily find yourself working many more hours than you did in your military days, or when you were an employee of a company.

This can often make you feel that the business is running you, rather than the other way around. That's why it's very important to have a clear-eyed view of the time, energy, and commitment that working for yourself will take. If your vision of being an entrepreneur is unrealistic and drastically out of sync with the actual day-to-day demands of your startup, then you can quickly begin to feel disoriented and lose your enthusiasm.

Mistake #2: Overspending due to image anxiety. Of all the traps you can fall into during your startup, being overly self-conscious and sensitive about your image is among the most serious. It can lead you to overspend, overpromise, and oversell yourself. It can drive you to move out of your home and into rented office space before you can really afford it, to buy costly equipment you can't really afford or to overspend on a flashy web site with lots of bells and whistles. Don't confuse image with professionalism!

Delivering on what you promise—exceptional performance and businesslike attitude and presentation—that's professionalism. This is what clients want. Whether you work out of a closet at home or out of an office on Fifth Avenue is far less important than the quality of the work you do. So don't get hung up on the trappings of success, or they'll trap you. Focus on finding new business and servicing your clients or customers at the highest possible level.

Spending too much on your operating structure can be a real money pit. Keep your system and equipment as simple as you can for as long as you can. Trade up when your client servicing needs outstrip your physical support systems—only at this point should you begin to think about investing more money to upgrade or replace your existing setup. Taking this approach may require some ingenuity and juggling, but it will allow you to grow at a steady pace while keeping your overhead down.

Mistake #3: Spending precious startup dollars on advertising. Experienced entrepreneurs will quickly caution you about advertising, especially in relation to the benefits it delivers to a startup. In her first year of building a decorating business, Crystal Johnson made a deliberate decision not to go the advertising route.

"I think it's a money pit," Crystal says of advertising. "Everybody was telling me to take out an ad and saying, 'We can bring you this or that audience.' But it just wasn't making any sense to me. I was saying to myself, 'I don't read this.' I was my target demographic, so I know what I would do and wouldn't do. I didn't feel comfortable writing checks for print ads when I didn't understand how they would work."

Mistake #4: Underpricing your products or services. Women actually have a higher success rate at running businesses than men, mainly because they tend to be very customer focused. Yet when it comes to negotiating the terms for performing a service or offering a new product, many women tend to undervalue their talent and experience. The result isn't hard to calculate; you can easily end up doing far more work than you're actually compensated for—not a winning formula financially.

"Women tend to undervalue their time and expertise," notes one small business advisor. "I also think that women may not think as big as they might when it comes to projections about the potential profits their businesses can generate." Studies consistently show that women tend to undervalue and underprice themselves. Male entrepreneurs generally ask for more money and for more from their employees.

Knowing how to price your product or service profitably is clearly a skill that every small business owner needs. But pricing may be a whole new world for you after being part of the military, and finding this information can be challenging when you are just starting out. This is definitely an area where mentors, industry trade associations, and groups like the SBA and SCORE can be especially helpful.

Mistake #5: Running yourself ragged. Burnout is bad for business! If you run yourself ragged, as many new business owners tend to do during their startup, then you're going to crash and burn, warns Lisa Druxman, the founder of Stroller Strides: "If you're really going to be the leader of a company, you have to be well enough to lead. And you can only do that if you take care of yourself. So you have to exercise and eat well; this is the fitness professional in me speaking!"

Build ways to re-energize into your day. Visualize yourself running your business smoothly and efficiently. Listen to inspiring tapes with advice from role models you admire and who have skills you need to acquire. Make it a point to exercise regularly and give yourself a reward when you complete a tough task or meet a big deadline. And be sure to always find time for hobbies that you enjoy and find relaxing. When you make renewal a part of your recipe for success, you'll reap many rewards.

There you have it—five success steps to take, and five missteps to avoid during a startup. Above all you're going to have to be persistent. You'll need to go over, under, around, and through many obstacles on the road to making your venture a reality. Successful business owners don't wait for opportunities; they go out and create them. But with help from mentors, guides like *Birthing the Elephant,* and with your own experience and ingenuity you'll have everything you need to succeed. Your dream awaits you!

Resources:

www.aceyourstartup.com
www.amexopenforum.com
www.business.gov
www.copyblogger.com
www.ducttapemarketing.com
www.entrepreneur.com
www.ewomennetwork.com
www.inc.com
www.indiegogo.com
www.kickstarter.com
www.gofundme.com
www.ladieswholaunch.com
www.launchwhileworking.com
www.makemineamillion.org/wvec
www.nawbo.org
www.SBA.gov

www.SCORE.org
www.smallbusinessprof.com
www.V-WISE.org
www.wbonetwork.com.

About the Author

Karin Abarbanel is an entrepreneur, author, and expert on startup strategies for women. A small business owner herself, she knows the demands involved firsthand. Her goal is to inspire and equip new business owners economically and emotionally. She is the coauthor of *Birthing the Elephant: The woman's go-for-it guide to overcoming the big challenges of launching a business* (Random House). Part portable success coach, part action guide to the launch cycle of a business startup, *Birthing the Elephant* takes women step by step through the first 22 months of a new venture, showing them smart moves to make and pitfalls to avoid. For more information and to order, visit: www.amazon.com or www.birthingtheelephant.com.

Karin was selected by The Hartford for its Small Business Pulse panel and has appeared as a guest expert on ABC TV's "Good Morning America," CNBC, WCBS, and Smart Money TV. She speaks widely on startup strategies and has a website focusing on startup strategies for women: aceyourstartup.com.

14: The Franchise Revolution

It's a Veteran Affair

A D A M   E D W A R D S ,   N F L   A L U M N I ,   C F E

The investigation into the franchise revolution and the role veterans play is among the most important inquires of our time. Why do most franchises flourish with innovation and others wither? What are the determinants that help a franchise achieve critical success early and often? At stake is nothing less than the economic vitality of towns, cities, and states where these franchise concepts operate.

The first explanation comes from analyzing the effect franchises have in our communities. Studies show that by 2020, 50 percent of all businesses will be part of a franchise system (IFA). This statistic is staggering and demonstrates the evolution of the franchise industry. To truly understand the upward trajectory of this industry, you must understand the group of individuals creating franchises.

The leader of a franchise must be an entrepreneur. These entrepreneurs must have a long-term commitment to their startup community. A franchise is simply a startup with a scalable model. The majority of franchises don't begin with the proverbial silver spoon advantage. A franchise begins with a determined entrepreneur intent on making a positive impact on his or her economy. Like any startup, they must be actively involved and willing to put the long-term fiscal health of the community ahead of their self-interest. This is a critical role; without the evolution of startups into franchises, the startup community will stagnate. Similar to other startups, a franchise takes a while to establish its brand. The seeds of a new concept are constantly being planted as others mature and become more recognizable in their communities. I term this the "franchise wave." It's a never ending cycle of innovation, evolution, and economic-maturation. Now let's explore the franchising industry itself.

According to Webster's Dictionary, a franchise is "the right or license granted to an individual or group to market a company's goods or services in a particular territory." The company offering the license is typically called the "franchisor" and the individual or group investing in the license is called the "franchisee." This allows multiple entities to operate their business under a recognizable brand name. Collectively, franchisees become the business beneficiaries of an established brand and the franchisors get their product and services into local, national, and global markets.

The franchise relationship is grounded in a sacred trust and mutual respect between the franchisee and franchisor. Each has a mission-critical job to do and greatly impacts the other. Like combat soldiers in a platoon, franchisees and franchisors completely depend on each other to execute their jobs to ensure mutual survival. This dependency has created a historical demand for franchisees that overwhelmingly possess these skills—hence the impact veterans have on the franchise revolution.

Consider this: There are approximately 2 million armed forces personnel in the U.S. military at any given time, and some 200,000 servicemen and -women separate from military service annually. A U.S. Census Bureau report found that former military members are one of the most successful groups of small business owners in the country. Veterans own 14.5% of businesses in the U.S. while comprising less than 8% of the nation's population. This has certainly caught the attention of franchisors and spawned the creation of VetFran. To honor those men and women who have served in the U.S. military, the Veterans Transition Franchise Initiative, known as VetFran, was developed to help them transition to civilian life. The idea of the late Don Dwyer, Sr., founder of The Dwyer Group, VetFran is a voluntary effort of International Franchise Association member-companies that is designed to encourage franchise ownership by offering financial incentives to honorably discharged veterans.

To date, over 500 veterans have become franchise owners by participating in VetFran and working with franchise consulting companies like iMatch Franchise.

Much has been said of late about veterans' excellent suitability for franchise ownership and their being highly desirable franchisee candidates for many franchisors. Reasons include veterans' discipline to follow operational procedures, willingness to work hard to reach specified goals, ability to function as a team member within a system, superior motivation, and leadership qualities. In order to participate in VetFran, a franchisor must be a member of the IFA and must offer a financial incentive to honorably discharged veterans. Since there are more than 75 different industries that use franchising as an expansion model, VetFran allows each company the flexibility to determine its own financial incentive offered to honorably discharged veterans. Some companies reduce the initial franchisee fee, others waive training fees, but the main idea is to help lower the upfront costs to veterans, since they are typically cash-strapped upon leaving military service.

One such participating franchisor is Express Employment Professionals, a leading provider of employment services. Express provides a full line of staffing services (temporary, flexible, evaluation hire, direct hire, and professional/contract staffing) and HR business solutions to individuals and businesses in nearly 600 locations in the United States, Canada, and South Africa. Express provides a sales-focused, business-to-business opportunity in one of the top-ten fastest growing industries in the US. Their franchise model allows you to develop solid, scalable, equitable business while maintaining a balanced lifestyle (www.expresspros. com). Consistent with other franchisors participating in VetFran, a 25% discount is applied to the franchise fee. This program has been so successful that Express Employment Professionals recently began to wave the entire franchise fee for qualified veterans. Fred Muse, Vice President of Sales, says that veterans are a good fit for their business: "As long as they have the necessary skill sets, their experience in handling extremely stressful situations makes them well equipped to deal with the stresses that often arise when facing common situations in our line of work, i.e., dealing with hard-to-please clients, or working to staff companies that depend on our expertise to stay in business."

Another franchisor very much interested in having veterans as franchisees is Comfort Keepers, which provides non-medical in-home care to thousands of people across the United States, Canada, and the UK. Executive Vice President of Franchise Development Jeff Bevis shared Comfort Keepers' tremendously effective method of identifying veterans amidst their prospective franchisees: "On 'Discovery Day' when we sit down with prospective franchisees, we ask point blank, 'Are you a veteran of the United Stated Armed Forces?' In almost every case, the veteran was not aware of VetFran until we asked." Comfort Keepers provides up to a total of $990 in credit toward startup costs for things such as promotional items and online training. Bevis says Comfort Keepers has found that "veterans are very aligned with following systems, procedure, and protocol. Their entrepreneurial spirit is alive with the sense of independence, but they know the importance of following a system."

The most recent trend is a good sign for veterans. Franchises are waiving their traditional requirement for previous experience. Liberty Tax is one of those brands making the shift, and the results are simply astounding. Liberty Tax is the fastest-growing tax service in the industry. Their focus is to bring in veterans of high caliber who are motivated to become the industry leaders and work in a team environment, similar to a platoon on the battlefield. Liberty provides ongoing support in operations, marketing, tax and technical areas. Veterans develop their exclusive territories by opening and operating retail store locations. Liberty Tax is an attractive franchise opportunity based on the seasonality of the business model. CEO John Hewitt is the only person who has founded two franchise tax companies that *Entrepreneur Magazine* has ranked on their Franchise 500.

Being a member of VetFran also provides access to private equity firms. BeneTrends is a preferred lender to veterans and offers a variety of financing options from loan programs. Some of these options help veterans access their own capital free of taxes and penalties, or at very low rates to buy a franchise or start a business. Financing is often a barrier to potential veteran business owners, and nonprofit organizations are now stepping up to match the support for our heroes. The Veterans Business Fund is a New York-based nonprofit organization that provides the supplemental capital needed to satisfy the equity requirements for obtaining a small business loan. The VBF provides capital to veterans in the form of a non-interest bearing loan with very favorable repayment terms. The VBF was established to help veteran entrepreneurs get equity financing to start a franchise or another type of independent small business. Veterans who have been previously denied bank financing because of insufficient equity capital are encouraged to apply for VBF financing. Getting a small business bank loan is particularly challenging for veterans, who are less likely than others to have access to capital in the form of home equity, investments or a 401k that they have been funding for years.

The VBF is managed by BoeFly, a New York-based marketplace that connects businesses borrowers with 2,400 lenders from around the country. This is BoeFly's first loan program targeted specifically to veterans. Veterans can apply for these loans for amounts between $5,000 to $100,000. These loans are typically financed over seven to ten years to keep payments low. The loans will carry a fixed interest rate of 1.5% amortized annually. Veterans pay back the equity financing including principal and interest to VBF, and then those funds are redeployed to other veterans who need similar financing to get bank loans. Initial funding of the loan program is being financed with charitable contributions from generous donors, individuals, corporations and foundations (www.franchise.org).

More and more veterans are coming to understand that franchise opportunities are a great way to start any type of business, but with so many options to choose from, the challenge is finding the right fit. With over 6,800 registered franchises it can be very overwhelming at times. Companies like iMatch Franchise apply experience in franchise operations, entrepreneurship, and opportunity-matching to help veterans connect with companies offering the means to accomplish their unique financial and personal objectives. Cofounded by Sarah Edwards, an 8-year veteran with the U.S. Army, she selected only the best brands that had a proven track record of success. Her firm represents over 400 brands, ranging from full-time to part-time, small to large and internationally known franchise concepts. You incur no cost or obligation.

The iMatch Process Overview:

Step 1: Let's get acquainted (1 hour)

- Clarify passion, interests and vision for the future
- Q&A on franchising industry
- Introduction to the iMatch Franchise process

Step 2: Self-Assessment Profile Review (1-2 hours)

- Core values
- Fiscal fitness
- Skill sets
- Passions & interests
- Lifestyle
- Career expectations

Step 3: Franchise Concepts Presentation (1-3 hours)

- 2 to 3 franchise concepts presented for best fit
- Top 2 franchise concepts selected to start franchise discovery process

Step 4: Franchise Matching Process (3 – 12 weeks)

- Introductions with selected franchisors
- Learn about franchise business process, core values, ongoing training and support, and track record of success
- Validate with other franchisees to envision franchise ownership
- In-depth look at franchisor experience, financial disclosures and legal documents
- Validation of franchise concepts with industry experts such as attorneys, CPAs, financial advisors and lenders
- Ongoing meetings with iMatch for continued guidance and support

Step 5: Final Franchise Match

- Finalize legal documents and funding
- Franchisee matched with perfect franchise
- Begin life as a "Franchapreneur!"

Now that I've given you an intimate look at the impact veterans have in the franchise revolution, it's time to decide if franchising is right for you. I term this the "No" decision and the "Yes" decision. It sounds simple, but here's my theory. Your research says "yes" but your emotions say "no." The decision seems perfect by all analysis, but your family and fellow veterans don't support it. You start to doubt the data and lack the confidence to make the final decision. Whatever the reason, it's valid and the responsible decision should be "no." On the other hand, your research says "no" but your emotions say "yes." The decision is not entirely clear. There's a lack of data and performance history, but you're fired up just thinking about the possibilities. Plus, your family and fellow veterans love the concept and support you. It's a valid response and the decision should be "yes."

Do or Don't: Simply trying is not an option. Making the choice to invest in a franchise doesn't require permission; it requires great leadership. Although it's a long, tough, and challenging journey, you're not in it alone. Remember, franchising allows you to be in business *for* yourself, but not *by* yourself.

About the Author

As a native Oklahoman, I'm a former collegiate and professional athlete who graduated from Oklahoma State University with three B.S. degrees in health promotions, business management, and criminal justice. I've also received a number of certifications, including Certified Franchise Executive, Certified Medical Representative, Certified Sales Trainer, and Corporate Management Development. I first entertained a future in business by starting a lawn mowing service at the age of ten. I was limited to my father's tools and the local neighborhood I lived in, but it was the experience that taught me the value of honest hard work. Since that time, I've played professional football (NFL), appeared on international stages, worked my way up the corporate ladder of Fortune 100 companies, and embarked on exciting entrepreneurial opportunities.

As a professional, I've been involved in several successful businesses. In 2002, after my brief professional athletic career with the Dallas Cowboys, I accepted a sales consulting position with one of the world's largest pharmaceutical companies, Johnson & Johnson, where I was recognized consecutively as its top national sales producer. In 2003, I partnered with a team of NFL investors on my first business venture in Oklahoma to create free football camps for inner-city youth. This initiative quickly developed into other locations, from Washington D.C. to Indianapolis and Pennsylvania, to name a few. In 2008, I became the minority share owner of a small virtual shopping company, modeled after QVC; this was my first successful exit. In 2009, I sponsored the creation of an international organization, Hunger Relief International, which currently feeds over 40,000 families annually in both Haiti and Guatemala. In 2011, I was appointed as the National Ambassador to a medical mission program named Passion to Heal in Nairobi, Kenya. Most recently, in 2012 I was selected as a Lead Mentor for Blue Print 4 Business, a high-tech incubator for tomorrow's leaders, and to partner with the NFL Alumni Association on The Venture Draft, where tech, athletes, and venture capital meet.

As an entrepreneur, my consulting firm, iMatch Franchise (www.imatchfranchise.com) has helped thousands of people get into business for themselves, but not by themselves. I've built my entire career around taking great care of my clients and building long-lasting relationships. By specializing in the franchise industry, I've worked extensively with the International Franchise Association to expand the veteran-friendly franchises my firm offers. In 2010, The Edwards Angel Investment Group procured the master franchise rights for Golden Heart Senior Care of Oklahoma (www.goldenheartsrcare-ok.com), netting 20 individual franchises throughout Oklahoma. Most recently, my partners and I created a national market for Waters Edge Wineries (www.watersedgewineries.com) with available locations throughout the US and other selected countries.

As a family man, I currently reside in Oklahoma and I'm married to my soul mate and business partner Sarah Edwards, who is an eight-year veteran with the U.S. Army. Outside of work, I mainly enjoy spending quality time with my two angels and giving back to my community and local church. I felt I had a solid purpose in life before the birth of my girls, but now I realize my purpose is to truly make this world a better place for them to grow up in.

15: How to Start a Home-Based Business

MEL COHEN, CFP®, RFC, RTRP

What Type of Business Do You Want to Be In?

Veterans leave active duty with a myriad of experiences that have laid the groundwork toward making them entrepreneurs. They have acquired skills and training as part of their service that can easily translate into a home-based business, or better yet, a future Fortune 500 company.

Determine what type of business you want to be in. Base it on your skill set, experience, knowledge, etc. Have goals and objectives for your business.

As a tax accountant, I have clients that are architects, attorneys, graphic artists, web designers, IT experts, SEO experts, SEM experts, app designers, craftsmen, and run businesses and ministries, all from their homes.

The reason many businesses fail is a lack of money and a lack of experience in the enterprise they start. Another reason for failure is a lack of management experience. If you left the service as an officer you have management experience. If you are an E-5 (enlisted) or above you have management experience. Each of these businesses will take very little startup money, and depending on your specific military background, you may have experience in your field of choice.

For 2013 Five Top Home-Based Businesses Are:

- **Freelance Writer** www.freelancewriting.com www.dailywritingtips.com/7-steps-to-becoming-a-freelance-writer

- **Blogger** www.freelanceswitch.com/freelance-writing/how-to-become-a-freelance-blog-writer www.becomeablogger.com

- **Craft Sales** www.ehow.com/how_5995907_make-crafts-sell-quickly.html
  www.usatoday30.usatoday.com/money/smallbusiness/colum-nist/abrams/story/2012-08-24/small-business-making-money-with-crafts/57250528/1
  www.squareup.com

- **Affiliate Marketer** www.youtube.com/watch?v=HuGJ3fdRHd4
  mattsmarketingblog.com

- **House Cleaner** www.infobarrel.com/How_to_Make_Money_House_Cleaning
  www.increasenow.com/starting-a-residential-house-cleaning-service

Tax Advantages

There are good tax advantages available for home-based businesses. I represent a husband and wife that converted the basement of their home to an office that they share. It takes up 25% of the square footage of their home. This allows them to write off utilities, maintenance, repairs, homeowners' insurance and other expenses that would not be deductible on their tax return if they did not have a business to write off. I formed a corporation for the attorney and an LLC for the architect. Each business pays rent for their share of the office to the couple. The rent is then deducted by the business to reduce their taxes. The income and the expenses are reported on the couple's Schedule E. The profit, if there is any, is not subject to the 15.3% self-employment tax. The expenses written off on the Schedule E usually offset the income, so little or no taxes are actually paid using this strategy.

The income received on the rental is offset by the prorated share of expenses that would not normally be deductible. This is a substantial tax savings for them. Learn more at www.irs.gov/Businesses/Small-Businesses-&-Self-Employed/Home-Office-Deduction.

Analysis

Freelance Writers and Bloggers are in the same field, which is writing. I have clients that are good writers and have learned search engine optimization (SEO) and search engine marketing (SEM) and have rates that range from $25 to $75 per hour. If you have a day job and you are good at it, use your skills in these areas to branch out on your own. Many bloggers have started with a minimal following and have grown to have hundreds of thousands of followers.

Craft Sales can feature a wide berth of products you make yourself and sell at flea markets, monthly events, yearly events and any gathering where there will be a lot of potential buyers. Also available are websites that specifically sell for you. If your sales reach a certain plateau it would be good to have your own website with an e-commerce store. That way you are not sharing your profit with a third party. If you don't have enough funds to have your own website, sell through Etsy: www. etsy.com/sell?ref=so_sell. No longer is there a need to set up a merchant account if you have an iPhone. You can process credit cards through Square at 2.75% per transaction. www.squareup.com.

Affiliate Marketing is a great stay-at-home business, especially if you like working on a computer. Affiliate marketing allows you to make money online from your site or blog by promoting other sites or products in return for a commission or a fixed fee per lead or sale. You earn a commission when someone follows a link from your site or blog to another site where they then buy something, sign up for something or complete a survey. You must sign up in advance with the company to see their fee schedule. Those that are computer savvy can make a nice living as an affiliate marketer.

The largest and one of the oldest affiliate programs is Amazon: www. affiliate-program.amazon.com.

Visit this site to see many more options: www.affiliateprograms.com.

If you want to have your products promoted by others use Clickbank: www.clickbank.com/index.html. Clickbank has paid out over $2 billion over the past 14 years. It is a great source for promoting your eBook or eProducts.

House Cleaning can easily translate into a full-time business as you acquire customers. You most likely have the materials needed to start this business in your house. Basic house cleaners complete the following duties: dusting, vacuuming and mopping all rooms in the house for a fixed fee ranging from $60 to $100. If you also do windows, waxing, polishing, trash disposal, etc., you can charge extra. You can ask questions on the phone about the size and scope of the cleaning project, size of the house, date, rate of pay, and travel. Be sure to cover all details so there is no misunderstanding.

You should take about two to three hours to clean the house. If you charge an average of $80 per house and handle three per day, you will earn $240 per day, which is $1,200 per week or over $60,000 per year.

This business is highly competitive, so you will need to do a little more to attract repeat business. I advised a client to put a live long stemmed rose in the downstairs bathroom or the kitchen sink with a small note that stated, "Thank you for allowing me to clean your house." This was a big hit and attracted many referrals. This, along with a thorough cleaning job, allowed the owner to prosper where others had not.

When Can I Leave My Job and Go Full-time?

A question I am regularly asked is, "When can I leave my job and go full-time into my part-time business?" Much would depend on your revenue stream. We can get accustomed to our full-time revenue and the added revenue from our startup business. It is best not to leave your full-time job until your revenue from your business reaches around 80%. Usually within the next year or two you can make up the difference by working full-time in your business.

How Do I Determine My Hourly Rate Compared to My Regular Job?

If you work in a service business where your company bills you out at an hourly rate, they most likely are working on a multiple factor of 3 to 3.5 times your hourly wage.

When I ran accounting firms we bought CPAs by the year and sold them by the hour. We would take the yearly pay and divide it by 2,080 hours, then multiply it by 3.25 rounded up to the next $5.00 increment. That was their hourly billing rate. This allowed us to pay the employee what he or she was worth while allowing the company to offer a wide range of benefits and make a profit for the firm.

Example: The CPA earns $40,000 per year. Divided by 2,080 hours, the CPA is earning $19.23 per hour. Multiply that by 3.25 and the billing rate for the CPA is $62.50. We would round that to $65 per hour.

Do not understate your worth. If you are that CPA or any other service provider and you pick up clients on your own, you want to bill somewhere in the $40-$50 range, more if feasible. You are offering your client a break from your standard rate set by your employer, but making well more than your current employee hourly rate.

You need to make sure you do not violate any company policy by acquiring clients on your own, regardless of the industry you are working in.

Resources

The SBA is a great free resource. They cater to businesses of all sizes and have a section on home-based businesses. Before I would go into business I would take their business assessment tool. www.web.sba.gov/sbtn/sbat/index.cfm?Tool=4.

SCORE is a part of the SBA. Here you may be able to find a counselor that has been in the same business you are trying to start, learn about financing options and be able to talk to a business professional. Details are at www.score.org.

The Internal Revenue Service will provide you with all of the forms needed and provide you with current tax laws at www.irs.gov/Businesses/Small-Businesses-&-Self-Employed/Small-Business-Forms-and-Publications. At a minimum you want to order Publication 17, Publication 334 and the "A Virtual Small Business Tax Workshop" CD, which is Publication 1066C. Also see www.irs.gov/Businesses/Small-Businesses-&-Self-Employed/Other-Government-Resources.

Other noteworthy sites

www.smallbusinessresources.com
www.entrepreneur.com/smbresourcecenter/index.html
www.sbrc.net

You may also check with your local colleges and universities, as they may have an incubator program where you may be able to acquire free advice, space for your business at a reduced rate and other free or reduced cost services. www.nytimes.com/2012/07/20/education/edlife/campus-incubators-are-on-the-rise-as-colleges-encourage-student-startups.html?_r=0.

Also check out your local Chamber of Commerce and look at their national site for information that may benefit you: www.uschamber.com/about/member-resources.

Write a Business Plan so you can get the thoughts out of your head onto paper. By putting them on paper, you will see the flaws as well as the opportunities. Go to www.sba.gov for a free sample plan. If you Google "Business Plans", there will be many free sites available.

One of the best commercial plans is Business Plan Pro. I have used them for years to write plans for a number of businesses for fees ranging from a few hundred dollars up to $2,500, depending on the complexity of the plan. Writing business plans for other businesses using Business Plan Pro is also a great home-based business. www.paloalto.com/business_plan_software. The same company also has Marketing Plan software: www.marketingplanpro.com.

Financing Options

If you are considering investors or having your business financed, a business plan is a must.

Now you have to make a decision: Are you going to give up **equity** (ownership), or will you finance the business through **debt** (borrowing money)?

I have counseled clients as follows: If there is a lot of risk in your business as far as the business succeeding, then equity may be a better route, as equity does not have to be repaid. Be sure you disclose any and all risks associated with the business so the potential investor can make a decision based on all of the facts and disclosures.

If the business has a high probability of success, then debt is the best route, and you will pay interest until the business creates the cash flow to pay back all of the loans, but you do not give up ownership. In the long term you will end up with much more money in your pocket.

The SBA is one option to explore when financing a business: www.sba.gov/sba-learning-center/search/training/financing.

Another source for business plans and financing: articles.bplans.com/financing-a-business.

Specific Steps

Define your skills. Know what you can bring to the table. You will need to determine if you have enough knowledge and resources to start your business now or whether you will have to receive more training.

Create a legal entity. I would not spend money on incorporating or forming an LLC until I was sure my business would be successful or at the least go into the following year. The main choices are: sole proprietorship, partnership, LLC, and corporation (S-corp or C-corp).

Register your business name if needed. If you use your own name or your legal entity's name, you do not need a separate registration. If you do not use your own name or a legal entity name, you may need to complete a Doing Business As (DBA) name.

You register with the Department of State in the state that your business is located. Not all states may require a fictitious name registration. See the SBA site for more detail. If you form a legal entity and use that name as your business, then you do not need a DBA.

Acquire a Federal Tax Identification Number (TIN). You can apply online at www.irs.gov. Before applying, you will need to determine the legal entity of your business. Once you acquire the TIN, you will not need to use your social security number. You will instantly receive your TIN from the IRS site by filling out Form SS-4 online.

Know your state's requirements. You can Google your state's name and Department of Revenue to find out if you will need a sales tax license or any local licenses or permits. If you plan on hiring employees, you will need to register with your state to withhold taxes, pay unemployment insurance, etc.

Owning your own business

Where there is a void, there is an opportunity.
Find a need and fill it.
Where there is no need for something, create one.

The Big Money

There are many of us here that earn a nice living being self-employed. We are entrepreneurs. We will always earn a living. The big money comes from creating something more than that, whether it is a new product, new idea or an improvement of the former two.

My hourly rate is very high, but my earning potential is limited by the hours I can or want to work. If you have a proprietary product you have no limitations on earnings, as the more you sell, the more you earn. If you make $1 per unit pure profit and sell a million of them, you have made a million dollars; if you sell ten million, ten million dollars.

Make sure you don't trade dollars. Selling a million dollars' worth of something with $990,000 of expenses serves no purpose.

If you sell a retail product the most important thing to know is the markup. What percentage am I making on each sale, and what dollars am I making on each sale?

Next is the turnover of the product. If they turn over too slow then you are sitting on unsold inventory, which costs you dollars. If too fast, you are out of stock too often and that also costs you dollars.

Make sure there is enough markup and turnover in whatever you sell. These are keys to success with a retail product.

Multiple Income Streams

Multiple income streams have been created and offer a great way for "wealth building."

If you sell other people's products and you can develop a good sales and marketing plan, you will make money every day, sometimes every few minutes.

I represent several authors. Every time a book is sold through their web store, Amazon, a bookstore or anywhere else, I am making money regardless of what else I am doing. I may be doing a tax return for an hourly fee, I may be giving advice as a business consultant, or I may be home with my family. At any point in a 24-hour day I will earn commission on their book sales whenever and wherever it happens.

As you become recognized as an expert in your business, you may be asked to write or speak for a fee. During your talk you will be making money while speaking if you have multiple income streams.

I often give talks on a commercial basis. I earn a speaking fee and still make money from the sales of products or books from clients I represent that are being made while I am speaking.

If I am looking for clients, at the end of the talk, I can usually walk away with new clients if I want to grow my business.

Marketing

You must learn marketing on your own or have the resources to pay someone to market your business.

Set your **Marketing Goals.**

Define your marketing budget. During the first year or two your budget may be 12–15% of your projected sales. This can cut back as your product or service gets well known. Once your business is established it should be 3–5% of annual sales.

Have an easy to navigate web presence that will allow you to make the customer experience easy and enjoyable for them. That first sale can create return customers forever. If the first sale is not a pleasant experience, the customer may never come back.

Look at the first sale as being worth several thousand dollars of **lifetime value** to your business.

If a customer spends $100 three times a year and does that for a period of ten years, then the lifetime value of that customer is $3,000 ($100 times 3 times 10). By not doing a great job on the first sale, the entire $3,000 becomes at risk.

You must have the ability to process credit cards, an easily under-standable ordering process, offer free reports to build your email list (which will later be used for marketing), and the introduction of new products.

All the marketing in the world will not replace quality. Make sure your products are defect-free, easy to use, and worry-free for the consumer.

Devote at least one to two hours every day marketing your business. Always have business cards with you no matter where you go, and be ready to give a one- to two-minute pitch on your business.

Successful products or services satisfy a need. Next in importance is satisfying a want, then a desire. Show the consumer why your product is better than your competitor's product in satisfying the need for the product.

Marketing Info Sites: www.powerhomebiz.com/marketing/general. htm

www.allbusiness.com/home-business-marketing-tools/16567886-1. html#axzz2A8YtJ16E

Part of marketing is having a large social network presence:

Facebook.com allows you to build a fan page, announce all events pertaining to your books, promotions, etc. You can post photos and links to your blog and other social media marketing opportunities.

LinkedIn.com is mandatory for all business type books and all nonfiction books. You can create discussion groups, provide comments to other ongoing discussions, and build a network of business professionals that can lead to the opportunities above.

Google.com allows you to post longer articles and video conferences, create interactive events, meetings, research, create private or semi-private circles.

Pinterest.com is an online pin board. It allows you to organize and share the things you love, which of course will relate to your business. Like Twitter, it allows you to re-pin photos you find interesting. Pinterest has over 12 million unique visitors per month. It is now #5 in all social network sites.

Twitter.com allows you to create a following of people in your niche. You can participate in chats, other discussions, drive people to your site and interact with like-minded followers. You should encourage people to retweet your tweets.

Youtube.com allows you to post videos, provide instructions, feature games that relate to your product or service provide tips and more.

Togather.com is great for authors or consultants that earn money from speaking.

Business Pluses

Your work hours are flexible, you can determine how many hours per week you want to devote to your business, and these can work around school, family responsibilities, church activities, and social engagements.

You are your own boss and don't need to take orders from anyone except the Lord.

You determine how much money you want to make an hour or a week.

You set how much you want to earn depending on how much time you devote to the business—that depends on how motivated you are, how hard you work, and how well you know your markets.

You gain knowledge of what it takes to run a business and how to interact with other business people.

You'll get connected with a lot of different people, whether they are friends, customers or entrepreneurs, who can assist you for years down the line.

Business Minuses

Many self-employed people feel isolated because they often have to work alone and lack the encouragement of interacting with co-workers and receiving good feedback from a supervisor.

Businesses often grows slowly, so you'll face feelings of discouragement while having to invent fresh business strategies and new outlets to market your product or service.

You won't have a fixed amount of income to depend on. You might make a killing one month, but do almost no business the next.

You're the decision maker and only you are responsible for any wrong choices made regarding the business.

You may need to deal with long hours, which may be overwhelming because of the amount of work involved (as well as managing family responsibilities and schoolwork).

You also need to do your own paperwork—like accounting, taxes, and keeping accurate record of materials' cost.

Although you are not accountable to a supervisor, you do have to deal with customers. If they are not satisfied with your product or service, you'll need to do what it takes to make them happy with your work.

How Do the Rich Think Differently than We Do?

Rich people think differently than we do in several major areas:

Money: We think in ways to get things.

To them money is a tool to invest to create more money for extras in life.

We look where we can spend it: cars, TVs, boats, vacations, etc.

When starting out, the wealthy drive what they own and watch what they have, and invest the dollars we would spend on luxuries.

Investing: We strive to retire comfortably.

Wealthy invest to create abundance: They learn, they study, and they practice.

We budget for clothes and living expenses.

The rich budget for investments to earn more and the rest falls into place. They see it as a way to gain abundance.

The rich believe money should work for them. We believe we should work for money.

Risk: We don't take risks because we are afraid to fail.

The rich feel if they don't take risks they have already failed.

Failing does not make you a failure, never trying does.

I have failed at several business ideas. Each failure taught me something. I learned not to make the same mistakes again. One of the biggest reasons businesses fail is over-optimistic sales or profit projections.

If you are starting a business make sure you have some experience in that particular field and you have adequate funding.

Wisdom is the key to abundance. Proverbs is loaded with writings on how to acquire wisdom. Read a chapter a day and mark all the wisdom passages with a W, all the money passages with a $, child training passages with a C.

The average person reads one book per year.

Wealthy individuals read two per week.

Listen to business and entrepreneurial MP3s or CDs while driving or doing something else.

DO SOMETHING! The first step is the hardest; after that big one, it gets easier.

Mel Cohen, CFP®, RFC, RTRP
Practical Tax & Financial Services, Inc.
1000 Pearl Road
Pleasantville, TN 37033-1796

www.practax.net
www.inspiredauthorspress.com
melcohen@hughes.net

PH 931 593-2484
FX 931 593-2494

All of the websites and the information provided are for general information only. If you need specific advice regarding your business, please consult your own accounting and legal professionals.

About the Author

Mel Cohen
Certified Financial Planner™
Registered Financial Consultant
Registered Tax Return Preparer

Mel Cohen is a consultant with hands-on experience. He regularly provides practical advice in business, book marketing, general marketing, finance, taxation, management, nonprofit organizations and barter.

Over 35 years of experience in retailing, wholesaling, merchandising, inventory control and turnover.

Over 30 years of experience in tax preparation and planning for individuals, partnerships, corporations, trusts and estates.

Over 25 years of experience in business startup and evaluation, business and marketing plans, and general business consulting for both nonprofit and for-profit organizations.

Current and Former Memberships, Affiliations and Associations

- College for Financial Planning
- Delaware County Chamber of Commerce
- Delaware Valley Society of the Institute of Certified Financial Planners
- Institute for Certified Financial Planners
- International Board of Standards and Practices for Certified Financial Planners
- Licensed Real Estate Professional
- National Association of Tax Practitioners and the National Society of Tax Professionals
- Financial Planning Association
- Rotary International

A biographical record appeared in the Silver Anniversary 28th Edition of Marquis *Who's Who in Finance and Industry*, as well as the 31st (2000/2001) Millennium Edition, inclusion in which is limited to those individuals who have demonstrated outstanding achievement in their own fields of endeavor and who have thereby contributed significantly to the betterment of contemporary society.

A speaker on marketing for the American Institute of Certified Public Accountants Firm Administrator's Conference.

Numerous radio and TV appearances on baseball cards, barter, and finance. Author of several local and national articles on taxation, business, marketing, and baseball cards.

Author and publisher of the book, *Secret of the Pros: How to Become a Baseball Card Dealer.* Editor-in-Chief of "Secret of the Pros, the Newsletter for Collectors, Investors and Dealers of Trading Cards."

Expert witness (plaintiff) for the largest class action lawsuit against major trading card companies that was filed to date in 1997. Was retained for other expert witness engagements by law firms representing insurance companies.

Designer of special Amazon promotions that have resulted in creating "Amazon Best Seller" status books. Achieved rankings in the Amazon Top 100 out of the over 20 million books on their website.

Example: *A Love That Multiplies* by Michelle and Jim Bob Duggar resulted in seven Top 100 rankings: Overall Sales, Movers and Shakers, Hot New Releases and the #1, #1, #2 position in its specific genre as well as a #12 Kindle rating in its genre. For three straight days the book was in the Top 50 in overall sales.

Military Service

Mel served aboard the USS Okinawa (LPH-3). Mel was on the ship during its first call to service for the Cuban Missile Crisis in October 1962 as well as the Cuban Missile Blockade in December 1962.

Later the ship earned seven campaign stars for Vietnam War service.

16: A Solution to Military Veteran Unemployment

Guaranteed Civil Service Jobs

WILLIAM A. "TONY" LAVELLE

A disproportionate number· of military veterans are unemployed. Thousands have served in Iraq and Afghanistan. Now that those wars are winding down, the military is downsizing, pushing tens of thousands of highly skilled and well-trained military veterans into the civilian job market. Corporate America has been slow to hire US veterans for a variety of reasons. In my opinion, the principal motive is that they are sheep and we soldiers are sheepdogs.

One Vietnam veteran, an old retired colonel, once said this to me: "Most of the people in our society are sheep. They are kind, gentle, productive creatures who can only hurt one another by accident. Then there are the wolves who feed on the sheep without mercy. And then there are sheepdogs. I am a sheepdog. I live to protect the flock and to confront the wolf!"

If you have no capacity for violence then you are a healthy productive citizen: one of the sheep. If you have a capacity for violence and no empathy for your fellow citizens, then you are a sociopath, a wolf. But what if you have a capacity for violence, and at the same time a deep love for your fellow citizens? Then you are a sheepdog: A warrior, someone who is walking the hero's path, someone who can walk into the heart of darkness, into the universal human phobia, and walk out unscathed.

The sheep generally do not like the sheepdog. He looks a lot like the wolf. He has fangs and the capacity for violence. The difference, though, is that the sheepdog must not, cannot and will not ever harm the sheep. A sheepdog's mission is to protect the sheep from the wolves.

America is made up mostly of healthy, happy, and productive citizens (sheep). Sheep don't like sheepdogs. Or they are just scared of sheepdogs, making it even harder for a sheepdog, a vet, to get a job. Not impossible, just harder.

OK, enough about sheep. What is my whiz-bang crazy idea to solve veterans' unemployment that guarantees all US veterans a civilian government job as soon as they get out of the service?

I mean full-time civil service employment, working for the federal, state, or municipal governments. By "guarantee," I propose that for every soldier who gets out of the service, there will be a civil service job waiting for him or her, if he or she wants it.

There are nearly a million US veterans out of work. The feds have about half a million civil service jobs. Add in all 50 states, 3,000 counties and nearly 20,000 incorporated cities. Looks like more than enough jobs. Of course, it will take time to implement. So I would like to see my program start immediately for newly separated service men and women. In 10 years every US veteran that wants a civil service job will have one.

Those vets that don't want a civil service job waiting for them when they retire or get discharged from the military, that's fine. Then they will work in US businesses and become valuable team members and leaders, or they will create businesses of their own.

How Would My Plan Work?

The Department of Defense (DoD) would establish a civil service personnel office for transitioning veterans. Their mission would be to track all civil service jobs that are open for hire and to place willing veterans into those jobs. A soldier, about a year before he is going to retire or separate from the service, submits a request to be transferred to civil service. The DoD would review the soldier's records of training and experience. Then the soldier is sent a list of available jobs. The solider picks the one he or she wants. The DoD will then plug him or her in for that job. The soldier's separation or retirement orders would show the soldier as transferring from military service to civil service. That soldier would report for work, just like transferring in the military. And he would keep his time in service and rank.

Example: Master Sergeant John Davis

- Air Force Sergeant John Davis is an aviation fuel supervisor at Travis Air Force Base. After eight years of active duty, he is transferring to the Air Force Reserves at Travis.

- Davis applies for civil service.

- He accepts a full-time position with the Port of Oakland to work at the airport as a fuel management safety supervisor.

Example: Corporal Luther Johnson

- Marine Corporal Johnson is 23 years old. He is a wheeled and tracked vehicle mechanic stationed at Parris Island.

- He is separating from the Marine Corps after four years.

- A year before his separating, he applies for a civil service job.

- The DoD gives him a choice of six different civil service positions in three different locations.

- He takes a position working for the California Department of Transportation as a master mechanic.

Example: Private First Class Dexter Lowell

- Dexter served as a helicopter door gunner in Vietnam. Then he got busted for dope and he finished out his tour as a cook.

- He did get an honorable discharge because the Army thought he was a heck of a cook.

- But Dexter spent most of his time unemployed and homeless.

- One day at the VA hospital for a doctor's appointment, he sees the DoD civil service office right next to the lobby.

- To make a long story short, the DoD got Dexter a full-time job working for the Forest Service as a journeyman cook at a camp in Alabama, Dexter's home state.

Example: Commander Sally Winters

- Navy Commander Winters retired from the Navy after 22 years of service as a personnel officer.

- When she put in her retirement papers, she applied to the DoD for civil service.

- She accepted a position as a personnel supervisor at the Air Force Personnel Center in San Antonio Texas.

FAQ (Frequently Asked Questions)

Q: Do you want only military vets to get all the civil service jobs?
A: No. Civilians can apply for civil service jobs. There are more civil service jobs that need filling that there are veterans to fill them. The total number of jobs in all federal, state, and local governments is about 2 to 3 million jobs. For all the civil service jobs that are not filled with a US veteran, a civilian can apply.

Q: Do vets have to take the civil service test and be interviewed for the job?
A: No, the soldier's records are reviewed by the civil service in lieu of testing. Copies of the soldier's performance reviews stand in for an interview.

Q: Can any military veteran just walk into a civil service job even without a test or interview?
A: Yes, that's the "guaranteed" part of the plan. After his or her records are reviewed and matched to the best types of jobs, based on soldier training and experience, the US veteran gets the job automatically.

Q: Is giving all the civil service jobs to the military fair?
A: Well, there are more civil service jobs out there than veterans can fill. If a civilian wants a guaranteed civil service job, with no testing or interview required, then he can join the military.

Q: What if the DoD can't match a military vet to any jobs?
A: You mean of the millions and millions of civil service jobs out there, the big computer can't match one soldier to one job? I guess that

possible, but this program is a guaranteed job for every veteran. I am sure the federal or some state or county government can find a good job for him.

Q: What if the soldier's job was as a sniper?

A: That's easy: Any prison that posts guards with sniper rifles in the towers can use him. He could also be a police officer or special agent SWAT team sniper.

What Can You Do?

My solution is straightforward: All federal, state, and local governments that hire and use civilian servants will hire all discharged or retired military members who want a civil service job. A soldier, say a year before he or she is discharged, would submit their request for transfer to the civil service. The military member would complete a "dream sheet" listing where in the continental United States (CONUS) they want to be transferred, as well as what types of jobs they are interested in and for which they are qualified.

Under My Plan Every Soldier Gets a Job After Military Service

I am writing to the 20 percent of you who will think this idea is worth your time to make it happen. You ever hear of "The Pareto Principle" (also known as the "80/20 rule")? 80 percent will sit on their butts, doing nothing. Maybe they will howl that I am of full of it. But those highly motivated "20 percenters" will show a little fortitude. This is a great plan. It's so simple and so good. I don't know why someone else has not already made it happen.

For those of you so motivated, what can you do? Start by writing letters and email to your elected officials. Start with emails to Congress. The name of the program is "Guaranteed Civil Service Job for All Vets." Say in the letter you want "Congress to legislate the creation of a program that will guarantee a civil service job to every veteran who wants one."

Every US veteran should be a member of at least one of the 40 or so professional military organizations that are members of The Military Coalition (www.themilitarycoalition.org). The Military Coalition is one of the most powerful lobbying groups in D.C. Join one of those groups. Write to them about the Guaranteed Civil Service Job program and what a great idea it is.

I got the idea when I was still on active duty. When I was about a year away from my retirement, I started my transitional training. I enjoyed and was comfortable working within a government environment, so I applied around Travis Air Force Base. I was lucky enough to be hired by the State of California as an adjunct professor of Criminal Justice at Cal State Sacramento. What a marvelous first job after 26 years of military service

What else can you do to help make this solution a reality? Write and email your state and local government representatives. Most states offer some type of veteran hiring preference, but none will guarantee a veteran a job as my solution does.

Since I have talked about my idea, I had one old Navy chief come up to me and tell me, "What kind of a civil service job can a moron with a bad conduct discharge get?" "Maybe we'll make him a garbage truck driver or a congressman," I said.

In closing, I would like to say it is disgraceful letting so many veterans go without jobs after they served their country. This book is about coming up with solutions to fix that. Let's all help get our G.I.s a job!

About the Author

William A. "Tony" Lavelle is a former military officer who served in the U.S. Army and Air Force. After his military career he was a faculty member at California State University. He left the public sector to found one of the first police dog service contractors that focused on explosive detection dogs (EDD).

His company has served Defense Security Service (DSS), government, and corporate clients in the U.S. and in Iraq for over nine years. At present, Tony is an anthropology researcher and author. Tony's most recent book, *The Manhood Test*, outlines his robust solution to stem the decline of manhood, and how to help boys reach manhood and to go on to live happy and successful lives as men.

Tony is still a service dog trainer. He has 15 years expertise as a professional dog handler of EDD Dogs. He is preparing to train his first post-traumatic stress disorder (PTSD) service dog. Tony is a Vietnam combat veteran afflicted with PTSD. He has been married for 38 years to the ever beautiful, wise, and tolerant Patricia Ann. His interests include scuba diving, teaching sailing, and studying Tai Chi.

P.S. I tried to give you a simple taste of my idea. It would work so well. US veteran unemployment would be wiped out! But as I said at the beginning, my idea is probably too far out of the box. Too many sheep would be whining, "Baa! Baa!"

*Editor's Note: Elected officials love to be seen as patriotic. They know that it gets them reelected. Find a United Veterans Council in your region and attend. Go to other major veteran organization meetings too. Get support for this idea. Have them sign a petition. Representatives from the Governor, Senators, Congresspersons, Assembly members, Supervisors and Councilpersons attend these veteran meetings regularly. Give them a copy. Tell them that the US veterans in their voting area are waiting to hear back from them about this. Put pressure on the people who have the power to make this happen! That is the American way.

17: A 'Brand' New You

J. TODD RHOAD

As if the journey into the military life isn't challenging enough, my re-entry back into the civilian world proved to be just as formidable. I truly enjoyed my years as an aircraft electronics technician on the Air Force's B-52 bomber and learned a lot of valuable technical skills that would be beneficial to many technical companies. However, the military has a tendency to build their installations in remote locations, and I ended up in such a place when I left the military to rejoin the private sector. It didn't take long to figure out that the skills I had weren't in high demand locally. As a young kid, I didn't have much experience to draw from and had never been in this situation. Far away from home, I had nowhere to turn for support or the development of a viable resolution. All I knew was that I had to reinvent myself. I needed a whole new me. It took a few years to build that new person, or personal brand, as we term it today.

My Story of Change

I started out on my new life by leaning on what I knew best, technical things. It was all I had, so it had to be the focus of my brand. Many senior enlisted guys told me I'd need to expand my expertise to get a better job in the private sector. I had already started taking college courses during my tour and decided that would be a good place to start to build new skills. As an avionics technician, electrical engineering became the obvious choice for my new pursuit of knowledge, skills and abilities. After talking with several professors, acceptance to an engineering program was granted. Now, the challenge was in paying the tuition and living expenses. The GI Bill did provide a small amount to me monthly. Unfortunately, my tuition was not included, so I took out loans to pay for my undergraduate degree. I also found some comfort in the Job Training Partnership Act (JTPA), started in the early 1980s to help disadvantaged youth and dislocated workers. Combining the GI Bill, JTPA and a part-time job, I managed to squeak through the program and graduate with a Bachelor's Degree in Electrical Engineering.

This wasn't the end of my academic career. During my undergraduate program, I focused on developing as many new skills as I could. Leadership was one of my top goals and something that most people believe the military is good at developing, so I jumped headfirst into as many leadership opportunities as I could find.

I became the Institute of Electrical and Electronics Engineers (IEEE) student chapter president for the university and used the position to make contacts in industry and other academic institutions. These connections paid off as I was offered a graduate fellowship to earn a Master's Degree in Electrical Engineering at another university, the Missouri School of Science and Technology. I struggled with this decision. I knew that a Master's Degree in Engineering would be a lot of work and would force me to continue my humble lifestyle. Did I really want to go back to school for two more years, or should I just take a job and start earning some money? I already had a job offer in hand. In hindsight, I think my decision to pursue the Master's Degree was one of the best decisions I've ever made.

My Master's Degree earned me the perception from others that I was an expert. Although I never would boast about that title, I would not refute it either. Having it made life much easier. After I graduated, I had several job interviews and hardly ever had to answer a technical question. They assumed I knew the answers. I can't tell you what a boost of confidence this was. I was now back looking for work. My new credentials made the search much easier because there was less competition. I had obtained some very specific skills that several companies needed. With several job offers in hand, I chose one and took a leadership role in a consumer products company, leading an engineering team. Two key factors in my background made this leadership position possible. First, I had demonstrated leadership skills in the military and in college. Second, I sought and earned a degree not too many people hold.

Life was great for a few years. However, it wasn't long until I got my first taste of how corporate America works. My company began to restructure itself. This usually means that someone isn't earning their bonus, so changes have to be made to fix that. I wasn't high enough up on the corporate ladder to be a big player in the restructuring activities, but I was high enough to hear the squabbling among the managers. It was a bunch of grown men jockeying for position. Everyone was looking out for their career and was hoping to avoid losing any power and to collect more. I didn't think this was right or what the leaders should be doing, but they were doing it. It made me realize that if they weren't looking out for me and my team, who was? The company made their changes. I couldn't see any logic to what they had done and certainly couldn't envision how this would best serve the company. It was at this time I realized that our goals weren't aligned anymore. I wanted to grow in my job; that is, in knowledge and responsibility. I didn't see any way this could happen, so I decided to leave the company and chase a dream I'd always had.

My dream was to become the expert people considered me to be. This dream took me to a position as a project engineer in a high-tech research and development company. Little did I know this company had many experts, most of whom held doctorate degrees. Building my brand as an expert would be challenging, as the competition was fierce. It took me several years to figure out what was necessary to establish my niche. I didn't want to compete with a Ph.D. These guys were young and smart.

So I decided that the only way to develop my expertise was to understand certain processes better than anyone else. I did this by reading a few technical papers from the latest journals in our field of study; then I asked many of the Ph.Ds. what they knew about each process. Once I found two or three processes they didn't know well, I would research them and study them in detail. I made myself the expert on each one. It just took time to understand what others had done, time and effort to experiment and gain more insight into what could be done. This small level of branding myself as an expert led to many new opportunities that would not have normally occurred. It led to publication of over 30 technical articles in just over three years. Once you put this on your resume, you look like an expert. But corporate life taught me another lesson, as this company restructured and moved to another state. I decided to pursue another career.

This time, I didn't just rely on my technical background. I contacted companies that dealt with the military (i.e., government contractors). This type of environment was perfect for me since I knew the military well. I am a veteran and I am technically literate. I won't dive off into another story of how this job played out, but it ended up with the company being sold twice within 18 months. As you can imagine, the company was in constant turmoil for years. That's not a great environment to grow your career in.

Having spent many years in small to medium enterprises, I am amazed that many of them actually remain profitable, considering all of the changes companies go through. It seemed no matter where I landed, I would end up in a company that changed. However, I didn't let this get me down. I went back to college to earn a Masters in Business Administration in the hope that it would give me better insight into all of this mass hysteria we call "business."

I wrote my master's thesis on the factors that affect career mobility. I decided to study a couple of fast-moving executives to see what they did to improve their careers. Then I did a little research to see what the experts had to say about their techniques. I combined my findings with my research and published the results in my first book. Little did I know that this was the beginning of a whole new transition. It wasn't long after my first book that I began to consult with others on career-related topics. At first, people just wanted me to help them make a transition (i.e., finding a new job), but it grew into helping executives develop strategies for achieving their career goals.

The Key to Transitions

Now that I've spent the past eight years or so helping others become successful in making transitions, I've grown into publishing ebooks on various career topics. I am also developing classes for MBA programs, and so much more. All of these new activities are used to reinforce my brand. If I want to stay in business, I have to communicate a brand message that says, "You'll get much more value than you'll pay for my services." This is no different for an individual in a company. If you don't deliver a high-value message, you may be forced to make changes. Whether you're retiring from the military and entering the workforce, or just returning to civilian life after a short tour, the name of the corporate game today is value. If you haven't developed your value statement or even considered how to build a brand, here are a few things you need to know.

• **Know Your Value**

While it may seem a little unusual to be asked what you are really good at, it is missed by many professionals. Often our desire to do certain activities impedes our judgment of how good we are at performing these activities. Therefore, it is useful to do a quick aptitude test to see if our natural tendencies fall in line with our desires. The Princeton Review (www.princetonreview.com) has a free five-minute survey that provides a snapshot of your strengths. Review your results and compare them to what you really want to do. Are there any discrepancies that you need to consider? Do you need to learn new skills? Consult with family and friends on your results and see if they agree with the assessment. A little feedback can save you lots of time and the embarrassment of learning such lessons on the job.

Another assumption we often make is that if our skills are needed at this company, then they will be needed at another company as well. I sure wish this was true. I could have saved years of time and a whole lot of tuition money. Unfortunately, the rate of change in businesses today is unprecedented. As organizations continue their quest for growing revenues, they change the company to aid their efforts. For example, Fortune 500 companies are filing near-record profits this year. However, they aren't hiring people because their revenues are low. By not hiring more people, the company keeps its costs low so profit margins remain high. Not only do you have a lot of competition in times of high unemployment, you also have companies who don't want to hire new people. With less people in the company, it is likely that you'll have to perform more roles to support daily activities. Maybe your previous company had more people so you could do just your own role. But as companies trim down in the size of their workforce, the more skills you'll need to develop. The more skills you have, the more value you have. Remember, your value statement is your greatest weapon to combat such challenges and to stand out against your competition.

So now that you know that company executives are searching for ways to grow revenue and reduce cost, how do you convince them that you have a high value? What have you done in the past that involves either of these? What can you do now? Look deep into your military, work and educational history to develop stories that highlight your ability to create value and reduce cost. Try to quantify it if possible. The more information you can provide, the clearer the value proposition you can make to a potential employer. Remember to include both past and future capabilities.

• Know Your Unique Selling Proposition

Once you know the value you can provide, you need to create a way to communicate it. A unique selling proposition (USP) is your statement of value to your potential employers. Words are the key to the mind and each word conjures up thoughts, ideas and emotions. As you walk through the process I present below, think about the emotions or ideas you want the recipient to think of or feel when you give them your USP.

Crafting and polishing your unique selling proposition is often challenging. However, if you know your value, putting it in words isn't too difficult. If you don't know your value, this will be impossible. Here's a simple six step process to help guide you in creating your own USP.

- Step 1 - Understand your target audience. Who are you communicating this to? Be sure that you mention who they are, so that they know you are talking to them.

- Step 2 - Solve a problem. People and companies have problems and need someone to help solve them. You need to communicate how you can help solve their problems. Remember, we discussed increasing revenues and reducing costs earlier.

- Step 3 - Three big strengths. You want to list the three biggest advantages of working with you. This is the central question any recruiter is thinking: "Why do I want to hire you?"

- Step 4 - Promise of value. Write down your promise of what you will do. Will you reduce costs or grow their revenues? Maybe you can develop products or expand their marketplace to areas they haven't considered.

- Step 5 - Combine all of your ideas. Write down everything that you understanding from the first four steps. Read it aloud to yourself. What emotions or ideas do you think of when you hear it?

- Step 6 - Refine your unique selling proposition (USP). <u>Combine everything you wrote down and shrink it to a single sentence</u>. This is your unique selling proposition. Examples: "When your package absolutely, positively has to get there overnight" (FedEx). "Melts in your mouth, not in your hand" (M & M's).

Test your USP statement on others to assess the emotional impact of the words you selected. Gather honest feedback and incorporate it in your USP. This is the message you will communicate to potential employers whenever you have the opportunity. Note their responses. Refine and repeat.

• Know the Battlefield

One thing many people overlook when it comes to career opportunity is where the battle is fought. When I was much younger, companies were family oriented. Companies would employ the family members of good employees because they felt that they would have the same values and ethics. In fact, my father worked for the same company for 34 years. He told a manager about my older brother and soon he was working at the company too. Unfortunately, companies don't really operate this way anymore. Business is global and companies need people who can speak to any part of the world. While great diversity does have great benefits, it is also challenging for the development of close personal relationships. People have a natural tendency to bond with those similar to themselves.

Securing employment through close relationships is still important, but it isn't as common as it once was. Today, headhunters are scouring the Internet to find potential candidates. If you don't have an Internet presence, you're at a huge disadvantage.

Facebook has over 1 billion members. That's a lot of candidates in one place. Naturally, headhunters will flock to it to identify potential hires. The Internet is a unique battlefield and one in which <u>being seen</u> is your main objective. If recruiters can't find you online, or if you don't have personal connections to the company, you don't exist.

The Internet is an easy tool to use. It's right at recruiters' fingertips. Therefore, they often go to this resource first. It is often used to verify information on resumes and to probe deeper into potential candidates. Therefore, the information you post on this battlefield must be professional, easily visible, accurate, interesting and consistent. Recruiters focus their efforts on screening applicants on the Big Three social networks: LinkedIn, Facebook and Twitter.

Facebook: Recruiters are using Facebook groups, advertising and corporate Facebook career pages to find candidates. You can use the BranchOut or BeKnown applications to map job openings to your network. You should also "like" a company, so that you can follow their updates and comment. Be careful what you post and make sure you keep it professional. Turn on your privacy settings to protect yourself.

LinkedIn: LinkedIn Recruiter allows recruiters to reach passive candidates by expanding the reach of their personal networks. They can contact candidates directly and manage a specific pool of talent. The best advice for job seekers is to fully utilize LinkedIn in your job search. Recruiters will only take you seriously if you have a complete profile. Take the time to fill out all sections as if you were creating a marketing brochure for a product (because that's what you are really doing.) You should also optimize your profile by adding specialty keywords to your headline, summary and throughout the rest of your profile. That way, when recruiters search for candidates with certain skills, your name shows up.

Twitter. Companies are using Twitter and other social network companies to post job entries via their own account page. They are also using third party companies, such as Tweet My Jobs and Twit Job Search, to promote their job listings. Job seekers should follow the companies they want to work for on Twitter and watch for job postings.

Building Your Profile

Now that you know your value, have a unique selling proposition, and know the tools recruiters will use to find candidates, it's time to develop your own brand. It begins with building a professional online profile. This is fairly easy. But it is very important. I can't reiterate this enough: Complete the profile on each of the social networks you setup. A partially completed profile tells people that you can't complete anything and that you are not a serious traveler on the web.

• The Photo

You need a good photo of yourself. Use the same photo on all of your profiles so that people can easily relate to you. Using multiple photos can cause some confusion, especially is there is a lot of time between when the photos were taken. Avoid the confusion and select a professional photo. You don't have to hire someone to take it, but if you can, you should.

• The Description of You

Anywhere you are describing yourself and what you do, be professional. Fill out the "About" section of your Facebook page completely. Use keywords in the "About You" section that reinforce the central ideas behind your brand. Much of this information will be applied to your LinkedIn and Twitter profiles. Describing yourself should be easy. If you've taken the aptitude test and discussed it with friends and family, you should already have a list of terms that describe you. Don't forget to include your USP. Recruiters will want to know what you have to offer and it should be clear in your description.

Recruiters will also want a peek inside your personality. You can take a free online personality test to gather information about your personality to share online. I wouldn't go too deep into who you are since the more information you share, the more you are judged. The information you share should be applicable to the types of positions you are seeking. I was an engineer early on in my career. I posted information that demonstrated I had great technical skills. I would list engineering awards I had won, technical papers I had published, and patents I was pursuing. These things are important to companies because it shows what I can do. And it presents value to the company, especially with regards to creating revenue (i.e., patents). Never forget your value statement. It should be communicated everywhere in your profile.

Expanding Your Brand

Establishing a great personal brand requires a little more effort than just identifying who you are on a few social networks. It requires a real contribution in your area of expertise. For example, I've added a new focus to my business. I am developing an expertise around professionals with a Master's in Business Administration degree, an MBA. If I just put a few phrases on my social network profiles that said I am the MBA 'guru,' but did not provide any evidence of it, no-one would believe it. I have to prove to others that I am the guru. There are two key considerations to expanding my brand this way: building tangible evidence of my claim, and validation of my level of expertise. Let's take a look at each of these.

• Building Tangible Proof

Because anyone can put anything on the Internet, it takes more than a few fancy words to convince anyone of its truth. To build your brand you need to create evidence. In making myself the guru of the MBA degree and how to create success with it, I began to create products to demonstrate my level of expertise. My first step was to blog about specific career issues that MBAs face. How did I know what issues they faced? I asked them on LinkedIn. MBAs responded with their challenges. So, I picked a few of them, did a little research, and then wrote several articles about my findings.

After I began to get a small following on my blog, I branched out to writing articles for career-related magazines on similar topics. I always kept my focus on the area of expertise for which I wanted to be branded, the MBA. In each article, I always referred the reader back to my blog. Why? I want people to see my work and refer it to others.

But I didn't stop there. I began writing ebooks to post on Amazon and Barnes & Noble websites. I enlisted support from MBAs from around the globe to not only help me create the ebooks, but to help market and advertise to their audience. Then, I go back to my social networking profiles and point my readers to my blogs, articles and ebooks. Once they see sufficient proof, the branding begins to take hold.

• **Validating Your Expertise**

To take it one step further, I use one of the oldest and most powerful techniques to show that I am the expert. This tool is called "validation." In my blogs and articles, I often interview well known experts in my field. In my ebooks, I ask many of these same experts to endorse me, lending instant credibility to my work. Once readers begin to associate my brand with that of the top experts, their perception of my expertise and success in the field greatly improve. It's branding by association. The important thing to remember is that for the validation to be effective, you must choose someone in your field and who is well known. Otherwise, it doesn't work well. This is a great method, but it does take some time to build. Most top experts are always busy as they get a lot of requests to support others. This technique is great but is also known by many people, so the competition for attention from the experts is a big challenge. However, once you get one expert to endorse you, getting others is much easier. Why? If a top expert thinks highly of your work, it must be good. Many times you'll get the support you seek just because of someone else who is supporting you. Don't overlook this method, as it is extremely powerful and can open the door to many new opportunities.

5. Summary

Today's business environment is extremely challenging. It's driven by value. Everyone is trying to communicate their value to someone. Those who communicate it best are afforded more security and opportunity. In our most recent survey, we asked MBAs if they felt personal branding was important to their career. Over 98% of respondents felt their personal branding efforts were important or very important to career development. Despite this feeling, only 49% of respondents spend "some time" on developing their personal brand and 47% are somewhat clear on what their brand is. It's very difficult to get someone to invest in you if you can't tell them why they would want to do that or what their return on investment will be. Just imagine you are a mutual fund that an investor is considering buying. This is what they want to see: past performance, trends, and return on investment. What's in your prospectus? Build a great brand so everyone knows what they get when they invest in you.

If you show the history of investment and the great returns investors received, you'll find that finding new opportunities are much easier to find. In fact, they will find you.

About the Author

J. Todd Rhoad is the Managing Director for BT Consulting, an Atlanta-based career-consulting company that focuses on helping high achievers grow and develop in their career and reach new heights on the organizational ladder. He is also the founder of MBAWriters, an international group of MBA students and graduates who share their expertise and experience through their writing. Todd also created the Henry Series of ebooks for MBAs, which provides solutions to many career-related issues MBAs face. He holds a Master of Science from the Missouri School of Science and Technology and an MBA from Indiana Wesleyan University. You can learn more about BT Consulting at blitzteamconsulting.com.

18: The Nitty Gritty of Getting Employed

SELDON B. GRAHAM, JR.

Veterans need to know the nitty gritty, not merely how to get a job, but to get the line of work they will love to have for the rest of their life. I believe that I have learned this secret by finding the right way to do it after doing it the wrong way a number of times.

I must give you the history of my military service as I have transitioned into civil life. In 1944 at age 18, I was a member of the Corps of Cadets at Texas A&M and was drafted into the Army. I went through infantry basic training at Camp Wolters, Texas. After basic training, I was extremely lucky to be selected for Infantry Officer Candidate School at Fort Benning, Georgia. After becoming a second lieutenant, I was assigned to the 20th Infantry Regiment in the Pacific. Again, I was extremely lucky because Japan surrendered and my regiment did not assault the Japanese beach just south of Tokyo as planned. Infantry second lieutenants have a very short life span on enemy beaches. I believe that the atomic bombs dropped on Hiroshima and Nagasaki saved my life.

So, when I was discharged from active duty in the fall of 1946, I got the first job that came along. I became a walking postal mail carrier with two deliveries per day. There was irony in this: from hiking with a pack in the infantry to walking with a mail sack in the postal service. It did not take me long to figure out that I did not want to do this all of my life.

Allow me to digress at this point. Do not take the first job offered without first doing your due diligence which I will provide later in this chapter. I have a good friend who took the first job offered to him as an agent in the Internal Revenue Service. I heard him complain about his job for the next 20 years until he retired. Life is too short to be in a job you do not like.

The way out of a civilian job that may not please you is to get more education. Once again, I was lucky to be offered the opportunity of a college education leading to a general engineering degree with a military obligation of active duty upon graduation. I quickly accepted.

Upon graduating with a Bachelor of Science degree from college, I served for three years in the Army in Germany. When I was released from active duty, I was once again a veteran searching for a job. This time I was somewhat smarter than the first time. I wanted to be employed as an engineer, and I also wanted to live in the southwestern United States. I am from Texas, and I liked living in Texas. I made a comprehensive study of what industry had the most engineers in Texas and the southwestern United States. I found as a result of this 1954 study that the petroleum industry had the largest number of engineers where I wanted to live.

There was one problem. I did not know anything about petroleum engineering. I found out that all the major oil companies had a training program for college graduates with engineering degrees. The next study I made was to determine which oil companies had the reputation for having a really good training program.

From that study, I discovered that one company, ARCO, had the reputation of having the longest and most comprehensive training program, which lasted 18 months. Since I knew nothing about petroleum engineering, I knew that I should first try to get into the ARCO training program.

When I made application for the ARCO program, I came upon a new obstacle. Before hiring new employees, ARCO gave the individual psychological examinations. After taking these exams, I was told that I was hired as an engineering trainee, so I assume that I did all right in these psychological exams.

Before I go any further, please let me critique what I did. Part of what I did was good, but part of what I did was not good. I focused on a job that I knew nothing about. The focusing was good. The research on the industry with the largest number of engineers was good. The research on the training program was good.

The bad aspects of what I had just done were that I had grossly neglected a self-analysis of whether I wanted to work in an office or out of doors, whether I wanted to be an individual player or a team player, whether or not I wanted to manage others, and many other personal questions. There is an easy way to do this, which I learned later. I will discuss this later in the chapter.

As it turned out, the training program allowed some personal choices. For instance, I was more interested in the study of petroleum reservoirs than I was in drilling offshore wells. The farthest offshore well I was on was drilling in a Louisiana swamp. I preferred the challenge of determining how much oil or natural gas was in a reservoir. After the training program, my permanent job was as an individual player in an office with no grime under my fingernails.

The next step in my self-education on job hunting was to learn the value of networking and mentorship. I attended an annual alumni dinner in a large city away from home. By sheer coincidence, I was seated next to an older petroleum engineer. When he learned that I was also a petroleum engineer, he told me that he was organizing an interstate natural gas pipeline and a member of his board of directors, a well-known Texas oilman, was in need of a petroleum engineer. He thought this might be a great opportunity and urged me to contact him.

I contacted this oilman and became his petroleum engineer. He issued me a Mercedes Benz as a company car, and I was introduced to every facet of the oil business: drilling wells, fracturing formations, making deals, buying producing properties, designing pipelines, making bank loans. After a year, I decided that I preferred the stability of working as a reservoir engineer for a major oil company, so I used my newly found art of networking to make the transition to Mobil.

At Mobil, I became a reservoir engineer who was an expert witness before state regulatory agencies. This was done in teamwork with a company attorney. After several years, I wanted to know why I lost cases on some unknown legal principle. I also wanted to be the person asking the questions at a technical hearing instead of the person answering the questions. I needed to become an oil and gas attorney.

The way out of a civilian job in which you are not fully satisfied is to get more education. I put my newly learned networking skills to work in order to get a part-time job as a petroleum engineer while going to law school. After all, I had to support a wife and three children while attending law school.

With networking, I was offered a position as an attorney with Humble (later renamed Exxon) before I graduated from law school. It was the proverbial offer that I could not refuse. I spent a career thoroughly enjoying being the attorney handling technical hearings for Exxon, until I retired, including the arbitration to determine the ownership of the Prudhoe Bay Field in Alaska.

After retirement from Exxon, I transitioned into a job as an attorney in practice for clients before the Railroad Commission of Texas, the agency that regulates the oil and gas industry in Texas. After that, I used networking skills to become "Of Counsel" in several major law firms.

It was at this point that I was selected by my local alumni organization to formalize the transition of Army officers into civilian life. In other words, I was to teach veterans how they should go about getting civilian jobs.

Many of these Army officers were retiring colonels and generals. My advice to these veterans had to be accurate and had to conform to the KISS principle of Keep It Simple, Stupid; namely, short, concise and to the point. The advice had to be proven successful in practice. In addition, it had to be in the form of "do-it-yourself steps."

So, here it comes. This is the nitty gritty of how a veteran can get a civilian job he or she will love.

Step 1 is to purchase the book *What Color Is Your Parachute?* by Richard N. Bolles. This is the focus book that I originally did not have. This book is updated almost every year. After finding out about this book, I have recommended it to every job hunter. Read it carefully, giving each subject thoughtful consideration. If after you have finished reading this book, you should be able to focus on professions or on industries in which you would love to work. If you have not focused after the first reading, then read the book again. This important first step of focusing is to find the net or nets that you will work in the next step.

Step 2 is networking. Network, the verb, in this context means to meet people who are in a particular business with the goal of providing a mutual benefit for all who are in the net. The best explanation of networking for veterans is to be found in a military organization of one of the ancient Greek cities. This military organization consisted of a number of companies, each one being "A Company of the Table." Each individual company ate together, thus the name, much like the company mess hall in the old Army, but also trained together, fought together, and risked their lives together. For that reason, a person could not join "A Company of the Table" unless every member of the company accepted that person.

Imagine that you are trying to join one of these "Companies of the Table" knowing that you first have to determine which company to try to join and that after you make the decision on which company to try, then every member of the company must agree with your joining. One member of that company can veto your joining. That will first require good networking with members of the various companies to narrow down the company you will try to get into, then additional networking with members of the company you selected.

I cannot overemphasize the importance of networking. Networking is the key to success. It is not an intelligence gathering operation trying to get output from others. It is all about trying to make friends with those in the business which you selected as a net. You must have some news and information to share with others in your net. The secret about networking is that the better you become at networking, the less you and others in your net realize that you are networking. It is from the net friends that you not only get clues about opportunities but also unsolicited recommendations. Veterans have been exposed to outstanding leadership in the military. Make use of that experience by sharing stories of that leadership with others in your net. Civilians can benefit from hearing a good leadership story too.

There are some common sense recommendations in networking. At a minimum, keep a diary or journal. List in it when and to whom you call, and with whom you meet, with the subject of your discussion. As you make friends with those in your net, they will suggest others for you to contact, thereby enlarging your net. Networking is an acquired art, so learn how to do it effectively. Your future depends upon it. A good networker becomes a "people person" who is in great demand in the business world.

A few words about resumes: I have never used a resume to get a job. Perhaps you might have better success with a resume than I did. Using a military resume in trying to obtain a civilian job is a tough challenge if not a lost cause. I do not recommend trying to write a military resume for a civilian job. No matter how hard you try, you cannot turn a military resume into a civilian resume that will persuade a civilian who is looking for an individual to fill a job. If networking is done properly, you can get a job without a resume. The personnel department may call you up after you are hired asking you to provide a resume for the company files.

Veterans, I wish you all of the best in your journey to find and obtain the job that you will love. I have given you the nitty gritty know-how, from 66 years of experience in obtaining jobs, as to how to get the job you will love. Go forth and do it.

About the Author

Brief chapter synopsis of "The Nitty Gritty Veterans Need to Know." Loving the work you do is vital, not only to your future success, but for your "pursuit of happiness" and "blessings of liberty." In order for a veteran to locate this work that he or she will love, the veteran will need to know and accomplish two actions. The veteran author of this chapter learned these two actions the hard way, mostly by error, and wants to expedite the job-hunting education of other veterans by providing advice based upon 66 years of experience in locating civilian jobs.

ROTC Cadet, Texas A&M 1943–1944
Drafted, US Army Oct 1944
Private, Infantry RTC, Camp Wolters, TX 1944–45
Officer Candidate, OCS, Fort Benning, GA 1945
2LT, 20th Infantry, Korea 1946
Postal carrier, Denton, Texas 1946–47

Cadet, USCC, West Point, NY 1947–51
1LT, 112th Infantry, Germany 1951–54
Engineer Trainee, ARCO, OK, LA, KS 1954–55
Reservoir Engineer, ARCO, OK 1955–60
Engineer, Vernon Neuhaus, McAllen, TX 1960
Regulatory Engr, Mobil, Corpus Christi, TX 1961–67
Engineer, RRC of TX, Austin, TX 1967–70
Counsel, Exxon, HQ Law, Houston, TX 1970–85
Attorney, private practice, Austin, TX 1985–86
Of Counsel, Reynolds Shannon, Austin, TX 1987–88
Of Counsel, Hughes & Luce, Austin, TX 1989–90
Attorney & Engineer, Austin, TX 1990–present
Who's Who in America
Colonel, US Army, Retired
West Point Association of Graduates
Legion of Honor Member, Society of Petroleum Engineers

Seldon B. Graham, Jr.
4713 Palisade Drive
Austin, Texas 78731-4516
(512) 452-4000
SelGraham@austin.rr.com

19: The Great Equalizer

DAVID J. RENZA, M.A.

In a sunny spring day in New York in 1988 I heard the news about an essay contest from my eighth grade English teacher. The two students who wrote the best would be chosen to place a wreath on the Tomb of the Unknown Solider in Arlington, Virginia. I wrote about the inspiration of two generations of relatives—my grandfather Constance who served in the Navy in World War I, my grandfather Ralph who was a Marine on Iwo Jima in World War II, my uncle who served as an officer in the Navy, and my father who served in the New York Army National Guard—and how their service inspired me to someday join the military. My essay was chosen as one of the two best, and I was granted the honor of going to Arlington.

The trip to Washington D.C. was inspirational. I had long been fascinated by presidential history, and to be in the backyard of that history was remarkable to me. Arriving in Arlington and seeing the eternal flame at the grave of President Kennedy gave me all the somber magnitude a 14-year-old boy needed to understand the importance of where he was. When we walked up to the tomb, the guard who would help us perform the ceremony was ready with his crisp uniform replete with ribbons and medals. Holding the wreath in my hands while Taps was played had me shaking with nervousness. Gently placing the wreath on the easel, I realized I wanted to join my family's legacy in the US military.

From the moment I placed the wreath on the tomb in front of my classmates, it was three years before I would finally investigate joining the service and making my dream of serving my country a reality. In my senior year in high school, after realizing my grades weren't quite high enough for the military service academies, I decided to join the Marine Corps and follow in the footsteps of my grandfather. I was excited about doing so, until I met a recruiter from the Army National Guard in Connecticut. He was no different than any other recruiter, except that he made me no promises of going anywhere glamorous, even though he had been stationed in some fascinating places. He made me no promise of doing anything overwhelmingly exciting, even though he had pictures on his wall of him doing all kinds of neat things, including parachuting out of a plane for airborne training. In fact, if it came down to it, he really should have come in last. Even his dress uniform didn't quite look as cool as some of the other guys.

So why did I take his pitch over everyone else's? He had a distinct advantage over every other recruiter in Connecticut, which was the magic of free tuition. It was simple, if I joined the Connecticut Army National Guard, I could go to the University of Connecticut at the same time and get free tuition while serving my country one weekend a month and two weeks in the summer.

I initially wanted to join the military service full-time, but the thought of still getting ahead of the game in college while still enjoying some of the military experience was intriguing to me. Some people wanted to join the service for their education money. I wanted to join for the education and the experience. This logically was my best opportunity to do both. As the only guy out there who promised me I could do both and get a degree in four to five years (with time off for training), he was suddenly the answer I had been looking for. My own path to education had been paved.

The title of this chapter is an excerpt from a quote referring to education by Horace Mann, considered by many to be the father of modern educational thought. In the 1800s, when Mann's vision for the future of education took shape, he was referring to a secondary public school education. College was still not a necessity, but one could argue that education then made the difference between living in prosperity and living in poverty. While the dawn of the industrial revolution was upon us, the country was still primarily agrarian, meaning that an education and the skills that went with it were truly a way of changing one's life.

As the 20th Century began, that changed considerably. Urban areas cropped up seemingly overnight, surrounding port cities at first. Eventually, with railroad systems in place, cities were built wherever an industry was ready to receive materials and had manpower to create products.

With a working class of immigrants suffering from subpar working conditions and pay, Mann's philosophy held true. That all changed after the
creation of laws and unions that made sure that factories were safe and
pay was decent. The automobile and banking industries helped create
modern suburbia, ensuring that no-one had to live in the city to work
anymore, while offering an opportunity for a house to boot. Factory jobs
often had skills that could be learned relatively quickly and didn't require
a college education. As companies grew at faster rates, the prosperity of
the post-depression America led to many jobs where someone could raise
a family comfortably and be guaranteed a steady job with decent pay as
long as they chose to work.

Stories circulated of white collar workers who started in obscure jobs
within the company such as the mailroom and, with the right amount of
drive and ambition, could "climb the ladder" to an executive's position
without anything beyond a public school education. In some respects,
Mann's statement seemed dated for all but the bookends of the 20th
Century. An education surely meant that you would have a chance at
some of the finer things in life. But for raising a family and living a
comfortable life wanting for nothing, an education was no longer a
necessary requirement.

Fast-forward to the new millennium. The employment landscape of
the United States has changed significantly. Foreign policy and investor profit has sent many of the factory jobs the workforce had counted
on overseas, and many of the once-thriving cities and suburbs have
fallen on hard times since these jobs left. Small businesses supporting
the workers and families have faltered. The factories that once housed
industry are at best "repurposed," at worst overcome with blight. In the
place of factory jobs that provided the opportunity of a decent lifestyle,
there are low-paying retail jobs. The absence of jobs that can sustain
a family has created an abundance of overqualified people working
two and three lower-paying jobs to replace the one higher-paying job.
People who had factory jobs once did their shift and then left. Their
workday was over.

The current overabundance of retail positions, "McJobs" as they
are called, force people to be concerned about things that never used to

matter to the factory worker: appearance, customer service and product knowledge. They never had to do these things before, and they receive very little compensation for doing so now.

Suddenly, with a recessed economy and tough job prospects, Mann's once antiquated quote has gained new significance. The aforementioned changes in the job market and economy have meant that an education is arguably now more important than ever. No place has this change in the job market seen more of a recent effect than with US veterans. The percentage of veterans who are unemployed was over three percentage points higher than the national average, over 12 percent (Bureau of Labor Statistics, May 2012). So the question becomes, how could such a group of individuals as trained and as skilled as veterans of our nation's armed forces suffer with a dearth of employment opportunities commensurate with their experience level?

The answer starts with the job market shift itself. As the level of jobs that once were worthy career options to veterans disappeared, so too did the ability of veterans to market themselves in the new economy. Many veterans leaving the service after initial enlistments in the past ten years joined on the impetus of the attacks from 9/11. These men and women joined the service as a way of making a difference and giving something back. The majority of them were motivated by fervent patriotism, since the draft was dissolved in the 1970s. Few joined for the Veterans Administration benefits.

Those who were coming upon retirement after Iraq and Afghanistan reached their peak in the middle of the decade. They joined the service during the Cold War era. Many entered the military at a time when a career military member's experience was revered by the private sector. A retired service member from any number of military occupations was virtually guaranteed a career when they were ready to leave the service. However, the downturn in the job market left both older and younger veterans on the outside of employment looking for higher paying jobs, settling for lower paying ones, or worse, falling into tough times of poverty and homelessness. This led to the current epidemic that nobody, much less a veteran of the U.S. Armed Services, should ever have to succumb.

With the shift toward employers seeking more qualified personnel and the technical nature of high-paying jobs, the desirability of military service as a sought-after experience for hiring has fallen to a near record low. Therefore, US military members leaving military service without certifications and college degrees find bleak civilian job prospects.

During the ramp-up of the fighting forces in the Middle East, the mantra of the military changed very quickly. Gone were the days of focusing on fighting during basic training and general training scenarios and working in your chosen occupation for 90 percent of your military career. The military era after 9/11 saw a drastic change in focus, particularly in the Army, which made up a large total of the fighting forces in the Middle East. With a new type of enemy, combat training came first and was often the focus of the training exercises. Additionally, the large need for ground troops in Iraq and Afghanistan led to a need for combat positions to be filled. These positions included occupations such as tankers, infantry and artillery whose skills did not necessarily transfer well to civilian occupations. Leadership training was also amped up and improved, often mimicking some aspects of management training outside of the military—but it still did little to stop this reality.

Many of our veterans are unfortunately also reeling from the trials and tribulations of life after battle. There are an increasing number of veterans seeking medical assistance for physical ailments and the results of Improvised Explosive Device (IED) explosions. Many of these lead to myriad injuries that make work in a traditional occupation difficult, if not altogether impossible. The consequences of these injuries are far-reaching. Being too close to a single IED blast, if they survive, can leave wounded veterans with considerable obstacles to overcome once they return.

As with all wars, some veterans are afflicted with post-traumatic stress disorder (PTSD). This can make some of the customer-oriented jobs that have surfaced in storefronts throughout the country a difficult proposition. Many veterans feel isolated and may come to the realization that a bustling work environment may not be best suited for them.

Another reason for unemployed veterans may actually be a positive: among the benefits of the current GI Bill, college tuition is largely paid for. Many US veterans have decided to attend school. Considering the above facts about the economy and the change in the employment landscape, this is a wise move.

The sacrifices of our US Armed Service members have led to the most robust veteran education benefit package in the history of this country. The education benefits that are available to veterans today are nothing short of extraordinary. At a time when colleges and universities are rapidly raising their tuition costs, the government has truly stepped up to the plate in historic fashion to make sure that veterans have to pay as little as possible to attend school. In addition to numerous states offering free tuition to their public universities, several benefit packages, including the new post-9/11 GI Bill, go a step further.

The post-9/11 or Chapter 33 GI Bill was initially referred to as the Webb GI Bill, so named after Senator Jim Webb, who enacted legislation for the benefit as a way to help the large influx of service members who served after September 11, 2001. As a bill honoring these brave men and women, it has some significant features. Not only will it pay for tuition up to a certain rate, but also some books, supplies, and in most cases also a stipend for living expenses, commensurate with the Basic Allowance and Housing (BAH) rates for active duty military. The most remarkable feature of this chapter of the GI Bill is a part that is actually not seen directly in the bill itself.

The Yellow Ribbon Program is an agreement between the Department of Veteran Affairs (VA) and certain universities to help pay for the remaining cost of tuition beyond the initial cost of the benefit. What makes this extraordinarily significant is not so much the fact that it enables veterans the opportunity to attend some flagship institutions at no cost to them, but that it also shows the universities' support for the influx of veteran students on their campuses. In return, these schools of higher learning are making a financial contribution to their success.

In past generations, veteran support on campuses wavered between reverence and disdain, depending on the institution and its location. But the overwhelming view of veterans on campus has never wavered. Military veterans are always viewed as different. While veterans on campus still stand out, they are more often than not welcomed as part of student bodies that grow in diversity on a seemingly daily basis. However, some veterans who are used to the close camaraderie of combat feel out of place on college campuses swarming with students' imaginative activities and events. While the typical teenager who just graduated high school may welcome such freedom, the US veteran student, particularly one just returning from deployment in a combat zone, may crave more camaraderie, structure and unity than found on a college campus.

However, in the Internet age a new contender for veteran education has emerged. Seemingly overnight, the influx of online and distance education has helped to make education a more realistic possibility than ever. The need for an education alternative for adults who are working and that find themselves needing an additional degree or certification in their particular field, looking for a career transition, or in need of new career alternatives, has made this a good option. These new alternative education opportunities can play perfectly into the hands of veteran students for whom, due to family obligations or any of the aforementioned ailments, attending school in a classroom may be a difficult task. Those who before could not consider going back to school now can. This can make a great compromise for veteran students who also may be intimidated by the traditional classroom experience, but may still understand the need for an enhanced education.

What about the need for trades? Not everyone is set out for reading the works of Chaucer in an English literature course. There are opportunities in trade schools too, and education for veterans at many technical schools is funded by GI Bill dollars. Jobs that once required little now require a certification or an Associate's degree in some cases. But many times getting a certificate in these fields will be enough to help you get the opportunity to get a job.

When I joined the service my goal was to complete my Bachelor's degree. The thought of returning to school for a graduate degree never crossed my mind. However, when I was in school, I happened to see a friend of mine from high school who said he was going to pursue his master's degree after he graduated, while I sought a job immediately. When I asked him why, he said, "Why not?" At the time it seemed a bit frivolous and unnecessary to me, but as it turned out, he was ahead of his time in his thinking. We were both studying history, and I didn't know it at the time, but he had made a move that would put him at a distinct advantage. Indeed, my friend has since stayed in his career field and moved significantly up in his profession of choice.

After working in the insurance and financial industries, I was called to active duty shortly before 9/11. When I returned from my deployment, I realized that I still had no idea what I wanted to do. My sense of perspective had changed greatly since I graduated from college. I decided that I had a unique opportunity to do what I loved to do. So I left my old life behind and started a new one writing for a small newspaper in Connecticut. I realized that I had a love for writing and a passion for history. After two years of newspaper writing, I decided to start working toward my graduate degree.

I started applying to graduate schools and was fortunate enough to be accepted by one of the top graduate schools in my own state—with free tuition to boot, thanks to my veteran status. I started in the summer of 2007. When I got to school, I and my fellow veteran students were stunned when we received bills to pay for the complete cost for tuition for the summer courses. When we asked why our veteran waiver was not used, we were told it was because the waiver can only be activated for fall and spring semester classes. We spoke to our program director, himself a veteran of the Marine Corps, who wrote a letter on our behalf informing them that our tuition waiver should not be denied because the program itself was created to be completed in one calendar year and we were not taking the courses by choice in the summer, but rather due to the design of the program itself. Thankfully, the request was granted and our waivers were again activated.

That turned out to be a watershed career moment for me, and one that served to underscore the importance of education. I was still going to graduate school to become a social studies teacher, but I realized that my true calling was to help other veterans discover the importance of learning about their education benefits when they have questions.

In some ways this epiphany had me traveling back to my time in my recruiter's office, and to college with my friend who went back to get his master's degree, and even back to that day in middle school when I wrote the most important essay I've ever written that helped me shape who I would become.

Because I used my decision regarding which branch of the service to join and based it on my own education goals, I feel I made the right decision. I also realized why my friend chose to get more education while he had the chance. He realized that he would have a distinct advantage in the workforce. The more educated you are, the more valuable you become to employers, your family, and yourself. As a writer, I have the ability to convey that to fellow US veterans.

Education can also give you time. While it's true that working toward a higher education is not easy, and in many respects it takes an inordinate amount of time, it's important to recognize the value of using that degree to leverage the type of lifestyle you desire. If one of your goals is spending more time with your family, traveling, or pursuing personal interests, it's important to recognize that having a degree can give you the opportunity and the means to pursue it. A report from the Bureau of Labor Statistics (BLS) states that your lifetime income increases exponentially with each degree you earn. This is of key importance to younger veterans who plan to have a family.

Another great and often overlooked benefit of education is the opportunity to network at a university. Your professors and peers in the classroom can be resources for you to overcome obstacles when seeking employment. With university growth, many academic programs in business and technical fields feature professors who teach part-time while working full-time in the field in which you aspire to be a part. These professors have many connections and can help you to get the proverbial "foot in the door" before you even have your degree in your hand. If a US veteran student makes a great impression on an instructor, it could truly pay dividends.

To veterans who have chosen to attend school, take two things into consideration: First, consider what career field you might like to pursue as early as possible. Knowing this as early as possible will benefit you in the long run.

Some veterans start in one program and decide it isn't right for them, or they transition to a new duty station and are unable change their focus to a different career path. This is part of the reality of veteran students who take courses at different times in their lives. Plus, family obligations, deployments and duty station changes can disrupt their education. These trends led to the reality known as the career student phenomenon among military veterans. School admissions staffs that evaluate their credits often have several transcripts worth of college credits that amounted to no particular direction. However, with more higher education options and cost measures currently in place, there is less of a chance that active military members or veterans who start school now will need to stop for more than a brief period for other obligations. This means that the sooner you determine the path you want to take, the quicker you will be able to finish. Taking a serious look at your future and what you want it to hold, where your priorities are, is of paramount importance. The sooner you make that commitment, the easier your road will become.

Next, the most critical step after determining what you want to do is to *start now*. Once you've made that decision, don't deviate from your path to the classroom. Once there, don't be deterred from finishing. Consider all of your education alternatives: Would you be better off in a part-time program completing your degree first before working? Or do you have family obligations that may require you to take a part-time or online program? Whatever your decision is, make sure you see your education through to the end, no matter what.

If you are new to considering a college education, you have the distinct advantage of a clean slate. Take advantage of that, and keep your goals and ambitions close in your thoughts. You will undoubtedly need them when times get tough, as they tend to do when you take on such a difficult task. Making a firm decision will help you stay your course.

The clock starts ticking on your veteran benefits the minute you leave the service. Waiting too long before taking advantage of benefits you paid into could mean that you lose them altogether. The same goes for still-active military members too. US military members have more education options and more education dollars at their disposal than their predecessors. US veteran students take classes while deployed in Afghanistan. The opportunity is there.

Want to stay in the service until retirement? Education is a virtual necessity even for enlisted military members to climb the ranks. Any improvement you can make in your education while you are in military service will only help you when you leave.

Education was always a priority for me. It made a difference in my life, and I hope to spend the majority of my career helping veterans realize it can truly be the great equalizer, as Horace Mann envisioned. Taking advantage of civilian education through veteran education benefits is the easiest way for many US veterans to obtain the career they desire after they leave the service.

Referral Services

www.credability.org 1-800-251-2227 – CredAbility is a nonprofit agency founded in 1964. They will help you lower your interest rates and create a debt management plan. CredAbility also offers counseling on foreclosure prevention, bankruptcy education and reverse mortgages. They also offer budget and credit counseling. Check out the education section for videos on dozens of topics.

www.995hope.org 1-888-995-HOPE (4673) – 24 hour hotline. Homeowners Hope Hotline is a nonprofit agency that offers advice and support on foreclosure prevention. They are a HUD certified organization.

www.militaryonesource.mil – Military OneSource is a free service provided by the Department of Defense (DoD) to active duty, Guard and Reserve service members and their families. They have comprehensive information on every aspect of military life, including deployment, re-union, relationships, grief, spouse employment and education, parenting and child care and much more.

www.annualcreditreport.com 1-877-322-8228 – Be sure to type in this full address to get to the proper site. This site allows you to request a free credit file disclosure, commonly called a credit report, once every 12 months from each of the nationwide consumer credit reporting companies: Equifax, Experian and TransUnion.

www.creditkarma.com – Free credit score. No hidden fees.

www.bankrate.com – Bank Rate compares rates on mortgages, credit cards, CDs, money markets, and various loan products.

www.irs.gov/advocate – Helps the taxpayer resolve problems with the IRS.

National Suicide Prevention Hotline: 1-800- 273-TALK (8255) – 24 hour confidential hotline. No matter how bad your financial situation is, take the time to talk it out with a caring person from this great service. You'll be glad you did.

www.ftc.gov/sentinel – Visit this site to get the facts on consumer frauds from Internet cons, prize promotions, work-at-home schemes, and telemarketing scams to identity theft.

www.consumeraction.gov – Federal consumer information center.

www.firstgov.gov – Government information.

www.ombudsman.ed.gov – The Federal Student Aid Ombudsman of the Department of Education helps resolve disputes and solve other problems with federal student loans.

www.score.org – Free counsel for small business owners, even in a one-person business. Retired business owners give one-on-one counseling in starting, growing, or managing a business.

www.business.gov – The official resource to help businesses find compliance information, forms and contacts from the government.

www.sba.gov – Website of the Small Business Administration, the independent agency of the federal government. The SBA counsels, assists and protects the interests of small business.

www.2-1-1.org – 2-1-1 is an easy to remember telephone number that, where available, connects people with important community services and volunteer opportunities. The implementation of 2-1-1 is being spearheaded by United Way and provides comprehensive and specialized information and referral agencies in states and local communities.

www.studentaid.ed.gov – Information from the US Department of Education on preparing for and funding education beyond high school.

Faith-Based Referral Services

www.newhopenow.org – New Hope Telephone Counseling Center: 24-hour counseling services.

1-714-NEW-HOPE (639-4673) – Suicide Prevention Hotline. Caring people are waiting to talk to you.

www.intouch.org/resources/all-things-are-new – Dr. Charles Stanley of In Touch Ministries posts 24 faith-based encouraging videos plus a free download titled "Overcoming Discouragement."

www.crossroadscareer.org – Crossroads Career Network helps people find jobs, careers and callings with online resources and career groups. For a limited time, download a free copy of their 80-page workbook, *Maximize Your Career*, which includes over 200 career resources.

www.crown.org 1-800-722-1976 – Crown Financial Ministries. For 35 years this nonprofit ministry has assisted thousands with in-person or online financial coaching. They offer more free online resources than I can mention here. Be sure to see the Crown Money Map.

www.careerdirectonline.org – The Career Direct® Complete Guidance System is an individual personal-growth resource designed to help you maximize your God-given talents and abilities. More than a simple career test, it analyzes four critical areas: personality, interests, skills, and values. Most other career assessments only analyze one or two.

www.medi-share.org 1-800-772-5623 – Medi-Share, Christian family healthcare

www.chministries.org 1-800-791-6225 – Christian Healthcare Ministries

www.family.org – Focus on the Family. Your one-stop resource for anything to do with the family—life changes, parenting, and marriage information.

www.soundmindinvesting.com – Austin Pryor's bestselling book on investing based on Biblical principles.

www.kingdomadvisors.org – A network of highly qualified Christian professionals. You can search the site for a professional financial planner, investment professional, attorney, accountant/tax professional, or insurance professional near you.

www.christianlawyerconnection.com – Website of the Christian Legal Society. Referrals can be selected by area of practice and geography.

www.resourceministries.net – Nonprofit consulting firm specializing in church administration.

www.integritymoments.com – Web home of Integrity Resource Center, a nonprofit ministry that teaches and equips business leaders to work with Biblical and financial integrity. They typically work with businesses and church leaders desiring to please God in their work or suffering due to financial difficulties in their business.

www.troubledwith.com – TroubledWith.com is a collection of articles, resources and referrals organized by topic around family issues and concerns. This site is provided by the Focus on the Family ministry.

About the Author

David J. Renza holds a bachelor's degree in history from Southern Connecticut State University and a master's degree from the University of Connecticut's Neag School of Education. He is a veteran of the Connecticut Army National Guard serving as a combat medic and working in retention helping soldiers with their civilian and military education towards career advancement. He is the assistant director of military admissions at Post University and is responsible for helping active military, veteran and dependent students navigate through the admissions process. He is the coauthor of *Military Education Benefits for College: A Comprehensive Guide for Active Military, Veterans and Their Dependents* (2010, Savas Beatie). He and his coauthor are tireless advocates for veteran education and will donate a portion of their proceeds from books sold from their website or publisher to the Wounded Warrior Project.

20: Do You Have a Financial Plan?

PATRICK MELLODY

You have served your country; therefore you have also served my family and me. We are forever grateful for your service and dedication to securing the greatest nation on Earth. My wish for you is that you will take your family's security as seriously as you do that of the United States of America.

Here are some basic steps that you can take to secure your family's finances. Protect them while you are with them, but more importantly, protect them when you are not.

- Update your will. Recently I came across my brother-in-law's will in my safe deposit box. It was dated 1986, which was the year he went into the Marines. I asked him if he wanted me to toss it out, since he probably updated the will now that it is 27 years later and he is married with children. He admitted that he had not updated it. In his state, if he and his wife both passed away without a will the children would go to the state. If there were a relative that wanted the children it would cost them about $10,000 in attorney fees and months of time to get those children out of the state system. I think the children's opinion of Mom and Dad would never be the same after such an experience. Since circumstances change in life, update your will so your loved ones do not go through a battle. They may love you now, but I have seen relatives curse a loved one that passed and left them in turmoil.

- Protect your family with life insurance. Term insurance is very inexpensive. Multiply your income by ten and purchase that amount. You can do it today. The loved ones you leave behind will be grateful that they have some time to get things figured out and downsize or replace your income. The last thing you want to do is force them into poverty if you pass unexpectedly.

- Create a "Just in Case" file. In case you do not come home someday, can your loved ones go to a single place and find all the paperwork they need? Items such as life insurance, wills, healthcare proxy, living wills, where to find any firearms and what to do with them, what bills you owe, where your bank accounts are, safe combinations and so on. For an excellent resource on this topic visit www.crown.org and purchase a book titled *Set Your House in Order*.

- Create and live on a budget. By this time you're probably thinking that this chapter is not very fun or motivational. This may be partly true, but your spouse or loved ones will have a sense of peace and security when you share with them that you love them enough to do your duty and secure and prosper the homestead. I admit no-one wants to have a budget. You will be happy to know that I have fine-tuned the budget process and made it as painless as possible. I have created two budgets, the "Crisis Budget" for when you need help now and a full-scale budget. The remainder of this chapter will detail the crisis budget. I have included a link at the end of this chapter to print out both budgets for free.

The Crisis Budget

I created this budget for a newly unemployed person or someone that is living on a reduced income. If you find yourself in a bind financially you need to survive this temporary crisis. Like a triangle, you have three points to protect: you need food, a place to live, and transportation. I'll help you list all of your spending that falls into the triangle. After we accomplish that we'll list your other spending that falls outside the triangle. Hope is on the way, because I will tell you about a service that will work with your creditors to reduce your interest rates and develop a long-term repayment strategy. It's a nonprofit organization that I've recommended dozens of times and they're fantastic. Your debts will not go away; they'll just become more manageable.

As you go through the Crisis Budget you'll most likely find that you can't pay all of your bills in full with your current income. If this is the case, you need to accept it and prioritize the funds you have coming in so you and your family can eat, have a place to stay, and a mode of transportation to get to work or find a job. You will survive this temporary setback.

The Crisis Budget is only six steps and then you're done. You can do it.

As you look at the Crisis Budget Form you'll see:

1. Calculate your monthly take-home income BEFORE the loss of any job, combat pay or overtime. This is to include all income from all family members whose income helped pay the household expenses. To find this figure, look at everyone's last pay stub without any severance included. Locate your net income (after taxes, social security, medical and so on). Multiply the amount by 52 weeks and divide by 12 months, which equals your monthly take-home income. If you were paid every two weeks, multiply by 26 and then divide by 12 months.

2. Deduct the amount of take-home income lost.

3. Subtract Total #1 from Total #2 and see your monthly income before any other assistance.

4. Enter your take-home income from the sources listed. Add total #3 and #4 together and place the amount in the box provided. This equals your new monthly spendable income.

5. Fill in your monthly food, housing and auto expenses in the boxes provided. Total them in the boxes provided.

6. Now we need to deduct your food, transportation and housing totals from your new monthly spendable income.

Remember that you may have to temporarily go back to the basics.

Food: Cut back to nutritious foods purchased on sale with coupons. Coupons are a pain, but they are the same as currency. Eating out, take-out and your local coffee spot may have to be temporarily cut back or eliminated. You can go back to the luxuries when you are able.

Housing: Housing costs include everything that is spent in the house: all phones, Internet, TV, utilities, taxes and your mortgage or rent. Again, cut out the luxuries for now. When you need to survive, one phone is fine. Life will go on with only having local channels with an antenna, and a thermostat change will not matter in the long run.

Transportation/Auto: Cut out unnecessary trips. Talk to your insurance agent about adjusting your coverage temporarily. If you have multiple cars, you may have to consider taking one off the road as long as it does not affect your ability to work or search for your next job. Please do not cut out the oil changes or anything to do with safety. I can't tell you how many people I spoke to that let their car run down and could not afford to replace it. The cheapest car you have is the one you own. If you live in a major city and don't own a car, protect the funds you spend for traveling by bus, subway, or taxi.

Also, if you are to survive, you should not add to your current debt. Do your best to live on what you have coming in. You'll only make things worse by going further into debt. Spend your money carefully and never pay retail price. Someone once said, "Money is like time: you only get to spend it once."

Now that you have completed the form, you know how much it will cost to keep your triangle protected. Your family's food, housing, and transportation are secure and hopefully there is some money left over. If you're facing major decisions in your life, you'll now know what it will take to survive this season of life. If there's not enough income to cover your triangle, even after you have reduced your luxury expenses, don't give up hope. I know a nonprofit organization that can help you.

The next step, after you've completed at least this form, is to contact CredAbility. CredAbility is a nonprofit organization that will help you create a debt management plan (DMP) that will address the debt obligations you may have trouble paying. Their web site is www.credability.

org. Click on "Our Services" and then "Debt Management Plan." Watch the short video explaining the service. If you decide to work with them, the additional forms at www.budgetsthatwork.com/forms will make the process go much faster.

As I mentioned previously, I have referred dozens of people to this organization and it helped them survive and then thrive. You can also call them at 1-800-251-2227. CredAbility also has services such as foreclosure prevention, and if you're far short of even your basic needs they offer bankruptcy education. Please exhaust all the referral services at the end of this chapter before considering bankruptcy. It's the last resort, and despite what they say on TV, it will not make all your problems go away; it will only create new ones. CredAbility is a nonprofit agency, but they do have an average charge of $35 to set up your account and a maximum charge of $50 if you have a lot going on that takes extra administrative time. It's the best money you'll ever spend, and you'll save it back right away. CredAbility already has preapproved arrangements with all the major credit card companies and lenders to lower your interest and payments. CredAbility does stress that they are not a debt settlement company. They suggest that you contact your creditors directly if you have funds available to settle your debt for a lower amount and close the account. They do not suggest paying some TV-advertised company to do what you can do yourself. I do suggest that you build emergency savings into your CredAbility plan. If you don't have savings, you'll fall into using credit again—and we all know emergencies happen all the time.

So there you are. You now know what income you bring home, where to spend it first and hopefully what you have left over for other bills. You have a place to go for help with those remaining bills and additional counsel. No-one has the power to erase all your debt, and eventually we all have to pay back what we borrow. I hope you'll find that the information in this chapter will keep you going until you get back on your feet.

Patrick Mellody's Budget Resources

Referral Services:

www.militaryonesource.mil – Military OneSource is a free service provided by the Department of Defense (DoD) to active duty, Guard and Reserve service members and their families. They have comprehensive information on every aspect of military life, including deployment, reunion, relationships, grief, spouse employment and education, parenting and child care, and much more.

www.credability.org 1-800-251-2227 – CredAbility is a nonprofit agency founded in 1964. They will help you lower your interest rates and create a debt management plan. CredAbility also offers counseling on foreclosure prevention, bankruptcy education and reverse mortgages. They also offer budget and credit counseling. Check out the education section for videos on dozens of topics.

www.995hope.org 1-888-995-HOPE (4673) – 24 hour hotline. Homeowners Hope Hotline is a nonprofit agency that offers advice and support on foreclosure prevention. They are a HUD certified organization.

www.annualcreditreport.com 1-877-322-8228 – Be sure to type in this full address to get to the proper site. This site allows you to request a free credit file disclosure, commonly called a credit report, once every 12 months from each of the nationwide consumer credit reporting companies: Equifax, Experian and TransUnion.

www.creditkarma.com – Free credit score. No hidden fees.

www.bankrate.com – Bank Rate compares rates on mortgages, credit cards, CDs, money markets, and various loan products.

www.irs.gov/advocate – Helps the taxpayer resolve problems with the IRS.

National Suicide Prevention Hotline: 1-800-273-TALK (8255) – 24 hour confidential hotline. No matter how bad your financial situation is, take the time to talk it out with a caring person from this great service. You'll be glad you did.

Faith-based Referral Services

www.newhopenow.org – New Hope Telephone Counseling Center: 24-hour counseling services.

1-714-NEW-HOPE (639-4673) – Suicide Prevention Hotline. Caring people are waiting to talk to you.

www.intouch.org/resources/all-things-are-new – Dr. Charles Stanley of In Touch Ministries posts 24 faith-based encouraging videos plus a free download titled "Overcoming Discouragement."

www.crossroadscareer.org – Crossroads Career Network helps people find jobs, careers and callings with online resources and career groups. For a limited time, download a free copy of their 80-page workbook, *Maximize Your Career*, which includes over 200 career resources.

www.crown.org 1-800-722-1976 – Crown Financial Ministries. For 35 years this nonprofit ministry has assisted thousands with in-person or online financial coaching. They offer more free online resources than I can mention here. Be sure to see the Crown Money Map.

www.careerdirectonline.org – The Career Direct® Complete Guidance System is an individual, personal growth resource designed to help you maximize your God-given talents and abilities. More than a simple career test, it analyzes four critical areas: personality, interests, skills, and values. Most other career assessments only analyze one or two.

www.medi-share.org 1-800-772-5623 – Medi-Share, Christian Family Healthcare.

www.chministries.org 1-800-791-6225 – Christian Healthcare Ministries.

www.family.org – Focus on the Family. Your one-stop resource for anything to do with the family—life changes, parenting, and marriage information.

www.budgetsthatwork.com – *The Unemployment Budget: Your financial survival plan*. A book to help the unemployed survive.

About the Author

Patrick Mellody is the author of *The Unemployment Budget: Your financial survival plan*. The book is designed to assist anyone living on a reduced income. Patrick has been a volunteer Crown Budget Coach for over seventeen years. In the book he uses real-life stories of people he coached to ease the reader through the budget process.

He has helped many individuals and couples create and live on a budget. After going through unemployment and extreme financial hardship, Patrick learned and fine-tuned the budget process and put that knowledge into a book titled *The Unemployment Budget: Your financial survival plan.*

There are two budgets in the book, the "Crisis Budget" and the "Unemployment Budget." The "Crisis Budget" is for someone that needs help today and the "Unemployment Budget" is a more in-depth version. The book also provides referral resources for ongoing assistance with the reader's financial and personal needs.

The book is available on Amazon or his personal web site: www.budgetsthatwork.com.

Patrick and his wife of 36 years live in upstate New York. They have three married children and eight grandchildren. Patrick leads small groups through the budget process and presents his dramatic personal story, as outlined in the book, to live groups.

21: Winning the War on Financial Illiteracy

JEFF MORRIS & GREGORY A. SPENCER

A Marine's Story – Jeff Morris

It was May of 1990, and I was just off unit deployment from Okinawa, Japan. I had saved over $5,000 during my time away from the States. I knew just what I wanted to do with it when I returned to the States: I was going to buy a car. I was off to my local Nissan dealer. $5,000 would be enough to get whatever car I wanted. I purchased a brand new champagne gold 1990 Nissan 240SX.

I wanted to purchase all of the accessories for the new car. In less than a month, I was able to purchase on credit a new fin for the car, 20-inch rims, a 16-speaker stereo system, and a cell phone for the new car.

I was a corporal with less than four years' experience in the Marine Corps. The items purchased on credit were easy to obtain for a young corporal; however, the payments for the items purchased would be difficult to make. Eventually I would be working a second job to make ends meet.

In most military communities there are places in town that give easy credit to those in the service. Often these businesses are predatory and can take advantage of the younger enlisted Marines and others in the Armed Forces. Understanding that most of these Marines do not have any formal money management experience or training, the interest rates offered are often exorbitant, and there are many details in the fine print.

As a result of money errors and poor financial choices, many in the Armed Services find themselves having to work second jobs and writing checks that cannot be covered with their current pay. These choices result in military personnel being reported to their respective commands.

Writing bad checks can end their careers. Eventually they could be locked out of traditional banking and have to start using alternative financial services with exorbitant fees, such as payday loan centers and rent-to-own stores. These establishments dig a deeper hole for those who are already in financial hardship, and the effect on relationships is enormous.

Financial stress is nothing new in the veteran community. My time in the Marine Corps in the late '80s and early '90s looked very similar to today's financial challenges that are in our veteran community. I enlisted in the US Marine Corps in 1986. Although the USMC did an excellent job preparing me for what I was to do while in the Corps, there was no financial boot camp. I was not equipped for the mission of properly and responsibly handling my money, especially at such a young age. I knew other young enlisted Marines, Guardsmen, and Armed Service personnel from every branch and of every background, race, creed, and color; we all struggled financially.

My Marine brothers and I had one thing in common: We experienced the same financial challenges from predatory credit card issuers. We piled on debt because we didn't understand the long term consequences, and we had poor spending habits. We were charter members of the "Spend Now and Maybe Pay Later Club." I found that this was systemic throughout all branches of service. Although more is being done to help military families, there is still much more work that can and must be done.

Now that I'm raising young children, I realize that veterans and active military are facing unprecedented economic issues. For most US veterans, battlefield readiness is no longer the major issue. For veterans it's a matter of family readiness, being able to position our families as best as possible to keep our spending in check, keep our debt loads under control, manage the use of credit properly, and have a retirement plan in place, even if we cannot contribute as much as we would like.

Too often the lack of basic financial education locks struggling veteran families out of banking services and products. These services and products are essential for daily living. While payday and title loans, pawnshops, cash advances, and other alternative financial services and products have offered temporary and expensive access to money, none have provided a pathway back to financial wholeness and economic health.

A Son's Story – Gregory A. Spencer

Some money messages from our moms, dads, siblings, and those that were influential in our lives include these messages: Shame, Guilt, Fault, Responsibility, Ignorance, Entitlement, and so on. I was the eldest of six kids, and we were in financial survival mode most of the time. My mother and daddy didn't talk about money to their kids. They fought and yelled about money. Financial illiteracy became the true weapon of mass destruction in our home. Because of my poor relationship with my daddy, I looked for other avenues to fill that void. Instead of drinking, doing drugs, and running the streets, I ran to the mall to "buy" my happiness, contentment, and relationships.

By the time I was 18, I was "possessed" by owning 23 credit cards. You name the card, I had it. I had the "power" to access over $120,000 in credit at age 18. Talk about a loaded gun. I spent, spent, spent without ever realizing that one day my catastrophic credit rating and debt load would cost me a job, relationships, and a home. When I graduated from college, I was recruited to join a financial services company that included a company car and expense account. I was so happy and proud. I called my mother and friends to brag about my latest accomplishment. I was offered the job on a Tuesday and was scheduled to start the following Monday. However, on that Friday, the job offer was rescinded after they ran my credit.

My past had caught up to me. I had allowed the errors of my ways to damage my credit. I would eventually learn that it's not about money, it's about relationships. Due to unfortunate money decisions that I had made seven years earlier, it was difficult to qualify to purchase a home as a newlywed. I was now 25 and strangely enough, it hit me that it was time to start growing up and take control of my financial life. But how? I learned that if you have a credit card, creditors really do expect you to pay the bill, especially when they send the bill to you in those pretty pink envelopes.

This tailspin also created serious relationship issues with many people, including God. I searched for the relationship that I longed for with my daddy but couldn't find it. I had professed that I wouldn't be disengaged like my daddy was with me, my siblings, and my mother, but I became what I said I wouldn't: an MIA dad. I was there, but I was not there.

We were invited to a new and growing church, New Venture Christian Fellowship in Oceanside, CA. I reluctantly went, but vowed never to return. I purposely arrived late so that no-one would greet me. I kept my arms crossed as I watched this guy on stage tell me about a person named Jesus. I left early so that I could skip having to put money into the offering plate. I had it all figured out, I thought. As the weeks and the months passed, I sat closer and closer to the stage. Eventually, I had my seat in the front row and God started to have me. I realized that because I hated my daddy, it was difficult for me to love a heavenly Father. I then started a journey of learning about God's character and the love of His Son, Christ, from the guy on the stage. I learned the art, blessing, and freedom of forgiveness.

Eventually I went to my daddy and asked him why he was the way he was. His answer shocked me. He held his head low, closed his eyes, and said, 'Son, that's the way I was raised. That's all I knew.' I asked for my daddy's forgiveness for my feelings toward him for over 25 years. He never knew that I harbored these feelings about him. I smiled and thought, *Unbelievable, I've wasted all these years being depressed, despondent, and hateful toward a person that didn't even know I had these feelings...what a waste!* I chose to forgive my daddy because that guy on the stage, now my pastor and good friend, Shawn Mitchell, told me that Christ first forgave me.

Are you living the way you were raised? Or are you choosing to live the way you should live? I wanted to be free from the slavery of hate. I also had to learn to be free from the incarceration of debt and poor spending habits. I had substituted the vice of hate for the vice of poor money management. During my journey, I was given a book authored by Dr. John Trent and Dr. Gary Smalley entitled *The Blessing*. One line that led to my spiritual freedom was to forgive and to love my daddy not for my daddy's sake but for the sake of the Father. When I read this revelation, it freed me and led to my repentance, forgiveness, and calling out to Jesus Christ to come into my heart to forgive me of my sins, and be both my Lord and my Savior. I was then able to start being a better husband and father to our three children.

Mathew 6:15 says, "But if ye forgive not men their trespasses, neither will your Father forgive your trespasses." I had to choose between loving the god of hate or being obedient to the God of love.

This former atheist was blessed, and has now served in ministry for over 20 years. In fact, my business partner, Jeff Morris, and I met while serving in lay leadership at our church. I got involved in mentoring male teens who were fatherless, counseled men who had daddy issues, served as a prayer partner, and worked in several capacities at our church. As a person seeking to get better with his walk each and every day, I also made a commitment to be a loving husband, nurturing dad, and obedient son to the Son.

In addition, I became a student of financial literacy and wellness education. My first clients were my children and immediate family. My three kids are in their 20s now, and I'm proud of the fact that they're on their own road to financial wellness and economic freedom. They have chosen to take control of their lives. The errors and sins of the father do not have to follow the next generation, as long as there are an executable action plan, accountability, a willingness to start fresh and learn new skills.

I had the privilege of leading my daddy through the sinner's prayer while he was on his deathbed in the hospital. He passed away two days later. I regret all of the years that we didn't have as father and son and I regret the years wasted, but I pray that he accepted the invitation to come to Christ and that we will rejoice in Heaven one day.

Helping the military community is a calling. It is a ministry. It is a responsibility to give back to those that have given so much to our country. I appreciate and respect the men, women, and families that serve and have served this blessed nation, including my father-in-law, brother-in-law, uncle, and brothers.

The Climate

Now more than ever, our veteran and active duty heroes need strategic tools to be battlefield ready, financially competent, and failsafe. An alarming number of men and women serving in our Armed Forces have family incomes that place them at or below the poverty line. This economic gap is unacceptable. While the active-duty spouse is serving overseas, many military families also find themselves in harm's way here at home because of the financial stress that they must endure.

One of the primary reasons for financial issues with military families is that military personnel are committing to relationships and marriage at a very young age. Cognitive science studies indicate that the cognitive reasoning (acquisition of knowledge, reasoning, and perception) portion of our brains is not fully developed until about age 25. This is one of the primary reasons that rental car agencies typically don't rent to those under 25. In addition, insurance is higher for those under 25, because at that age you still believe you're invincible and you think little of planning for a future, especially for males. You're living life in the moment.

An article from the Centers for Disease Control states that "48 percent of couples who marry before 18 are likely to divorce within 10 years. Only 24 percent of those who marry after age 25 will divorce within 10 years. That doesn't mean half those teen marriages last forever. That means only half of them even make it to their tenth anniversary. So it is not surprising that young age and first marriages have been found to predict a higher rate of divorce in the military population too, especially among the young enlisted men and women. Considering how many stressors a young military marriage must face, that fact alone ought to be enough to convince us that everybody in the military ought to be single until, say, age 25 or 30!" But that is not going to happen.

The question remains of who is going to tell an 18-year-old kid you're too young to marry, but you're old enough to be a man or woman and go to war. This is not the romanticism that we saw portrayed by John Wayne in movies about the Greatest Generation that went to war during World War II. This is a world that is seeing more stressors than ever before.

Those partners and spouses left behind are young, isolated, and typically without the education and job prospects they would have if they were older and had received more education. When you add being based far away from family and a baby or two to the mix, it's a game changer that escalates and magnifies all family and financial issues.

The Issue

Military families are dealing with the ever-increasing challenge of financial hardship. Reports and studies indicate that these issues include the lack of an emergency fund, no savings, an inadequately funded retirement, the lack of a sufficient college fund, late fees, foreclosure, and bankruptcy issues. These things dramatically impact lifestyle as well as the physical, emotional, and mental health of military personnel and their families.

Financial stress may be at its highest when a veteran and his or her family is transitioning from military to civilian life. Financial stress is also a reality for disabled veterans as well as homeless veterans.

Errors and poor financial choices can haunt a veteran when he or she is in the transition stage of his or her career. A poor credit score may play a role when a veteran is looking for employment as was in my case. A prospective employer may not look favorably on someone with credit errors when making a final decision to employ or not to employ.

Should veterans not get the help and services they need to be productive in the civilian sector, they could easily end up separated from loved ones, despondent and homeless. The Secretary of Veterans Affairs and retired Four Star Army General Eric K. Shinseki stated that there are more than 68,000 homeless veterans on the streets every night. Financial stress is a major contributing factor in divorce, separation, spousal abuse, child abandonment, workplace violence, dishonorable discharge and homelessness.

The majority of us, whether we served or not, were never taught to be financially literate. We shoot from the hip and hope that one day things will work out. No competent military unit would go on an important mission without first developing a plan of action and considering all of the possible scenarios. But we do this with our financial lives each and every day.

Financial Stress for Military Personnel Is a National Security Issue

A Matter of National Security and Family Health

The last thing a soldier needs on the battlefield is to be distracted by financial problems at home. These issues can eventually lead to broken families and can affect our armed services' ability to focus on the battlefields of the world. Military personnel that are dealing with financial stress and that don't find or seek relief could impact our national security as well as the security and wellbeing of their own families.

Military Challenges

"The majority of middle-class military officers say that someone in their family has experienced a mental or physical health problem within the last year directly linked to economic uncertainty. Those officers who work with financial experts, however, have lower odds of developing these mental or physical problems, the study revealed." Source: First Command Study

"Fewer than half of all military families interviewed say they have an emergency fund in place big enough to support their needs for at least a three-month period. Additionally, more than two thirds, or 68 percent, report feeling 'stressed out' about their financial condition, with debt being one of the leading factors." Source: Military Authority Blog

Suicide

"Due to financial stress and other issues, nearly one in ten spouses surveyed had actually considered suicide—a number that closely parallels the percentage of uniformed service members who have considered taking their own lives." Source: Military Authority Blog

Military and Family Issues

Military personnel and their families deal with an enormous amount of pressures, stressors, and challenges that those in the civilian sector never have to deal with on a daily basis, including:

- Preparing for long deployments
- The rigors of constantly training for battle

- Leaving family behind to function while away
- Separation from loved ones and children
- Relationship challenges with family members

The Solution

At-risk military families must be provided unbiased financial literacy and wellness education programs. These classes must be designed for those that need support, perspective, coaching, and an action plan. These programs will educate, empower, and encourage. They will give military families hope, help, and a simple success plan.

To win the financial war, you need much more than workshops that teach you how to create a budget, manage bills, pay off credit, eliminate debt, and plan for retirement. The truth is, it's really not about the "How To." It is about the "Why Do." The first thing you need to figure out is why you make the money decisions that you make. Once you understand your money personality type, you will be better equipped to deal with the mechanics of money management. The bottom line is that in today's society we have to choose to self-educate ourselves. There are many good TV shows that talk about money, as well as resources available to military families. The problem is that we typically choose not to take advantage of the abundance of the free services available to us.

So the question remains: Are you in the group that is doing well, or are you like most, struggling to make ends almost meet? How strong are your financial habits? Do you make saving money and cutting debt a priority? Or does money slip through your fingers in spite of all your good intentions? Below are a few helpful tips for managing your money, accumulated from many sources.

Tip No. 1: Understand that people typically purchase due to emotion, not logic. Establish specific goals for things you really want. Saving as a matter of principle just doesn't provide the necessary motivation for most people. You must have definite goals, things you really wish to have, as opposed to merely want.

Tip No. 2: Set definite deadlines for reaching your financial goals. Be realistic about how much will be required to reach your goals. How soon will you need the items that you seek to purchase?

Tip No. 3: Pay yourself first. It is fundamental to every financial plan. When you make out the checks to pay the bills, don't put yourself last. You may never get there. Make that first check out to yourself or to your charity of choice. There is nothing wrong with investing in others as well as yourself, first.

Tip No. 4: Get your money out of sight and out of mind. Automatic savings tools such as bank drafts and the Thrift Savings Plan are an excellent means to this end.

Tip No. 5: Establish specific accounts for each separate goal. If you have two or more basic objectives, establish two or more accounts to achieve them.

Tip No. 6: Stick with your plan. The best plan in the world is useless if it's not activated or if it's abandoned. If your goals are meaningful to you, you must stick with your original plan.

Tip No. 7: Hire a financial coach or find free advice. Military families who use a financial planner or coach contribute more to their savings and investment accounts. Planners serve the role of a coach, encouraging and inspiring their clients to embrace positive financial behaviors and to stick with their long-term plans.

Tip No. 8: Take advantage of resources provided by organizations such as the Family Readiness Centers for military families.

Tip No. 9: Understand that today is a new day. There is no need to beat yourself up over the shames, mistakes, and decisions of the past. Learn from those experiences and take steps toward financial freedom.

Tip No. 10: Realize that you first have to understand "Why Do" you make the money decisions that you make, not the "How To." Yes, it is important to know how to balance a checkbook and how to spend responsibly, but if you choose not to first understand why you make those decisions, you will be back where you started.

Military families without a financial plan are twice as likely to feel financially stretched as those with a plan. By saving more and cutting debt, people feel less stressed and more optimistic about their financial future.

These are common sense tips, but when it's all said and done it's really never about money. It's about healing self-relationships and family relationships. It is about a "hopelistic" approach to healing the financial wounds of the past so that you can move toward a future that will allow you to be financially successful.

Winning the financial war for yourself and your military family is a continual battle. The key is tapping into the free resources available through the military, websites, and reputable community-based organizations focused on serving the unique needs of the military and at-risk communities.

About the Authors

Jeff Morris is the Co-founder & President of SpendSmart, Inc., (dba SpendSmart.org). Jeff is a disabled and honorably discharged Marine Corps sniper. He earned many commendations as a sergeant and has a passion for serving, supporting, and educating the military and their families. Jeff is a Certified Master Money Coach and a Certified Credit Expert. Jeff is a sought-after speaker and workshop presenter in the area of financial wellness education. He is the creator of the SpendSmart Financial Wellness System™ and is also the coauthor of *Invest in Your Debt*™ and *The CEO Mindset*™.

Gregory A. Spencer is the Co-founder & CEO of SpendSmart.org. Greg is an experienced educational technologist and is a former school teacher and principal. Spencer is a Certified Financial Literacy Instructor and is the coauthor of *Invest in Your Debt*™ and *The CEO Mindset*™. Greg is a sought-after speaker and workshop presenter in the area of financial wellness education. He is the creator of the MoneTude™ concept, a coaching program that helps clients understand their dominant money personality type. He also cowrote *Discover Your Inner Strength*™ with NY Times bestselling authors Dr. Stephen Covey and Dr. Ken Blanchard.

About SpendSmart.org

SpendSmart, Inc., (dba SpendSmart.org) is a 501(c)(3) Financial Literacy and Wellness Educational Nonprofit. SpendSmart.org has established a relationship with HirePatriots.com and others to serve the military community more effectively. SpendSmart.org has created a unique financial wellness workshop series called Operation SpendSmart™. The mission of SpendSmart.org is to provide workshops, webinars, and financial wellness coaching services to the military, at-risk and underserved communities, students, families, companies, and organizations.

Recognitions & Awards

- The White House – The Presidential Citizens Medal Award, Nominee
- CNN Heroes Award Finalist
- GuideStar – Valued Partner Seal of Approval
- Classy Awards – Small Charity of the Year Award Finalist
- Great Nonprofits and GuideStar – Children and Families Award Winners
- Financial Planning Magazine – National Pro Bono Team Award Winners
- California State Assembly – Community Service Award Proclamation Recipient
- San Diego Business Journal – CFO & CEO of the Year Award Finalists
- Ernst & Young – Entrepreneur of the Year Award, Finalist

Free Offer

Please email us at Info@SpendSmart.org to receive our free Operation SpendSmart™ Newsletter. This online military newsletter will provide important tips on how to save, spend, become debt-free, and improve your credit. You can call us at 888.965.5554. We also offer free introductory workshops and webinars for groups.

We have created over 30 workshops for the military, at-risk communities, athletes, students, the faith-based community, families, law enforcement, first responders, companies, and others. Operation SpendSmart™ workshops have been specifically designed for the military community.

You Can Help

Since 2009, SpendSmart, Inc., (dba SpendSmart.org) has been serving communities. As a 501(c)(3) Educational Nonprofit, we accept tax-deductible donations, sponsorships, gifts, and in-kind services that will allow us to better serve our military and at-risk communities. Please support our efforts.

- Tax EIN #: 80-0484810.
- Visit us at: www.SpendSmart.org
- Email us at: Info@SpendSmart.org
- Follow us at: twitter.com/spendsmartorg
- Like us at: www.facebook.com/SpendSmart.org
- Call us at: 1.888.965.5554 / 1.760.415.1071 / 1.760.390.6009
- Write us at: 825 College Blvd., Suite 102 – 322 - Oceanside, CA 92057 USA

You can also volunteer your time and inquire about serving on our advisory board as well to help us make a generational difference in the lives of military families.

22: The Reality of Unemployment for Our National Guard

TED DAYWALT

In 2007, the veteran unemployment rate for 18 to 24-year-old veterans started rising rapidly. Studies show that this rise in the young veteran unemployment rate was a direct result of the Department of Defense (DoD) call-up policy implemented in January 2007. The call-up policy caused employers not to want to hire members of the National Guard and Reserve (NG&R), and this is what led to the high unemployment rate in young veterans: The National Guard and Reserves is largely a young person's branch of the US Armed Forces.

The new policy stated that an NG&R member could be mobilized for up to 24 months and then be demobilized and allowed to return to a civilian working life. But it also allows for these just demobilized troops to be mobilized a second time. The NG&R can serve actively a total of 48 months in any 60 month period. In practice, most members of the NG&R have been called up for only 12 to 18 months and then released back to the civilian workforce. Many have then been recalled again or volunteered for another call-up when they could not find employment. Veterans serving in the NG&R are having the most difficult time finding meaningful employment, due to the constant call-ups and deployment schedule.

My interest in the NG&R was heightened when the 20 to 24-year-old young veteran unemployment rate doubled, going from 10.4% in 2006 to 22.3% in 2007. That increase was the initial warning bell that there would be significant increases in employment problems directly related to the changes in the NG&R call-up policy.

Solving a problem requires effective analysis. One must define and identify the problem and its causes. Without understanding the sources of problems, well-meaning solutions will not work, or worse, they will not address the problem at all. Unfortunately, defining the real reason for young veteran unemployment was clouded by politics. Incredibly, the official Department of Defense position from 2007 to 2012 was there were no unemployment problems in the NG&R.

At the Pentagon press conference when the new policy was announced, titled "Pentagon Abandons Active-Duty Time Limit," the Associated Press quotes Dr. David Chu, Under Secretary of Defense for Personnel and Readiness: "The fact that some NG&R with previous Iraq experience will end up spending more than 24 months on active duty is no big deal." In a discussion with a former head of a Reserve force, I was told that not one of his Reservists was having a problem finding a job. He was parroting official Department of Defense policy. But it was a flawed policy, because at the time many Reservists were having significant problems finding employment due to the call-up policy. The same issue affects the National Guard.

I know those at the Department of Defense are acutely aware the NG&R unemployment problem exists, but for various bureaucratic and political reasons, they have been trying to pretend it doesn't. They have been kicking the can down the road for someone else to deal with in the future. That might be good for a bureaucrat's career, but the young members of the NG&R, especially those who have families to support, should be given better treatment. These US Armed Services members are being made to suffer from bureaucratic policies, and that is not fair.

As the last six years have demonstrated, the current policy has had long-term negative consequences for members of the NG&R. The root to this problem is that the Department of Defense did not fully understand that corporations have a fiduciary responsibility to their corporate shareholders to run a profitable operation. Companies cannot succeed without their most important asset, their employees. For anyone in business this is just common sense, but those making the decisions at the Department of Defense on how to utilize the NG&R seem to be either ignorant of or ambivalent to corporate America's needs.

When looking at overall veteran unemployment, it helps to understand that there are three groups that comprise the post-military service veteran employment and unemployment picture. The first group would be those who have transitioned out of active duty. This group is frequently referred to as 'veterans.' The second group is comprised of the Federal Reservists of the Army, Air Force, Coast Guard, Marine Corps and Navy who are separated and in the civilian work force. The third group is the NG&R. While all three groups are veterans, it helps to make these distinctions when analyzing the unemployment issue.

Of the three groups, the NG&R has the most unique and severe problems. Unlike active duty component members, when NG&R return from war, they are demobilized and do not have a source of income. The fortunate ones have or can find a civilian job. Given the bias against hiring NG&R members due to the call-up policy and high operation tempo, NG&R members have problems maintaining a continuum of service with a civilian employer. This leads to financial difficulties and a host of family and personal problems for the National Guard participant.

Complicating the issue is that when NG&R members demobilize, they do not have ready access to resources, as active duty members do, to deal with employment search, mental illness issues, physical healthcare and family counseling. They live at home, not on a full-time, active-duty US military base with a myriad of immediately available resources.

Historically, the NG&R system has been very effective. It has worked due to the outstanding support of corporate America, municipal and state governments and small business owners. But that support has been strained as a result of the many call-ups of the NG&R over recent years in support of overseas operations.

Veteran Employment Problem Is in the NG&R

Chart #1 provides annual unemployment rates for the last eleven years. Note that the 20 to 24-year-old veteran unemployment rates start to rise rapidly in 2007.

Year	Nonveteran	Veteran	Nonveteran	Veteran
	20–24	20–24	25–29	25–29
2000	7.2%	8.0%	4.2%	3.0%
2001	8.3%	9.6%	5.0%	4.2%
2002	9.6%	11.2%	6.5%	5.8%
2003	10.0%	11.0%	6.6%	6.8%
2004	9.4%	13.6%	6.1%	7.2%
2005	8.7%	15.6%	5.8%	6.5%
2006	8.1%	10.4%	5.1%	6.5%
2007	14.5%	22.3%	5.1%	6.4%
2008	11.6%	14.1%	6.5%	6.1%
2009	14.6%	21.2%	10.6%	12.1%
2010	15.4%	20.6%	10.7%	14.9%

Chart #1: Nonveteran versus Veteran, 20–24 and 25–29 Years Old
Source: BLS CPS veteran report

From the above Bureau of Labor Statistics (BLS) Current Population Survey (CPS) data, the 20 to 24-year-old veteran group's unemployment exceeds the nonveteran group starting in 2007. And there are various reasons why the overall unemployment rate of the 20 to 24-year-old group is high, including education, skill levels and the lack of work experience. But there is an overriding reason why the veteran unemployment rate for this age group is greater than other US veteran age groups.

If a person is on active duty, they are not classified as unemployed by BLS. (Those 18 to 24-year-olds are still finishing out their obligation. They are gaining marketable skills wanted by civilian employers.) But if a person is in the National Guard and does not have a civilian job, they are classified by BLS as 'unemployed.'

The large differences in unemployment rates for 18 to 24-year-old veterans continued into 2011. Chart #2 is the CPS data for 18 to 24-year-old veterans unemployment compared to nonveterans by month throughout 2011:

Month	Nonveteran	Veteran	# Veterans
January	18.10%	31.90%	67,000
February	17.20%	28.60%	59,000
March	16.10%	28.80%	57,000
April	15.30%	26.80%	50,000
May	16.30%	31.90%	60,000
June	17.10%	26.20%	53,000
July	16.50%	19.80%	39,000
August	16.30%	30.40%	66,000
September	16.30%	35.60%	83,000
October	15.40%	30.45%	71,000
November	15.30%	37.90%	95,000
December	14.60%	31.00%	74,000

Chart #2: Nonveteran versus Veteran, 18–24 Years Old
Source: Bureau of Labor Statistics

Note the number of unemployed veterans for each month, especially in November. But the active duty military did not release 95,000 18 to 24-year-olds in one month. To have so many "unemployed" in the 18 to 24-year-old age group, the majority of the participants would have to be in the National Guard and the Reserve.

From the inception of the Federal Reserve in 1903, there was a partial call-up of the NG&R for World War I, a full call-up for World War II, and a partial call-up for the Korean War. Of the 37,000 members of the NG&R who fought in the Vietnam War, most were volunteers.

Since the 1991 Gulf War, there have been nearly one hundred call-ups of the NG&R. This has put a tremendous strain on the NG&R system and the relations of those NG&R components with their employers.

Since 2007, employers of the NG&R feel disenfranchised. They had no input on the Department of Defense's use of their National Guard employees, and they have no practical ability to replace the absent employee who is called up for long periods of time. This is especially burdensome to small and medium-size employers and to employers in rural areas.

This higher pace of deployment activity has put a tremendous strain on the National Guard citizen soldier system and on the relations of those military participants with their civilian employers. This has placed a significant number of National Guard members in the tenuous position of trying to serve two masters at the same time.

The problem of who "owns" the employee has been around since 1903. While the Department of Defense considers members of the NG&R to be their assets on loan to civilian employers, the reality is the NG&R component members belong to the civilian employers and are on loan to the Department of Defense or the NG&R unit.

The increase in NG&R unemployment also explains why there has been an exponential increase in veterans applying for unemployment benefits since 2008. The result of the current call-up policy has had unintended consequences that are not favorable, either for employees or companies.

Evidence that there is a trend of declining support by employers for employees who participate in the NG&R comes from Workforce Management Magazine and the Society of Human Resource Management (SHRM). Both have conducted surveys.

Given a company's fiduciary responsibility to its stockholders, the current policy regarding the use of the National Guard puts human resource (HR) managers in a quandary. One senior vice president of human resources of a major company explained it to me this way: "If I have three final candidates for a position who are all equally qualified; and one mentions they are active in the National Guard, with the new call-up policy, that person is not likely to be chosen as our candidate."

Another senior HR executive at a major company commented to me that, in light of the policy, they will continue to support current employees who have been activated, but will no longer hire new employees who are in the Guard or Reserve. I have heard this same sentiment from many HR managers. Many employers are upset they were not consulted by the Department of Defense. They no longer support the system.

I want to reinforce that I have found corporate America to be very supportive of the military. Corporate America understands the importance of having a strong military to protect our freedoms and our free market economy. Without a strong military, our freedoms and economy would be at risk. However, they cannot go broke supporting the military, which is what the Uniformed Services Employment and Reemployment Rights Act (USERRA) does regarding the National Guard.

Anecdotal information indicates that the National Guard is singled out more than their US military branch counterparts. A big part of the reason for the National Guard being singled out by employers is they are activated not only for wars, but also for state emergencies. This policy causes them to be called away from their civilian employment much more than their Federal Reserve counterparts. Now we find employers have been terminating members of the NG&R under the guise of the recession.

Companies have learned that if they lay off an employee under the guise of the current recession, before the employee has orders in hand, the company can subvert or circumvent USERRA. I have received reports of this activity nationwide from Department of Labor (DoL) veteran representatives, ESGR representatives and directly from the affected NG&R members.

Conclusion

81 percent of military occupations have a direct or very close civilian equivalent. Any person who has spent a year or more on active duty has marketable skills wanted by civilian employers. The military has engineers, nurses, lawyers, accountants, store managers, telecommunications technicians, truck drivers, food service managers and more. And all military members possess, to some degree, intangible skills such as leadership, process improvement, problem identification, troubleshooting, managerial/supervisory administration, and project management.

It is very encouraging to see how companies are employing US veterans, especially wounded warriors; companies like Walmart, Home Depot, Humana, BNSF Railway, American Airlines and many others. They are making special accommodations to hire our wounded warriors too. It is a positive change from the 1970s, when veterans would apply for a job and not mention having served in Vietnam, as their Vietnam service frequently would work against them.

There are potential solutions. They include helping US veterans purchase franchises, giving civilian certifications and licenses and college credit, compensating employers when NG&R members are activated, hiring more veterans to federal agencies, providing strong mentoring programs, creating state level programs, and providing more career fairs, especially for the NG&R who need it the most.

The bottom line to be derived from the above information and data presented on NG&R unemployment is: Employers want to hire veterans. In my 14 years of working with employers, I have found the American business community to be extremely pro-military.

Business people understand that without a strong military, their businesses could not exist. The United States has learned this the hard way since we disarmed after World War I, but this has been the record of humanity since the dawn of time. Those who will not protect what they have are subject to losing what they have. As the Latin phrase "si vis pacum, para bellum" so aptly put it: "To have peace, prepare for war."

America is fortunate to have a truly operational NG&R. But in order to keep the system effective and operational, employer support is necessary. And that is currently missing for the National Guard. A more balanced way to utilize the National Guard needs to be found.

About the Author

Since 1999 Ted Daywalt has been the President of the Veterans of Foreign Wars and sponsored VetJobs (www.vetjobs.com). Ted spent 28 years in the Navy (7 active, 21 in the Naval Reserve Intelligence Program) and retired as a Navy captain. Ted has held senior management and C level positions in the steel, electric utility, importing, biomedical waste and recruiting. He earned a B.S. from Florida State University, an M.A. from the University of California and an M.B.A. from the Goizueta School of Business, Emory University.

23: How Soldiers and Their Families Protect You

WILLIAM A. "TONY" LAVELLE

I am Tony Lavelle, a military veteran, a "lifer" with 26 years as a soldier. For those civilians who have never had the privilege to serve in America's Armed Forces, please read this essay. While many Americans make us feel respected and appreciated for what we do, I am frustrated that a large number of Americans do not really understand us and our job. Sir or ma'am, before we begin, I must confess that my talk can tend to be a bit salty sometimes, especially when my blood is hot. But I will attempt to restrain myself for this audience, because a good soldier is never intentionally disrespectful.

When I use the term "soldier," I am talking collectively about the elite group of men and women wearing a military uniform that are defending our nation around the world. "Soldier" includes all veterans of the US Armed Forces now discharged or retired.

Walk in a Soldier's Boots

"A U.S. soldier has undergone extensive surgery to amputate both of his arms and legs after he stepped on an improvised explosive device (IED) while on foot patrol in Afghanistan. Despite his horrific injuries, Army Staff Sgt. Travis Mills' first thought was not for himself. It was for the three fellow soldiers who were also injured in the blast."

The part of this story that resonates with me is the initial action this soldier took after the bomb blew his arms and legs off: Staff Sergeant Mills' first thought was to make sure the soldiers under his command were OK.

Recently, I heard some congressional staffer publicly remark at a budget hearing that soldiers make too much money, and that they should not have a retirement program better than all other US workers. For her sake and any others like her, let me respond (or explode, whatever comes first). Most Americans are clueless regarding a soldier's life. But now that the budgets are tight, these particular civilians are whining in greater numbers that the compensation and benefits for soldiers are more generous than some other civil service jobs. Civilian budget gurus say that a warrior's job is no different than serving our country as other civil service employees. Do you really believe a soldier deserves nothing more than what a prison cook gets paid? That point of view shows complete ignorance. Furthermore, it is insulting to all US soldiers and their families.

Before shooting your mouth off as to why we dogface soldiers do not deserve our pay and benefits or how overcompensated we are, you should walk in our boots for just one battle. What you will see and hear and do will terrify you! It may even cause you to have nightmares for the rest of your life.

Only those who have taken the soldier's oath, donned the uniform, and served under command are able to understand.

What other civil service jobs require an employee:

- To work in a job environment that is so hazardous employees are often killed or wounded.

- To obey every order of every supervisor. Disobedience can lead to being put in prison, or even executed if the refusal to immediately comply occurs during combat.

- To be brave. You must be able to advance towards the enemy while that enemy is trying to kill you. Again, cowards who run away can be tried, imprisoned and executed.

- Watch his co-workers die or be horribly wounded.

- Never quit, no matter what. Endure monsoon rains, bad food, disease, thirst, little ammunition, poisonous snakes, and booby traps for weeks.

- Live for months or years in a combat zone, far from home and family, and do it again and again.

What other civil service jobs require a supervisor:

- To deliberately send his employees into a hazardous work environment knowing that some will be killed or wounded.
- To send vehicles, aircraft, and millions of dollars of equipment into a hazardous work environment, knowing that ALL of it may be damaged or destroyed.
- To write plans that include expected casualties, the number of employees that will be killed, wounded, captured, or missing in action.

Is there any other civil service job like a soldier's? What we do is different from any other job. We are willing to sacrifice ourselves and so are our families. We never run away from battle. We show bravery, leadership, and loyalty. Sergeant Miller sacrificed his limbs; I was nearly killed several times during my time of service.

Oh, that great retirement! I think the average military twenty year retirement is $1,700 a month. And I believe statistics show that over 80% of those US veterans are disabled.

Tell me, what job can you think of that is a similar occupation to soldiering? Police, firefighters? About 150 policemen per year get killed in action in the U.S. That is also a tremendous sacrifice and they deserve our greatest honor and respect. But they can walk off the field at any time they choose. If that were true in war, perhaps we wouldn't have any. But it is not true. In the last ten years, American soldiers have averaged 900 killed per month.

Staff Sergeant Mills, for his two arms, two hands, two legs and two feet, will get about $4,000 per month plus medical and mental health care for him and his family. Does $48,000 a year seem like a lot to you? I think he should get $14,000 per month. That may be able cover his special house, lifetime medical care, and a special vehicle. If Staff Sergeant Mills' sacrifice and loss of limbs and his noble first thought for his troops do not also make you teary eyed, then perhaps I'll never persuade you.

Before I get off this soapbox, let me say something else that may help civilians better understand the service of military family members. Military spouses and kids sacrifice extraordinarily, subsidizing their warrior in uniform. Families must move every two to four years, sometimes to a foreign country (OCONUS). They frequently must change schools. Military spouses often need to seek a new job. Did you know that most military kids will attend over ten different schools by the time they graduate high school? Most military kids don't get to graduate with their friends.

Plus, money in military families is always tight. Rates of divorce, clinical depression, and domestic violence are higher for military families. Most families survive. Some do not. Is any of this listed in the job description of another civil service position?

A Military Casualty: *Operation Desert Storm*

*Note: The names, location, and timeline below are fictitious to protect the privacy of the victims and their families.

Airman First Class Doug Miller was a 20-year-old, two-year US Air Force veteran from Radcliff, Kentucky. He was married to Sara Miller, the 1989 Homecoming Queen from Radcliff High School. The Millers were married in 1989. In 1990 Doug joined the Air Force, and Sara had a daughter, Jess.

After Doug completed his military training in 1991, the Millers were transferred to Kaiserslautern, Germany, where Doug was an Emergency Medical Technician in the Lanstuhl Hospital. Germany was a high-cost location. The Air Force contracted some apartments for airman families in the villages around Ramstein Air Base. The Miller family was assigned to a ghetto, a welfare project apartment, occupied by unemployed foreign guest workers, and American lower enlisted rank Airmen and Army families. It was about 30 minutes from the base. They could not afford a car, so they used public transportation and friends' help.

Desert Storm in Kuwait was in progress. So after 61 days in Germany with his family, Doug got orders to a field hospital in Saudi Arabia, for six months to a year. 19-year-old Sara and 1-year-old Jess were left in the ghetto 20 miles from Ramstein Air Base. About a month after Doug flew to the desert, the German Police notified the American Military Police that two bodies were found in an apartment of an American military family, 20 to 30 minutes from base.

Sara killed her baby, and then committed suicide. An Air Force Security Police lieutenant arrived to find Sara and Jess in the bedroom, lying side by side on the bed, wearing identical long dresses, holding hands. Sara had given Jess poison in her milk bottle. When the baby was unconscious, Sara drank the poison in orange juice. They had been dead about six days. The medical examiner's report showed both to be malnourished. It seems like Sara was unable to afford groceries after Doug left for Saudi Arabia, and so instead of letting her child suffer, she took both of their lives.

Also, Sara Miller's suicide note said she was "scared [expletive]" living so far from home. They had no money to call home. They had no cell phone or land line in their apartment. She felt abandoned. She was depressed and overcome with anxiety. Sara said in her note why she was scared. Some of her neighbors were selling drugs day and night on her floor, and there were many "scary guys" hanging out all day.

I have told these two different true stories because I would like those who have never served to get to know US veterans better, and to better understand how dangerous it is for the soldier and his or her family.

This book is part of a noble effort to help military veterans return to civilian life with a good plan to support their families or start families, for them to be able to go to college, start a business, or just work in a good job that makes enough money and benefits for the veteran to live decently.

How Can You Help?

- Read this book.
- Write to your U.S. congressman and senator. Tell them you want the very best for America's soldiers.
- Join a US veteran support organization.
- Hire a US veteran.
- Thank a US veteran and their family members in a meaningful way. They deserve it.
- Never say bad things about US veterans again.

About the Author

William A. "Tony" Lavelle is a former military officer who served in the U.S. Army and Air Force. After his military career he was a faculty member at California State University. He left the public sector to found one of the first police dog service contractors that focused on Explosive Detection Dogs (EDD). His company has served Defense Security Service (DSS) government and corporate clients in the U.S. and in Iraq for over nine years. At present, Tony is an anthropology researcher and author. Tony's most recent book, *The Manhood Test*, outlines his robust solution to stem the decline of manhood, and how to help boys reach manhood and to go on to live happy and successful lives as men.

Tony is still a service dog trainer. He has 15 years' expertise as a professional dog handler of EDD Dogs. He is preparing to train his first post-traumatic stress disorder (PTSD) service dog. Tony is a Vietnam combat veteran afflicted with PTSD. He has been married for 38 years to the ever-beautiful, wise, and tolerant Patricia Ann. His interests include scuba diving, teaching sailing, and studying tai chi.

24: How You Can Help

TORI BAIRD

Every chapter of this book has given readers excellent advice forged in the fire of experience. From sergeants to generals, CEOs, hiring managers, business owners and business builders—almost all US veterans—we have heard from the best how to find a job, why companies should hire them and how to hire them. Plus, we have heard the personal stories of these men and women and have been captivated with their struggles and successes. Whether a civilian, a veteran or the wife or child of one, this has been an entertaining and enlightening use of your time. All of our authors thank you!

Below is a list of good things for any of us to do. After that there are some stories about the veterans we have met and become friends with by doing so.

1. **Pray for veterans and their families.**

2. **Share this book.** Help local veterans by giving this book to them.

3. **Educate** your friends, relatives, clubs and community about the value of veterans by letting them know about the book.

4. **Take action.** If you are looking for employment or starting a business, apply the wisdom in these pages. Contact the authors. Check out the lists of resources within the chapters. If you are a business or hiring manager, please do the same.

5. **Become involved with a local veteran group.** Many welcome patriotic civilians.

6. **Volunteer** to help US veteran community programs. Pitch in for their events, parades, job fairs, celebrations and memorials.

7. **Donate** to a US veteran nonprofit. There many great ones!

To close this book, here are some vignettes about US veterans and their families that my husband and I met while building HirePatriots and our Patriotic Hearts safety net for them across the country. We have added some comments from those that hired them from our unique job board. You can personally meet the US veterans in your community too. Please contact us about getting a local HirePatriots job board started in your area.

Cement Between the Cracks

I met Greg during one of our first job fairs at Camp Pendleton. He told me about his long search for a full-time job that would support him, his wife and his four young children. Greg had been a Navy Petty Officer through several wars. He was on track to retire with a nice pension. But with 18 years under his belt and 18 months to go to retirement, he injured his thumb on the job and was forced leave the service. His hopes for a pension were dashed.

Eventually Greg got an interview with a company that needed a laser technician—the job Greg did in the Navy. They hired him right away. That job enabled Greg to buy a house for his growing family. But a few years into that job, the economy sputtered and Greg was laid off. The layoff was devastating for Greg. His beautiful home went into foreclosure. Their dependable family van had to be returned to the dealer. He now drove an old junky car that broke down often. Once again Greg came to our job fair. Ever hopeful and uncomplaining, he began a job search again. But interviews were few and far between.

Greg picked up jobs several times a week from our One Day job board. Some of these jobs were regular. Every weekend he worked on a ranch. He manned a photo booth at county fairs. There were a host of other jobs he picked up that just required a few hours. He shared with me about how these jobs he was taking from our site were a "Godsend" for his family. He could not imagine how they would have survived without them.

He helped an elderly widow move. Then he stayed and put everything away where she wanted it and cleaned the house. She was so pleased that she told her friends to hire Greg too. These one day jobs were keeping him afloat as he looked for that next job. Eventually Greg found a full-time job as a generator mechanic. It paid about $15 an hour and there was plenty of overtime. It wasn't quite enough to cover all his bills though, so he still picked up one day jobs to make ends meet.

But the decline in the economy forced Greg's company to downsize. "The last one hired is the first one fired," was their standard procedure. This time Greg, his wife and four children went homeless. They moved into a tent at the campgrounds on the Camp Pendleton Marine Base. There they stayed for the better part of a year. When Pacific storms or the California "Santa Ana" winds came the tent collapsed. His wife and children would huddle in the car as Greg struggled to erect it once again.

One day a US veteran who worked for a large nationwide company back east called us looking for a service technician. My husband and I made a warm introduction, and Greg was hired. This job paid very well and provided Greg with a company car, computer and phone. Things were looking up. The downside to the job was that Greg traveled around the country fixing machinery and only saw his wife and kids on the weekends. But financially things were better.

Recently, I called Greg to check on how they were doing. He was very sad. His son has been diagnosed with leukemia. They need to find a larger apartment. His son requires a very clean and stable environment. He will be on chemotherapy and bone marrow transplants for two to three years. On top of that terrible news, Greg also shared that he was hearing grumblings at his plant that layoffs were on the horizon. Not long after, the ax fell on his head once more. So Greg is picking up one-day jobs again.

The one day jobs provided through www.HirePatriots.com have truly been the cement between the cracks for Greg and his family.

Mentoring

Several years ago Mark and I were preparing to put on a military job fair. We needed help in calling companies on our behalf to invite them to the fair. We posted a job on our website, and later that day, a savvy young former Marine sergeant by the name of Sally bounded up the stairs of our office and knocked on the door.

Mark introduced himself and quickly proceeded to describe to Sally what the job entailed. He didn't have much time to properly train her. The job fair was fast approaching. He handed her a script and a call list and directed her to start making calls.

It wasn't going well. Sally was nervous. I walked over to Sally, put my arm around her and we started again. These things are easy for Mark. He has been doing it for decades. But I know how hard it is at first to call someone you have never met. After a while, she got the hang of it. From then on no matter what task we gave Sally, she excelled. She was our Girl Friday. She fixed our computers when they broke, did the books, filed, called companies, set up and served at job fairs, created flyers, banners and signs for our hiring events, marriage retreats and welcome home parties, and even fixed some of our furniture. But that seems like only one percent of everything she did. Sally was invaluable and kept our engines running.

She was such a doll. She was married to Michael, a handsome active duty Marine sergeant. They both took one day jobs off of our site. Residents frequently called us to let us know what a delight Sally and Michael had been. I would respond, "We know!"

Soon Sally was pregnant with twin boys. And far too soon she moved far away to begin her new life in a new state. Mark and I sorely miss Sally. Our company has never run quite so well as when Sally was by our side.

We lost touch with Sally for a while as life absorbed all of us. Then she called not too long ago. Sally told us about the successful marketing business she had launched in her state. She told us how working with HirePatriots had mentored her. She watched us brainstorm on how to do this or that and she learned that you can build a business by the seat of your pants. You just figure it out. It might be scary. You might fail a lot. But just like in the Corps, you just keep going until it works.

We talked for hours. We didn't want to get off the phone. We wanted her to pack up her family, jump on a plane and come back to HirePatriots. Dear Sally, we miss you so!

Making a Friend

My husband and I became friends with a disabled veteran who was taking one-day jobs off our website. Jon was colorful. He wore a cowboy hat, boots and belt. He wasn't a cowboy. He just liked the clothes. "They fit my personality," he told us.

Jon had served tours of duty in Iraq. He had fought in many battles. He had developed little regard for the accuracy of those that tried to lob mortar shells into their base regularly. They made big holes in the desert and blew up a few fig trees, but very rarely did they hit anything that caused injuries or important destruction.

One day Jon and his best friend were given an assignment to paint a wall It was common for mortars to explode in the vicinity throughout the day. Jon and his buddy would joke about what a lazy aim the enemy had. But one day their aim improved.

A shell landed very close by. A large wall of concrete slammed against the wall they were painting. Jon turned to his buddy to exclaim—but that young Marine was in death throes. Jon tried to run to his friend, but he did not realize or even feel that the explosion had torn off much of his back and legs too. He fell to the ground, unable to come to his fellow Marine's aid.

Back home, it took a long time to heal. There were multiple surgeries. By the time we met Jon, he was on a waiting list for surgery number 16. The only complaints he had was that his pain pills no longer worked and that it was taking the Veterans Administration (VA) much longer than they had promised for his next surgery. There are hundreds of pieces of tiny metal slivers embedded in Jon's body. When they float into joints or between ribs and such, they cause him immense, constant pain. He will probably be having these operations for the rest of his life.

He told us that the best thing he could do to endure was to work and to focus on that. It was the only thing that helped him to cope with the agony. That is why he first came to HirePatriots.com. He needed to work—not so much for money, but to keep his torment at bay.

As we got to know Jon a little better he became a friend. He would visit us with his wife and daughter. We had barbecues and shot the breeze. We tried to stay away from mentioning the war or his injuries. When it did slip into our conversations, his wife's countenance quickly turned to concern and worry. We all would change the subject as soon as possible. Those memories were too fresh and may always be. They would cause a darkness to fall over Jon's face, and he would become irritable if they continued too long.

Mark was on TV or radio several times a month in San Diego. Jon's knowledge of veteran issues and his usually eager and fun personality allowed Mark to have him take his place sometimes. Everyone loved his military jargon and humor.

He came to our home often just to hang out. Sometimes he said very little. He would sit on our beach-view balcony for hours. Mark and I guessed he needed a place to be alone and away from his family for a while. We were honored to be chosen as his safe place, and we did not disturb him when it seemed he needed space.

It has been a few years since those days. We moved and our paths do not cross very often anymore. We miss him. But he still uses our job board regularly. Talking to patriotic people and working for them is still his best therapy.

Last year, on his own volition, Jon held a coffee fundraiser for HirePatriots.com and raised $500. Thank you, dear friend.

When Your House Is on Fire!

Paul, a Force Recon Marine, also got a job at the ranch Greg worked on during the weekends. "Doc" owned the property and especially liked Paul. The elderly Doc and he enjoyed talking together. The Doc and his wife became like Paul's second family. He would stay on their property in the tack house when he did not have to be back on base.

But one night just as Paul was getting off duty, a horrible fire started near the ranch. Doc and his wife had to evacuate. Homes were burning down and Doc's livestock were being threatened. Paul's first instinct was to head for the ranch immediately, but he could not get there. The fire departments had closed all roads in that area to traffic. So Paul and another Marine that he had brought with him walked for several miles, avoiding fire and police, until they got to the ranch. The flames had already reached within a hundred yards of Doc's property. It was going to be the next victim of the towering inferno that caused some buildings to burst into fire before the flames even reached them.

It was very dangerous and they really should not have been there. But they worked tirelessly for more than 36 hours, keeping the house and outbuilding wet enough to keep them from burning. They also corralled the horses and kept them safe until animal rescue arrived. Without a doubt Paul and the other Marine with him saved the Doc's property and animals.

Creating an Employment Safety Net for Veterans

Too many of our veterans struggle to make enough to sufficiently support their families! Food distribution services arrive at our bases regularly to help feed their enlisted families. Then there are our National Guard and Reserves, as well as transitioned US veterans, who are underemployed and unemployed. Our mission is to provide a HirePatriots Day Job board in communities all across America. These jobs are a lifesaver for veterans.

Of course, it all starts with a community having a HirePatriots job board of ours to use. So we look for business sponsors in each area to help us get it started. The reward for them in public relations, branding and media attention is great. But nothing is better than the joy of helping out US veterans. Check out these comments from those who have used HirePatriots.com and see: www.hirepatriots.com/news-and-blogs/entry/what-people-say-about-hirepatriots-job-program.

But most of all our veterans need us to pitch in. Just posting a day job whenever you need an extra hand makes a big difference. Let's all do it. And let's spread the word. Let's make sure that whenever our local US military, veterans and their families need to earn some extra money to keep afloat that there are day jobs posted for them in our area.

About the Author

Tori Baird is the proud and happy wife of Mark Baird. They both believe in Jesus Christ as the one and only Savior. He is the Creator and giver of life. They are entirely certain that nothing they have done or accomplished could have been done without Him.

About the Contributing Authors

The publisher would like to offer our
sincere thanks to all of the contributing writers to this book.

Notes From Some of Our Contributing Authors

Karin Abarbanel

Karin Abarbanel is an entrepreneur, author, and expert on small business and startup strategies for women. She is coauthor of *Birthing the Elephant: the woman's go-for-it! guide to overcoming the big challenges of launching a business*, an action guide featuring startup stories and frontline advice from successful entrepreneurs.

Karin was selected by The Hartford for its "Taking the Pulse of Small Business" panel and served as Avon's spokeswoman for its "Corporation to Cottage" initiative. She has appeared as a guest expert on TV, radio, cable and print—and has been featured on ABC TV's "Good Morning America," CNBC, WCBS, and SmartMoneyTV. Karin speaks widely on a range of startup topics, including "7 Success Secrets of Women Entrepreneurs," "Lean Launching in a Tough Economy," and "Winning the Small Business Mind Game." For more information, visit: birthingtheelephant.com and aceyourstartup.com.

Mark Baird

Mark Baird is called to serve US veterans and their families. He uses his education, experiences and resources to assist veterans with finding careers, starting a business, counseling, marriage retreats, and job placement. And he allies his nonprofit, Patriotic Hearts, with other veteran causes so as to provide a comprehensive, holistic curriculum. His primary endeavor is to end US veteran unemployment for perpetuity. Mark Baird is the founder and CEO of HirePatriots.com, a pastor and author.

Tori Baird

Tori Baird is the loving wife of Mark Baird. She has been crucially instrumental in building HirePatriots and its 501(c)(3) nonprofit Patriotic Hearts. Tori focuses on assisting HirePatriots business members and volunteers. In particular, she helps them to become media spokespeople on TV, radio and press. She and her husband are popular public speakers at events and on TV and radio. She trains them to do what we did. She makes introductions to CEOs and hiring managers on job seekers' behalf. She also creates marriage retreats for US veterans, and works with the volunteers that want to pitch in. She shares her husband's passion and concern for US veterans and their families. And because she has so many conversations and relationship with veterans, her heart is entwined with theirs.

Doug Beabout

Doug Beabout is a principal partner of Career Talk Guys, a Service Disabled Veteran Owned Businesses (SDVOB) enterprise dedicated to teaching job seekers how to identify the job they desire and the employer they want without the frustrations that many experience. Job seekers master an empowering and actionable process proven by thousands of successful hires. Doug and his partner, Kevin Sutton, transform employers into talent attractors in an effective, but unconventional manner. While people struggle to find work, employers struggle to find people. Doug and Kevin have mastered the means to bring both together successfully. They provide practical and actionable solutions that result in people finding work and companies finding talent. They bring over 50 years of effective experience in career consulting and industry performance improvements.

Seldon B. Graham, Jr.

Seldon B. Graham, Jr., is a World War II veteran who served during the Korean War and the Vietnam War. His father was a veteran of World War I, and his paternal grandfather was a veteran of the Civil War. Graham is an engineer, attorney, and transportation energy expert who lives in Austin, Texas with his wife of 60 years, Patricia. A grandson is an Army captain and Apache helicopter pilot in Afghanistan. Graham is a member of a number of veteran organizations such as the Veterans of

Foreign Wars, American Legion, and Military Officers Association of America. Graham wrote the 2005 book, *Why Your Gasoline Prices Are High,* which is the history of how the United States got into this foreign oil imports mess.

Mel Cohen

Mel is a consultant with over 35 years of hands-on experience. He regularly provides advice in business, book marketing, taxation, nonprofit organizations and barter. Mel designs special Amazon promotions that have resulted in creating "Amazon Best Seller" status books and has achieved overall sales rankings in the Amazon Top 100 out of their over 20 million books.

Mel had a Biographical Record appear in the Silver Anniversary 28th Edition of *Marquis Who's Who in Finance and Industry* as well as the Thirty-first 2000/2001 Millennium Edition, inclusion in which is limited to those individuals who have demonstrated outstanding achievement in their own fields of endeavor and who have, thereby contributed significantly to the betterment of contemporary society.

Ted Daywalt

Since 1999, Ted Daywalt has been the president of the Veterans of Foreign Wars sponsored VetJobs (www.vetjobs.com), a premier military employment site on the Internet. From 1971 to 1978 he served on active duty in the Navy as a line officer and intelligence officer. He was then transferred to the Naval Reserve Intelligence Program, from which he retired as a captain (O-6) with 28 years of service. Ted held senior positions in the steel, electric utility, importing, chemical and recruiting industries. Ted is an in demand speaker and is regularly cited and interviewed in the press, including USA Today, 60 Minutes, Military Times, PBS, NPR, CNN, and FOX News. Ted testifies regularly before Congress on veterans and economic issues. Ted earned a BS from Florida State University (1971); an MA, International Relations, University of Southern California (1977); and an MBA from the Goizueta Business School, Emory University (1980)

Crystal Dyer

As the president of Professional Coaching Consultants, Crystal is an organizational development consultant and an active advocate for the military community in many ways. She's a veteran of the Army's Chaplain Corp, a proud military spouse, the mother of three boys, an entrepreneur, professional speaker, author and philanthropist. Crystal uses every resource in her arsenal to make a positive impact on those who serve this country and those who serve beside them. As a board member of several nonprofit organizations, Crystal provides strategic guidance so that much-needed services are always available to support veterans, spouses, and gold star family members. Her goal in life is to work herself out of a job by helping to eliminate veteran unemployment and military spouse underemployment one client at a time. For more information, visit www.crystaldyer.com.

John Eynouf

My journey from soldier to entrepreneur is not necessarily the typical one and is certainly not over. The experiences I have from my time in the military and all the amazing places and schools I got to go to have given me a unique foundation from which to build future success. The leadership training and skills I adapted while serving my country fueled my passion for becoming an entrepreneur and starting my own company (www.readyupgaming.com). I would never be able to be where I am today if it weren't for the love and support of my wife and family. I am thankful to be able to give back to other vets through HirePatriots.com. After reading my story I know you will see that if I could survive and overcome, so can you!

Josh Galle

Josh Galle, is an Operation Iraqi Freedom (OIF) Veteran and served two combat tours in Iraq with the United States Marine Corps as a Noncommissioned Officer. Since being honorably discharged from active duty in 2008, he has served as a national veterans advocate, especially on behalf of his fellow wounded warriors and disabled veterans. He shares an honest and personal perspective from both sides of the national crisis of veteran unemployment, and has been an instrumental leader in the design and management of national recruiting programs for several Fortune 500 companies, leading to the hiring of thousands of veterans. He now represents Humana, headquartered in Louisville, KY, a company that has an ongoing initiative to hire military veterans and spouses nationally. If you are a military veteran or spouse seeking employment please visit: www.jobs.net/jobs/Humana-Veterans. To connect with Josh visit his LinkedIn profile:www.linkedin.com/in/jgalle.

Tony Lavelle

Tony Lavelle, a Vietnam vet who served 26 years in the Army, then the Air Force, is an anthropology researcher and author for the Gallantry Group Press (www.gallantrypress.com). His first book, *The Manhood Test*, straightforwardly defines what a man is, laying out a simple path any boy can follow to reach manhood and carry out the duties and responsibilities expected of a man as a mature and responsible adult, and a loyal and involved citizen. Tony's new book, published later this year, is titled, *A Training Manual for Men: How to Woo Woman and Find a Good Wife*. This book offers a solution, laying the groundwork to train men to find a good woman to marry.

Patrick Mellody

Patrick Mellody is the author of *The Unemployment Budget – Your financial survival plan*. The book is designed to assist anyone living on a reduced income. Patrick has been a volunteer Crown budget coach for over seventeen years. In the book he uses real-life stories of people he coached to ease the reader through the budget process. There are two budgets in the book, the "Crisis Budget" and the "Unemployment Budget." The "Crisis Budget" is for someone that needs help today and the "Unemployment Budget" is a more in-depth version. The book also provides referral resources for ongoing assistance with the reader's financial and personal needs.

Patrick's book is available on Amazon or his personal web site: www.budgetsthatwork.com.

Jeff Morris / Gregory Spencer

Jeff Morris and Gregory A. Spencer are the Founders of SpendSmart, Inc. (SpendSmart.org); a 501(c)(3) financial literacy and wellness educational nonprofit. SpendSmart.org provides unbiased, fun, and transformative financial literacy coaching and workshops. The focus is to help people learn how to live debt-free and stress-free. The firm has been nominated for the Presidential Citizens Medal for their commitment to serve military families, students, and at-risk communities. Jeff and Greg experienced financial hardships, which eventually birthed SpendSmart.org.

Morris served six years in the Marine Corps. He served in the infantry, was trained as a sniper, and was also a ceremonial sergeant. Jeff is a Certified Master Money Coach and a Certified Credit Expert. Greg has served as an educator and success coach. He is a Certified Financial Literacy Instructor and a Certified Financial Crisis Coach. Spencer's family has served in the Marines, Army, and Navy.

Cesar Nader

This book would not have been possible without the leadership and passion of Mark Baird and his lovely wife Tori. Together they have devoted a lifetime to support veterans and their effective transition from the military with their nonprofit organization HirePatriots.com. I would also like to thank a few people who made my transition a more effective and successful journey: Brig. Gen. Tom Draude (USMC ret.), Lt. Col. James Van Zummeren (USMC ret.), Lt. Col. Gabe Patricio (USMC ret.), Lt. Col. Scot Seitz (USMC ret.), Lt. Col. Joseph Paschall (USMC ret.), Maj. John Stanton, Capt. Corey Taylor, Francis Hesselbein, Marshal Goldsmith and my wife Melanie Nader. Last but not least, I would like to thank the U.S. Marine Corps for taking a 19-year-old Hispanic boy who did not speak clear English and molding him into the leader I am today. I will never forget I will always be a United States Marine.

Kevin O'Brien

Kevin O'Brien is the managing partner of Veteran Recruiting Services. He is a pioneer in the virtual career fair space has been instrumental in bringing together hundreds of industry leading employers with more than 200,000 active duty, guard/reservists, veterans, and military spouses since 2011. Employer partners who have worked with the VRS team have hired more than 15,000 veterans and military spouses. VRS has also recently launched a veteran-friendly employer index by industry called VetFriendly (www.vetfriendly.com) in support of the First Lady and Dr. Biden's Joining Forces Initiative. A regular contributor to Fox News on veteran's employment, and a Huffington Post blogger, O'Brien and his team have committed 100 percent of their focus on ensuring that all veterans and military spouses can secure meaningful employment. Kevin resides in Doylestown, Pennsylvania, with his business partner and wife Nicole and their two sons Gavin and Aidan.

John Phillips

John Phillips was a lieutenant colonel in the US Army. And as a major executive in a Fortune 500 company, he founded the Military Veterans Business Resource Group. He is also the author of *Boots to Loafers*. It guides veterans on a journey through the transition process and the transformation process or rebranding those veterans must undergo in order to survive in the "new normal" of the private sector. John's book focuses on US veterans landing a job and building a new life outside the gate. *Boots to Loafers* guides them through the process of successful reintegration.

Mona Singleton

Mona Singleton is a United States Coast Guard veteran. She served a four-year tour of duty as a radioman 2nd class. She is an author, certified corporate business coach, and project management professional. She is an excellent leader, coach and mentor and is best known for her energy and enthusiasm.

Her new book, *Lead with Your Gifts: Why Who You Are, Not a Label Defines You* as a Leader, is due for publication in summer 2013. For more information about Ms. Singleton visit www.monasingleton.com.

Carl Vickers

I would like to start off by saying that everyone has an inner passion that drives them. It is why they get up in the morning and pushes them through the last sip of coffee for the day. However, if it were not for the support of my wife Lisa, all this would not be possible. Through my time in the military and throughout our travels she has always told me that to be great at something you must love it and truly enjoy your work. Her wisdom and insight has been spot on. In addition, my parents who have always told me I can do anything and stood behind me through all those ups and downs as well. Thank you!

Index

Resources and Websites

Sample Resume:

Available: June 1, 2013

Military Transition Person
1234 Proud to Serve Street, United States. USA 123456
// 555-123-4567 // MTP@gmail.com

OBJECTIVE: Seeking a position in Quality Assurance or Maintenance Management, so a company can use my management, quality assurance, multi-platform avionics, and logistics experience to increase the safety and efficiency of its operations.

CAREER SUMMARY:

Secret Clearance with current Special Background Investigation

Strong and extensive quality assurance and maintenance background. Expertise in the logistical support of a diverse range of aircraft. Avionics experience on EA-6B, E-2C, P-3B platforms and associated systems. Repeated success in identifying, evaluating and resolving problems with large-scale, complex operations, often within heavily regulated environments. Proficient in guiding highly skilled, cross-functional teams; able to build solid relationships with upper-level executive leaders and achieve consensus across multiple organizational levels and the achievement of goals despite limited resources and tight timeframes.

Excellent trainer, mentor, facilitator, coach, and problem solver.

CORE SKILL AREAS:
Management and Training

- Established and enforced Naval Aviation maintenance policy, including aircraft modification, upgrade, and rework/repair scheduling.

- As combat aircraft manager for 55 aircraft and four squadrons, set the scheduling and modification for 34 aircraft at three maintenance facilities. Overall effort resulted in a 98% mission success rate and a 20% improvement in equipment availability.

- Produced annual savings of $67,000 and 54 man-hours by establishing micro-miniature electronics repair facility at Fleet Readiness Center New Orleans.

- Expedited $37 million in maintenance funds to purchase 6 new aircraft, 41 aircraft conversions, and 16 major avionics upgrades, while minimizing impact to deployed squadrons and maximizing combat readiness for Operation Enduring Freedom, Operation Iraqi Freedom and Joint Inter-Agency Task Force Counter-narcotics exercises.

- Developed and implemented training program to improve team members' knowledge for job performance and advancement opportunities, leading to 15% increase in advancements.

- Provided over 800 man-hours of training and guidance to 8 squadron program managers and 41 intermediate level program managers during 47 separate readiness inspections.

Quality Assurance and Analysis

Enforcement and inspect maintenance program, process, and materials under the guidance of the Naval Aviation Maintenance Program, Code of Federal Regulations, OSHA/NAVOSH and Naval Air Force CSEC 6.0 evaluation system.

- Key leader and coordinator for seven multi-agency aircraft inspections, enabling four navy aircraft squadrons to meet overseas operational obligations ahead of schedule.

Employment Related

www.americasjobexchange.com
www.beknown.com/landing
www.bradley-morris.com
www.branchout.com
www.cameron-brooks.com
www.careerbuilder.com
www.dice.com
www.gijobs.com
www.H2H.jobs
www.Hero2Hired.org
www.hireheroesusa.org
www.HirePatriots.com
www.indeed.com/military
www.jobs.net/jobs/Humana-Veterans
www.jobs.oriongrassroots.org
www.JoiningForces.gov
www.lucasgroup.com/recruiting-military
www.monster.com
www.recruitmilitary.com
www.uschamber.com/hiringourheroes
www.tweetmyjobs.com
www.twitjobsearch.com
www.veteranrecruiting.com
www.veteranrecruiting.jobs
www.vetfran.com
www.vetjobs.com
www.warriorstotheworkforce.com
www.westillserve.com

Finances

www.995hope.org
www.annualcreditreport.com
www.bankrate.com
www.budgetsthatwork.com

www.credability.org
www.creditkarma.com
www.crown.org
www.SpendSmart.org
www.soundmindinvesting.com
www.studentaid.ed.gov
www.ombudsman.ed.gov

Military Sites

http://missioncontinues.org
http://joiningforces.uso.org
www.acap.army.mil
www.esgr.mil
www.militaryonesource.mil
www.taps.org
www.themilitarycoalition.org
www.vetsuccess.gov

Networking Sites

www.kingdomadvisors.org
www.linkedin.com
www.facebook.com

Crowdsourcing Sites

www.accionUSA.org
www.GoFundMe.com
www.Indiegogo.com
www.kickstarter.com

Business Sites

http://articles.bplans.com/financing-a-business
www.aceyourstartup.com
www.apps.whitman.syr.edu/vwise
www.becomeablogger.com
www.benetrends.com
www.business.gov
www.consumeraction.gov

www.dailywritingtips.com/7-steps-to-becoming-a-freelance-writer
www.ducttapemarketing.com
www.ducttapemarketing.com/blog/tag/copyblogger
www.ehow.com/how_5995907_make-crafts-sell-quickly.html
www.freelancewriting.com
www.entrepreneur.com/smbresourcecenter/index.html
www.etsy.com/sell?ref=so_sell
www.firstgov.gov
www.freelanceswitch.com/freelance-writing/how-to-become-a-free-lance-blog-writer
www.ftc.gov/sentinel
www.imatchfranchise.com
www.increasenow.com/starting-a-residential-house-cleaning-service
www.infobarrel.com/How_to_Make_Money_House_Cleaning
usatoday30.usatoday.com/money/smallbusiness/columnist/abrams/story/2012-08-24/small-business-making-money-with-crafts/57250528/1
www.irs.gov/Businesses/Small- Businesses-&-Self-Employed/Home-Office-Deduction
www.irs.gov/Businesses/Small-Businesses-&-Self-Employed/Other-Government-Resources
www.irs.gov/Businesses/Small-Businesses-&-Self-Employed/Small-Business-Forms-and-Publications
www.ladieswholaunch.com
www.makemineamillion.org
www.makemineamillion.org/event/wvec/home
www.marketingplanpro.com
www.nawbo.org
www.new.ewomennetwork.com
www.nytimes.com/2012/07/20/education/edlife/campus-incubators-are-on-the-rise-as-colleges-encourage-student-start-ups.html?_r=0.
www.paloalto.com/business_plan_software
www.powerfulyouwomensnetwork.com
www.powerhomebiz.com/marketing/general.htm
www.sba.gov

www.sba.gov/content/express-programs
www.sba.gov/content/veterans-business-outreach-centers
www.sba.gov/sba-learning-center/search/training/financing
web.sba.gov/sbtn/sbat/index.cfm?Tool=4.
www.sbrc.net
www.score.org
www.smallbusinessresources.com
www.squareup.com
www.uschamber.com/about/member-resources
www.veteransbusinessfund.org

Personal Resources

www.bignet.org PS
www.careerdirectonline.org
www.crossroadscareer.org
www.crystaldyer.com
www.family.org
www.intouch.org/resources/all-things-are-new
www.newhopenow.org
www.careerdirectonline.org
www.princetonreview.com
www.professionalcc.com
www.returningheroeshome.org
www.studentveterans.org
www.troubledwith.com

Other Websites

www.baseguide.com
www.blitzteamconsulting.com
www.chministries.org
www.irs.gov/advocate
www.medi-share.org
www.integritymoments.com
www.christianlawyerconnection.com
www.resourceministries.net
www.affiliate-program.amazon.com

www.affiliateprograms.com
www.clickbank.com/index.html
www.mattsmarketingblog.com
www.youtube.com/watch?v=HuGJ3fdRHd4

The Authors Have Agreed To Answer Questions on Their Respective Chapters

Karin Abarbanel: kmja_w@hotmail.com

Mark Baird: www.hirepatriots.com

Tori Baird: www.hirepatriots.com

Doug Beabout CPC, CSP: Doug@CareerTalkGuys.com

Mel Cohen, CFP®, RFC, RTRP: melcohen@hughes.net

Ted Daywalt: tdaywalt@vetjobs.com

Crystal Dyer: info@professionalcc.com

Adam Edwards: adam@imatchfranchise.com

John Eynouf: JE@readyupgaming.com

Josh Galle: Jgalle@humana.com

Seldon B. Graham, Jr.: SelGraham@austin.rr.com

LTG (ret.) Don Jones: info@professionalcc.com

William A. "Tony" Lavelle: tony@gallantrypress.com

Patrick Mellody: patrick@budgetsthatwork.com

Jeff Morris: Info@SpendSmart.org

Cesar Nader, U.S. Marine, Retired: cesar@cesarnader.com

Kevin O'Brien: kobrien@veteranrecruiting.com

LT Col (ret.) John W. Phillips: johphillips@bellsouth.net

David Renza, M.A.: dj.renza@yahoo.com

J. Todd Rhoad, MBA: todd.rhoad@blitzteamconsulting.com

Kristina Saul: ksaul66@gmail.com

Mona Singleton: coachmona@yahoo.com

Gregory A. Spencer: info@SpendSmart.org

Carl Vickers: cvickers@peoplescout.com

Books by the Contributing Authors

Birthing the Elephant: The woman's go-for-it-guide to overcoming the big challenges of launching a business
Karin Abarbanel and Bruce Freeman

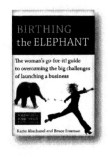

Surviving the ups and downs of entrepreneurship takes more than just a great idea. It means facing a host of challenges, from giving up a paycheck to mastering marketing and other unfamiliar skills. While other guides focus on business plans or management, *Birthing the Elephant* breaks new ground by charting the emotional ups and downs of launching a start-up, and offering practical advice for weathering them.

Birthing the Elephant features inspirational stories and how-to tips from successful entrepreneurs, including cosmetic mogul Bobbi Brown and Liz Lange, the maternity wear pioneer. It provides a step-by-step supportive road map for:
- lean launching in a tough economy.
- substituting brains for bucks.
- do-it-yourself marketing strategies
- avoiding cash-draining pitfalls

For information, **visit: www.birthingtheelephant.com.**

Career Soup
Career Talk Guys, Doug Beabout, CPC,CSP and Kevin Sutton

There is a talent storm brewing on the horizon. Employers express universal failures at seizing critical people. Many are having a difficult time hiring qualified people for uniquely different types of positions, across most education and skill levels. A *Wall Street Journal* article stating, "Some Firms Struggle to Hire Despite High Unemployment" is proof in the press that Recruiters and job seekers alike, need education in a proven process so the best get together.

Several companies reported they have had difficulties and do not understand why with so many people unemployed, that the U. S. Dept. of Labor projects a talent shortfall by 2013 of twenty million+ people that are trained and experienced.

What's needed isn't a long-term fix; it's the mastery of getting the opportunity and candidate each party seeks by applying a proven and well taught process. Come by **Careertalkguys.com/12.html** where great solutions and help can be found.

Why Your Gasoline Prices Are High

Seldon B. Graham, Jr.

Seldon B. Graham, Jr. is the author of the book, *Why Your Gasoline Prices Are High*, order directly at **www.iuniverse.com/Bookstore/BookDetail. aspx?BookId=SKU-000030339** or from any bookstore. He is also the author of the booklet, Gas-Oil Ratio Calculation, published by the Oil and Gas Division of the Railroad Commission of Texas, as well as a number of technical articles in legal periodicals.

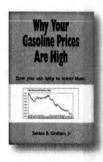

The Unemployment Budget – Your Financial Survival Plan

Patrick Mellody

People often ask me how I became a "budget nerd". Truth is like most people the last thing I wanted to do was have a budget but circumstances forced me into it. It wasn't until my income was drastically reduced that I even considered living on a spending plan. My motivation was either go broke or try to work with my creditors while I searched for a fulltime job that would get me back to normal.

In my book I tell my full story and the stories of others like us that went through tough times. By the end of the book you will have a spending plan and referral resources to keep you going until you find your next job. You can find the book on Amazon. Thank you for your service. **www.budgetsthatwork.com**

The Military Veteran Career Transition System (MVCTS)
Cesar Nader

It takes months to transition civilians to become "basic" military professionals in the U.S. Armed Forces. To transition out from the military, the mandatory requirement is a one-week Transition Readiness Seminar (TRS) and completion of the DD form 2648 - Preseparation Counseling Checklist.

An effective Career Transition Program for veterans should be a more complex and developed process that is done in phases. It should address the four quadrants of the transition process: military, personal, professional and family. It should also be tailored and scaled to the age, family composition, stage of military career and long term chance of success of each individual who transitions. The MVCTS book is about this process and how to navigate each phase, assess the needs of each quadrant, involve those in your transition circle (spouse, children, family) and complete an effective transition that will have a long-lasting effect on your next career choice. **www.cesarnader.com**

Lead With Your Gifts, Why Who You Are, Not A Label Defines You As A Leader
Mona Singleton

It's no surprise the world is starving for wise, gifted leaders. Unprecedented and unpredictable global changes are prompting the need for next generation leaders to bravely and reliably navigate through tough and turbulent times. To lead effectively, servant leaders must play a variety of "serving" roles rather than many of the traditional roles of the past.

Lead With Your Gifts, Why Who You Are, Not A Label Defines You As A Leader is a new book by Mona Singleton written for the extraordinary men and women who are willing to step up and serve when times are tough, not just when leading is easy. What makes ***Lead With Your Gifts*** special is that Mona provides a fresh perspective into how leaders can leverage their gifts to contribute in more powerful and productive ways. Look for the book at **www.leadwithyourgiftsbook.com** in the summer of 2013.

How Inspired Authors Press LLC Started

About three years ago I was told about a woman who was a victim of domestic violence for over nine years. I stated the victim should write a book about it. She wanted to, but didn't have the skills or finances to do so.

After coaching her on writing, I agreed to finance the project. *Found Missing: A True Story of Domestic Violence, Murder and Eternity* by Linda Slavin released. This book launched IAP. The original goal of **Inspiredauthorspress.com** was to serve as a marketing consultant to the Publishing marketplace specializing in Amazon promotions. These promotions moved books from a sales ranking in the millions to reaching the coveted Amazon Top 100 in overall sales out of Amazon's 21 million plus books. We handled an Amazon Promotion for Michelle and Jim Bob Duggars' book, *A Love That Multiples* that kept the book in the Top 50 in overall sales for almost three days.

An American Crisis: Veterans' Unemployment/Stand by Them/How You Can Help/Solutions followed. It is a book that will be a solution to helping the over 850,000 unemployed veterans find employment or start businesses **www.veteransunemploymentbook.com**. The book is a collaborative effort by an Army general, a Congressional Medal of Merit recipient, a wounded warrior, a military spouse and others contribute insightful chapters for the purpose of getting veterans back to work expediently, or assisting them in becoming entrepreneurs. The USP is "Buy a Book-Help a Veteran." One of our marketing strategies is to have organizations and other groups purchase books in large quantities to give away to unemployed veterans.

From inception to release was a total of six months. The book debuted on Amazon http://amzn.to/Xgvwcp in February of 2013 and has had two separate Amazon Top 100 genre rankings during prerelease, an accomplishment we are proud of. The goal with *An American Crisis* is to offer an updated version every 12-18 months with an additional group of experts. IAP will continue to offer marketing advice, speak on book marketing and manage Amazon Promotions for clients.

Mel Cohen, CFP® , RFC, RTRP
Inspired Authors Press LLC
931 593-2484